MARY E. ANDERSON, M.F C.C.
LICENSE #MFC 28838
P.O. BOX 1400
OCEANSIDE, CA 92051

What Do I Do When...?

a handbook for parents and other beleaguered adults

juliet v. allen

Impact Publishers
POST OFFICE BOX 1094
SAN LUIS OBISPO, CALIFORNIA 93406

WHAT DO I DO WHEN...?

Copyright © 1983 by Juliet V. Allen

Third Printing, July, 1988

All rights reserved under International and Pan-American Copyright Conventions. No part of this book may be reproduced, stored in a retrieval system, or transmitted in any form or by any means, electronic, mechanical, photocopying, recording or otherwise, without express written permission of the author or publisher, except for brief quotations in critical reviews. Permission is hereby granted for reproduction of the child behavior charts only in quantities needed for individual family use by the purchaser of this copy.

Library of Congress Cataloging in Publication Data

Allen, Juliet V., 1922-
What do I do when--?

Bibliography: p.
1. Child rearing--Handbooks, manuals, etc.
2. Parenting--Handbooks, manuals, etc. 3. Family--Handbooks, manuals, etc. I. Title.
HQ769.A48 1983 649'.1 83-12903
ISBN 0-915166-23-2 (pbk.)

Design and cover by Tess Taylor, San Luis Obispo, California

Child behavior charts by Emily Stuart, Salem, Oregon

Printed in the United States of America

Published by **Impact Publishers**
POST OFFICE BOX 1094
SAN LUIS OBISPO, CALIFORNIA 93406

Acknowledgements

''If we could learn from mere experience, the stones of London would be wiser than its wisest men,'' observed George Bernard Shaw. That's one way of saying that experience is not enough. We need other people to give meaning and direction to our lives, and I have been very fortunate, both personally and professionally, that the paths of some very generous people crossed mine.

The adventure of becoming an applied behavioral analyst requires the cooperation and sharing of those researchers who develop the procedures that may appear to be deceptively simple, of those who serve in personally supportive ways, and of the clients who come for consultation. Among some special people are Helen Crisp, Ph.D., who encouraged my entry into the field of psychology, and Sybil Bullock, M.A., both of whom have provided good-humored encouragement and intellectual stimulation throughout the years. Appreciation is expressed to Diane De'Armond, Ph.D., and Lawrence D. Simkins, Ph.D., for demanding the best when I was a student at the University of Missouri, Kansas City; to Montrose M. Wolf, Ph.D., and Edward Christophersen, Ph.D., for giving me the opportunities to see, hear, and learn and who serve as models of professional excellence, rigor, and commitment; to Carole Carlson des Lauriers, Ph.D., and Paula Rohrbaugh, Ph.D., who were very special mentors in broadening my horizons.

Some others who contributed to this work in various ways were Helen Miller, MSW, who gently but firmly prodded me into writing; Dr. Clement Vickery, psychiatrist, and June Stryker, MSW, whose more psychodynamically-oriented approach always proved to be constructively invigorating and stimulating; Richard H. Horner, MSW, Child Guidance Supervisor, and Ruth Shirley, Ph.D., Director of the Marion County Health Programs, both of whom encourage creativity within a bureaucratic setting (no mean feat when coping with policy and budget dilemmas); Marilyn Herb, M.A., and Sandra Asher, M.A., co-leaders and idea generators in numerous parent training groups; Emily Stuart, artist who understood; and Jane Tyler, author and secretary, who with good humor and enthusiasm typed and critiqued my first manuscripts submitted to the Salem *Statesman-Journal* (Gannett Press), which generously provided the space to publish the weekly ''Child Guidance'' columns that provided the underpinning of this book.

A very special thank you to Robert E. Alberti, Ph.D., publisher, who gave a vote of confidence and who, with Margaret McGrath Porter, M.A., took the time and energy to edit the material that is presented.

Learning from books and associates is one thing. Learning from a family is another. For that opportunity, I am grateful to my husband, Bob, my daughters, Gloria and Janet, my sons, Richard and Kenneth — all of whom presented numerous joys and critical challenges throughout the years and sensitized me to the need to view fallibilities — including my own — with humor and tolerance. They show their loving regard by their commitment to their own lives and careers and by giving high priority to the enjoyment of life and to be caring and compassionate human beings.

As Charles McCabe, the columnist, once observed, ''If there's any point to life at all, it is that it should be embraced joyously.'' That's the purpose and premise of this book.

J. V. A.

The author and publisher gratefully acknowledge permission of the persons and organizations noted below to quote or adapt copyrighted material from the resources noted. Readers are reminded that it is a violation of the Copyright Act to reproduce copyrighted material without express written permission from the author(s) or publisher(s) involved.

Thanks for permission goes to...

...Salem (Oregon) *Statesman-Journal*, Edward P. Bassett, Editor. (Most of the material in this book is based upon my "Child Guidance" columns which appeared in the *Statesman-Journal* in 1981 and 1982.)

...H & H Enterprises, Inc., Lawrence, KS, for material on Attention Span, Bedtime, Cars and Kids, Television, and Mealtime which were adapted from *Little People*, by Dr. Edward Christophersen, copyright © 1977.

...Dr. Edward Christophersen, Kansas University Medical Center, Kansas City, KS, for the material noted immediately above, and for information relating to anticipatory infant training and shopping.

...Teaching Research Infant & Child Center, Monmouth, OR, and Nancy J. Johnson, Dixie L. McKinley, Dr. Bud Fredericks and Dr. David Grove, for the "Bugs Me Chart" on page 31.

...*Journal of Applied Behavior Analysis*, Lawrence, KS, for the "Job Description" on pages 39 and 40. From "Modification of behavior problems in the home with a parent as observer and experimenter," R. V. Hall, S. Axelrod, L. Tyler, E. Grief, F. C. Jones, & R. Robertson, copyright © 1972 (5:1, 53-64).

...Chicago Community Child Guidance Centers, Inc. for "Memo from Your Child," on pages 74 and 75. 1963.

...McGraw-Hill Book Company, New York, for material on Praise, Mild Social Disapproval, and Ignoring which was adapted from *Effective Parents, Responsible Children*, by R. Eimers and R. Aitchison, Copyright © 1977.

...San Francisco *Chronicle*, for Charles McCabe's column "On Being Unworthy," page 133. Copyright © San Francisco *Chronicle*, 1968.

...*Family Life Education: Parent/Child Homework Assignments*, Planned Parenthood of Santa Cruz County; Network Publications, 1983, for "How Well Do You Know Your Son/Daughter" and "How Well Do You Know Your Parents?" pages 205-208.

...Research Press, Champaign, IL, for material relating to reasoning, adapted from *Parents Are Teachers* by Dr. Wesley C. Becker. Copyright © 1971.

...McGraw-Hill Book Co., New York, for material relating to Dressing Problems, adapted from "Behavioral Problems in Children" by E. H. Christophersen and M. A. Rapoff. In G. M. Scipien, M. U. Barnard, M. A. Chard, J. Howe and P. J. Phillips, (Eds.) *Comprehensive Pediatric Nursing* (2nd ed.) © 1979.

...Masters Agency, Capitola, CA, for the cartoons. Copyright © by artists Al Kaufman, Betty Swords, and Brad Anderson which appear on pages 3, 26, 48, 81, 87, 107, 120, 192.

Publisher's Note

This publication is designed to provide accurate and authoritative information in regard to the subject matter covered. It is sold with the understanding that the publisher is not engaged in rendering psychological, medical, or other professional services. If expert assistance or counseling is needed, the services of a competent professional should be sought.

Contents

A Few Words of Encouragement for Parents

Notice over the piano in the Old West bar: "Please do not shoot the piano player...He is doing his best!"

The children are finally in bed. The house is in shambles. The dishes are piled high in the sink, a mountain of clothes has to be sorted, and you're sitting at the kitchen table sipping a cup of cold coffee. Your mother told you there would be days like this! You didn't believe her then but you do now!

Someone once said that "Experience is the worst teacher: it gives the test before presenting the lesson." The problem with children is that each is a unique personality, and there's no manual that comes with them. You want to protect but not stifle them — to train but not intimidate them — to love but not spoil them — to teach them to have a conscience but not to make them feel guilty. You want them to have compassion for others but not to be "taken in" by others — to be independent and self-sufficient but also caring, considerate and cooperative.

That's a big order. In fact, maybe you can't do all of that. After all, your kids will also be making their own decisions as to the kind of people they want to be, and they will be influenced by others. Nevertheless, there are some things that you *can* do that will help you feel better and more self-confident — and good feelings are contagious!

One thing you can do as a parent to make your job easier is to concentrate on just three main goals for your children: *social skills, integrity,* and *responsibility*. If they grow up with those, you know they'll be able to handle just about anything well!

This book is full of help for you to accomplish those three goals. The recommendations I give come out of the "behavioral" school of child psychology, in which the basic premise is that almost all behavior is learned. If you think about it, that's wonderful news. If what your child has learned is creating problems, new behaviors can be learned! You see, there is hope!

You'll need to know something about a couple of basic principles of human behavior. As a parent, you can learn to put those principles to work for you. They are really quite simple. The hard part is learning to *use* them consistently to develop your child's social skills, integrity, and responsibility. I have summarized those principles for you in the first chapter, "ABC's of Child Behavior." Be sure to read it first, whatever problems you're trying to solve!

It can help to think of your role as a *parent-teacher* whose job ends when your child "graduates into the real world." Good teachers use certain skills, and you'll be learning some key skills in this book. As you apply them to solving the problems you may face today, you'll see how they can be used to deal with tomorrow's challenges as well.

But you are more than a parent and teacher. You are a *person*, with feelings and needs of your own. Do not neglect yourself, and don't ever lose the "kid" in you. Hang on to your sense of humor; that's your humanity and the most important lifeline when things go wrong. Life is meant to be enjoyed. (I don't know who suggested that if something is fun, it must be sinful; I hope no one ever took that seriously!) Teach everyone in your family to share the responsibility for household chores. Don't let yourself become a servant; if you are one, take steps to change that (the chapter on "Chores" will help). Even a two-year-old can learn to pick up toys!

Take time for yourself. Enjoy life in your own unique way — go out with friends, pursue a hobby or career, plant a garden, read. Find something to smile or laugh at every day — if only at yourself.

Are you fallible and imperfect? Great! Welcome to the human race! Don't punish yourself for honest mistakes. That's part of your humanity. Besides, if you were perfect, you would set your kids up to have unrealistic expectations of the world! (And who could stand to be around you?)

Sometimes, of course, you just have "one of those days." When it happens, I like to pull out a list of "touchstones" for support. I pin one up over the sink or on the refrigerator until I get back on the track of enjoying myself and my family. Here's a starter list; you'll find more scattered throughout the book:

Life is hard by the yard. By the inch it's a cinch.
Let me have the courage to be imperfect.
I can change my feelings by changing what I tell myself.
No one can upset me without my permission.

Most of us need all the help we can get. If at times things seem beyond your own capacities, don't hesitate to seek some professional counseling. None of us know all the answers. I've included some ideas about getting professional help in the "More Resources" section at the end of the book.

One final note of introduction: I've written this book to offer aid and comfort to parents — and other beleaguered adults — who are having a tough time coping with specific child behavior problems. Because the emphasis here is on problem solving, it may sound as if children never do anything right. Please be assured that I consider being a parent one of life's most rewarding challenges. My own children are now grown, and I have many occasions to reflect on the joy and learning they brought me while they were growing up. They enriched my life. (I also have occasions to remember the pain of not knowing "what to do when," and how too few times the words, "You're fantastic" and "I love you" were spoken.) In fact, it is largely for those reasons I have written this book. I work every day with parents who are having a tough time feeling the joy and expressing their love because the problems seem overwhelming. I hope this helps you get back in touch with the joy!

© Masters Agency, Capitola, CA

"What ever happened, Ruth? You used to be a fun person!"

ABC's of Child Behavior

WHAT DO I DO WHEN...I don't know the first thing about the way children pick up good (and bad) habits?

I hope you read the "Few Words of Encouragement" I shared on the preceding pages. Most of us start out as parents not knowing how children learn. One of the most important jobs of parenting is to find out how, and to use that knowledge to help our children become better adults.

Three Basic Principles

Let's take a look at the basic principles of behavior. I'm going to oversimplify somewhat: you needn't be a psychologist in order to be an effective parent!

First — and most important for parents — *we humans try hard to do those things that bring us pleasure and attention!* If your little Luke has a choice between washing the dishes and going to see the latest episode of the "Star Wars" movies, which will he choose? The problem is that you want the dishes done — a real pain to Luke! How do you resolve that? You'll get one effect if you nag or rave or complain. You'll get another if you simply say: "Fine! After you do the dishes, you can go to the show."

Another child whines a lot (not yours, of course!) What happens if the parent gives Susie a cookie every time she whines? What would happen if Susie were ignored every time she whined and got a cookie only when she asked politely?

The second principle is pretty much the other side of the same coin: *We avoid doing those things that inconvenience us, bring us pain, or seem to have no results at all*. "Ahah!" you say, "Then spanking and yelling should be incredibly effective!" Wrong! If pain brought change, the world would be populated by peaceful, loving people who are courteous and cooperative. Look around you. What do you see?

The message is that consequences must be carefully considered in terms of what you are trying to accomplish. We learn to dislike and avoid those people who bring us pain, and you don't want to alienate your children. For example, Luke comes home from school two hours late with no excuse. You won't help the situation by spanking or yelling at him. You can teach him that misbehavior costs if you simply say, "You've lost TV privilege for tonight. Go and do your chores and get ready for dinner."

The third key principle of behavior you need to be aware of as a parent is that *the way we interpret a situation determines our behavior.* What *really* happens is not nearly as important as what you *think* happens in terms of deciding how you will react. We all view the world through our own unique set of filters: values, beliefs, attitudes; and we behave according to those ''filtered'' interpretations. There is no special magic in the universe about an eight o'clock bedtime, or eating everything on your plate, but if you *believe* those are important values, your children are in big trouble if they don't go along!

Anger, fear and other emotions are also subject to conscious control by our thoughts. In fact, attitudes and thoughts are always in the pathway between an event and the way one feels about it.

Luke may be angry with you because he wanted to see the ''Star Wars'' movie instead of doing the dishes; at least a part of that anger comes from Luke's *belief* that he should be able to go to the movies when he wants to, and that it's ''not fair'' that he has to do dishes instead. One of the toughest jobs we have as parents is to teach our kids that life is often ''not fair.'' They'll be a lot happier if they learn to use rational thoughts to help themselves feel happier, instead of angry and depressed. Examples: ''Mom fixed a great dinner; the dishes are my share.'' ''The movies will be there tomorrow night.'' ''I don't like it, but I can handle it.'' Luke will be happier telling himself those things, instead of ''Mom is mean and unfair.'' More on this subject in the ''Reasoning'' and ''Anger'' chapters.

''Grandma's Rule''

You will find your parenting role less confusing if you learn to use one more pretty simple idea, known in many families as ''Grandma's Rule: ''*When you do what I want you to do, then you can do what you want to do.* To apply it consistently is not so simple!

Parents have to learn how and when to praise, to punish, and to ignore.

''Oh!'' you may say, ''But that's controlling! Isn't that totalitarian? Isn't that manipulative?'' No, I do not want you to become an authoritarian or heavy-handed parent. However, *someone* will be in control. Is it going to be you, or your child? Or, better yet, how about *cooperative* control? If you make a practice of being very open and honest when you praise, ignore, punish, or negotiate, your child is aware of and involved with the process. There are no secret agendas. Your goal is to do what is in the best interests of your child, to equip him or her with the social skills, integrity and responsibility needed for coping in a difficult world. Your guidance provides the standards that will serve well during those times when your child, alone, must make critical decisions.

Freedom, Feelings, and Rewards

"But," comes your next protest, "doesn't the emphasis on behavior ignore the total personality? What about freedom and self-expression and feelings and perceptions?" I return the question to you. Who can be free for self-expression and good feeling about self and others when indulging in self-defeating behavior? Help your child to be free by knowing what to do when, by developing competencies, by learning to assert, not aggress.

Ann Sullivan, who trained Helen Keller and released her from the prison of ignorance, was a wonderfully effective behaviorally-oriented teacher. If you have a chance to see the motion picture, "The Miracle Worker," on TV, watch it. It is a heart-warming story and an excellent portrayal of the procedures I advocate in this book: using consequences and enforcing rules. It poignantly shows that loving is not enough. There must be more. Children must be *taught* to be loveable by being socially competent, honest and responsible.

Some of the ideas suggested here will involve material payoffs in addition to praise and attention. "Now you've done it!" say you, "That's bribery! I refuse to bribe my child. Kids have to learn to do things without expecting something in return!"

I agree: kids do have to *learn*. And parents must *teach*. I am not asking you to bribe your child. Bribery is payment to do something illegal. Be assured that no material rewards can replace your attention and praise. Those remain the most powerful rewards of all for young children. Sometimes, however, material rewards must be used to get the attention of a child (remember the story of the farmer and the mule?). Material rewards can, as noted in the "Chores and Allowances" chapter, help build independence and self-assurance. Susie and Luke — and your children — need the opportunity to *earn* what they get. They will do many things graciously and cooperatively — with an enthusiastic and sincere "Thank you" as the only "payment." (When it comes right down to it, do you think of your paycheck as "bribery" to get you to come to work and do a job?)

One more caution about rewards: you as a parent do not always have control of what your child finds rewarding. Particularly as children grow older, they enjoy the attention of peers (ask any junior high school teacher!) and other results of their behavior. So start early to teach the values and behaviors you want your child to grow up with, and be as consistent as you can.

Punishment

Punishment is always a critical issue in childrearing and everybody has an opinion. You may protest: "What do you mean I shouldn't hit my kid? That's the only way to teach them. That's how I was raised!'' No one can stop you from spanking your child, of course, but you won't like the effects in the long run! I discuss that in the ''Discipline'' chapter. The point is to use discipline constructively, and striking a child can only be destructive — for both of you. Somerset Maugham said it best, I think, when he wrote: ''It is not true that suffering ennobles the character; happiness does that sometimes, but suffering for the most part makes men petty and vindictive.''

One more important point about punishment. Quite often throughout this book you'll see references to ''Time Out.'' The procedure called ''Time Out'' is one of the single most effective tools for parents to come along in the past twenty years. I describe Time Out and its use in the ''Discipline'' chapter, but let me take a moment to introduce it here, since it comes up so often.

I mentioned a few paragraphs back that there are many different things each child finds rewarding, and that the rewards are unique to each child. What's more, it is very tough for parents to completely control the rewards their children are gaining at any moment. Susie may be getting a stern reprimand from you while she sprays the dog with the garden hose, but she's also delighted by the dog's reaction and the laughter of her onlooking peers. Time Out is a way to remove Susie from as much external stimulation as possible for a short time (usually five minutes). Escorting or sending her to a dull ''neutral corner'' can be strong medicine — it's b-o-o-o-oring! Time Out is just that: *so* boring Susie will quickly learn to avoid it. What's more, it's more powerful than the ''usual'' punishments parents use.

Read more about Time Out in the ''Discipline'' chapter. For now, just keep in mind: Time Out is boring, but never hurtful. It is a painless way to teach your child behaving is better than misbehaving.

Summing Up: ABC...DE

We humans are complex beings: spiritual, social, economic, philosophical, intellectual and much more. Body chemistry and genetic inheritance get into the act too. But don't let those complexities get in your way. The basic principles in this chapter will go a very long way in helping you master the tough job of raising a child:

Here's a quick summary of those key ideas:

...People seek pleasure and attention, so praise a lot.

...People try to avoid pain, discomfort and boredom, so use discipline that teaches and does not alienate. Time Out is an excellent example of such a method.

...People act according to their interpretations of situations, so learn how to control your thoughts.

...''Grandma's Rule'' (first do what I want, then you can do what you want) has many helpful applications. Most of my recommendations in this book are based on it.

I've included suggestions for your further reading on the subject of raising healthy children. I urge you to visit a library or bookstore and look up those materials!

> ***We are none of us wise. We are all on the way to wisdom.***

Aggression

WHAT DO I DO WHEN my son is aggressive? He's only six, but he picks on other kids at school, and the neighbors are complaining also. He's always been kind of fiesty and high-spirited. Maybe others don't understand him?

I hope that you are not one of those parents who mistakenly believes that "it should all hang out," that kids should be encouraged to freely express their hostility. This faulty reasoning says, "we mustn't do anything to repress their natural spontaneity" or build "internal conflicts that may fester and contaminate their delicate psyches." Don't you believe it!

Please note:

...Psyches are *not* all that delicate.

...Aggression breeds aggression.

...Control — not expression — of aggression is the only way civilized people can live together.

As witnessed by the increasing number of acts of violence in our society, aggression is one of the most serious problems confronting you as a parent — and everyone else — in the rearing of children.

Although there may be genetic factors that contribute to aggressive *tendencies*, aggressive behaviors are *learned* very early in life in the home, school, and community. The most critical factor in this learning appears to be the *child-rearing practices of the parents*. Very punishing parents rear very aggressive children — as do parents who do not set limits. The buck stops at the door of the home. That is, with you and with me.

Let's begin with a *positive* step...and begin *early*. Help your young children learn to respect others — including animals. Encourage consideration for rights, sensitivity to feeling, cooperativeness, and esthetic appreciation. Although we parents are only part of a total system, we are the child's first experience of society. Our parenting skills largely determine how our children will relate to society.

Do not encourage — or ignore aggressive acts by children in the mistaken belief that they will "grow out of bad behavior." Begin training your children very early in life that aggressive acts will not be tolerated. Show and encourage kindness and gentleness — and that can start by showing the toddler how to treat the dog, Fido, and the cat, Samantha. Remember how powerful your attention is, and use it to discourage aggression. Abuse is never "cute" or acceptable, however young the child may be who inflicts it. Work cooperatively with your child's school to bring about constructive change if your child displays coercive behavior — yelling, teasing, hitting, tantrums, and non-compliance. Such problems are easily identified very early (see the "School Behavior" chapter).

Some parents set the stage for aggressive behavior by being permissive and indulgent. Others, sad to say, accomplish the same thing even more efficiently by reacting to misbehavior in highly punitive ways (yelling, slapping, hitting, sarcasm, put-downs). The "I'll learn him or kill him" approach is very costly for everyone and almost insures disturbed behavioral problems.

Conduct problems have implications for later delinquency, and they must be dealt with as soon as possible — with non-aggressive discipline. If you believe that "All my kid needs is a firm hand, and I'm giving it to him!", you may find the "firm hand" coming back to haunt you when your child becomes a teenager. If you react to early nuisance behaviors by hitting or screaming, you will find that you are only adding to the problem. You may even be teaching your child to be aggressive (especially if that is the only attention the child receives). It is easy to learn that strength and brutal power are intimidating persuaders.

We probably know more about the effects of physical punishment than about any other aspect of human behavior. We know that it damages the parent/child relationship, that punitive parents gradually lose their power to influence and may find themselves becoming increasingly fearful of their own creation. Supportive peers, often described as "undesireable influences," gain control; or the child may become a potentially explosive isolate. Such a youngster may feel like a "loser" and relate to losers, who, in turn, teach the child more self-defeating behaviors.

"Time Out" — an alternative, constructive disciplinary procedure described in the "Discipline" chapter — is very effective, but must be used consistently and immediately. Get to the problem as soon as possible. Problems which persist into the teenage years are far less manageable.

To be forewarned is to be forearmed. "...Those parents who punish their children physically and express dissatisfaction with their children's accomplishments and characteristics have the most aggressive children," says Dr. Leonard Eron (1982), a psychologist at the University of Illinois who has followed the progress of more than 1,400 children during the past 25 years. Rejection and physical punishment, particularly on the part of the mother, appear to be highly related to training sons to be violent.

The best predictors of a child becoming an aggressive adult, notes Dr. Eron, are: rejecting and punitive parents; watching violence on television (identifying with violent characters and perceiving stories of violence as "the way the world works"); day-dreaming about fighting, killing and hurting; and behaving aggressively against people, animals, and property.

The need to use nonphysical punishment and set limits has been noted. Several other factors have been found by recent research to contribute to the likelihood of aggressive behavior in children. The following summary may help you prevent unnecessary aggression in your own family:

Please *monitor television programs* that are viewed by your children. (You always have the option of pressing the "off" button!) Extensive viewing of television violence clearly increases the possibility of encouraging serious real life violence. There is also evidence of increasing aggression on the part of girls, who are now exposed to more aggressive models on television. (Apparently, they were less impressed a few years ago when girls were depicted as victims.)

In addition to monitoring the TV programs that enter your home, you may want to write letters to advertisers who sponsor violent programs and refuse to buy their products, as recommended by the National Coalition of Television Violence (an organization supported by concerned citizens and mental health specialists).

Do you approve the motion pictures your children go to see? I urge you to do so. The most grotesque and obscene violence appears in the *blood-and-horror movies*. Viewing robberies, rapes, and raw, brutal murders serves to "numb" both children and adults to the real-life horrors of violence. Films often demonstrate how to commit violent crimes and convey the message that human life is cheap and that pain and suffering are irrelevant. They may stimulate disturbed viewers and generate fears and anxieties in others, who start thinking of themselves as potential victims.

Even comic books should be reviewed by parents. They are another primer that serves as an important model for aggressive behavior. It has been estimated that more than 75 percent of all children in the United States between 6 and 17 years of age read comic books: "the most violent material in most newsstands." New York psychiatrist Dr. Fredric Wertham observed:

> "The atmosphere of crime comic books is unparalleled in the history of children's literature of any time or any nation. It is the distillation of viciousness. The world of the comic book is the world of the strong, the ruthless, the bluffer, the shrewd deceiver, the torturer and the thief... Force and violence in any conceivable form are romanticized... Trust, loyalty, confidence, solidarity, sympathy, charity, compassion are ridiculed. Hostility and hate set the pace of almost every story."

Do not permit your children to have access to a weapon. According to psychologist Dr. Leonard Berkowitz of the University of Wisconsin, because the gun is associated with killing and hurting, it serves as a cue that triggers murderous thoughts and feelings — even muscular reactions. Anger increases the probability that a person will react to the cue and behave impulsively and tragically. A gun in the house may be an invitation to mayhem, particularly if any family members have volatile tempers. Tragedy has resulted from curious children finding and experimenting with revolvers. Psychological studies reveal that, instead of being neutral and innocent, the gun, by its very presence, often suggests a deadly solution to a problem, particularly to someone who has lost self-control.

When a gun is in view, according to many careful studies, people tend to be nastier in what they say, harsher in their judgements, and more punishing toward others. Even normally well-behaved people seem to become uninhibited and stimulated by the sight of a gun.

Children act more aggressively when they play with toy guns (and, contrary to popular belief, toy guns do not "get it out of their systems").

Drivers become more hostile toward another driver who openly displays a rifle in the car. Motorists stopped for traffic violations are found to be more hostile toward the policeman if he carries a visible revolver in his belt than if he does not have a gun in sight.

J. Edgar Hoover, former director of the FBI, who was

not known for pacifist views, maintained that the *availability* of firearms was an important factor in the rising crime rate. He noted that easy access to weapons obviously makes it easier for a person to commit murder if he or she wants to do so.

If your child of any age is behaving aggressively and hurting others, take steps to curb those actions immediately. If you make an honest effort to follow the guidelines in this handbook and still don't see results, get some professional counseling. You owe it to yourself and to your child. Don't wait until your child does things that lead you or others to dislike him or her. You won't want that to happen, but such things *do* happen when "small" aggressions are ignored.

Incidentally, if you *do* decide you need help, you should know that *traditional psychotherapy* (talking, group, or play therapy) is *not* effective with highly aggressive children. Highly structured programs may have to be designed by your counselor with your cooperation. I strongly recommend that you seek out a qualified *behaviorally-oriented* therapist. More on professional help in the "More Resources" section at the end of the book.

Anger

WHAT DO I DO WHEN both my child and I have difficulty controlling our anger?

"When angry, count ten before you speak; if very angry, a hundred," advised Thomas Jefferson. Mark Twain was less conservative and suggested, "When angry, count four; when very angry, swear."

More recently, Dr. Laurence Peter warned, "Speak when you're angry – and you'll make the best speech you'll ever regret!" As I noted in the chapter on Aggression, "Let it all hang out" is *not* the way to go!

Here's a situation you could easily work yourself up over: Your son, Phillip, has borrowed the car to run an errand. He promised to be back in time so that you could go to your dental appointment. He is now 15 minutes late; you're starting to build up a good steam of anger, moving beyond mere irritation at being inconvenienced. As you wait, you begin to reflect on all that you've done for him, starting with diapering days, moving on through the school years. By the time he *does* show up, you have concluded that King Lear was right: ''How sharper than a serpent's tooth it is to have a thankless child!'' When Phillip walks through the door with a sheepish grin on his face, you have revved yourself up to really let him have it with both barrels!

Why *not* bop him one? Should you merely smile and greet him with open arms? Not at all. You have the alternative of deciding to be irritated rather than enraged or tolerant. Advise Phillip that his coming late means that he can't use the car for a week (a month would be ''overkill''). In that way, you *both* win: you avoid guilt for blowing your top and a migraine headache; Phillip is again reminded that commitments are important. (Of course, if you didn't really want to go to the dentist in the first place, it will be a lot easier to contain your anger!)

We Create Our Own Anger

Almost 2,000 years ago, Epictetus observed that ''People are disturbed not by things, but by the views they take of them.'' That insight is just now beginning to penetrate!

You (and I and everyone) are always talking to yourself in your head. The trick is to *pay attention*! There is no little person in there chattering away. That's *you*! Your thoughts may be disconnected, but you are continually telling yourself how you feel, giving yourself instructions, making predictions, drawing conclusions about yourself and others, and interpreting events. You can talk yourself into a first-class fit of anger about almost anything and anyone — water dripping from the tap in the kitchen sink, Phillip's lateness, the stranger who cut in front of you on the freeway.

The other side of the coin — the good news — is that you can also calm yourself by talking sense to yourself: ''I'm really irritated at Phillip, but I am *not* going to go ape and give myself an ulcer because he's inconvenienced me. I'd like to pop him one but losing the car privilege for a week will impress him more than anything I can say or do.''

Our ''self-talk'' reflects our expectancies and beliefs about our world and experiences. Two sons may respond very differently to being restricted for the weekend. Kevin may react with fairly good grace. Kyle, given the same circumstances, may literally tear up his room! Two teenage girls, rejected after auditioning for a high school musical, respond like night and day. Mary becomes severely depressed, angry, and withdraws from all activities. Margaret is disappointed but decides to work harder at her singing or dancing lessons.

Why do those differences occur? It's because each person has different interpretations of how the world works — and how it *should* work. We really don't know why some people are more prone to irrational thinking than others.

Anger is usually triggered by a sense of injustice — something has happened that *ought not* to have happened according to an individual mental ''rule book.'' The problem is that ''the way things ought to be'' is a form of wishful thinking and is *not* pre-ordained by some universal law! Kyle and Mary believe it is unfair for them not to get their way. Kevin and Margaret, while disappointed, recognize the reality that life doesn't always work as we would like (you win some and lose some).

Lewis Carroll's Tweedledee aptly phrased it: ''...If it was so, it might be; and if it were so, it would be; but as it isn't, it ain't. That's logic.'' And what ain't so is that we will *never* be disappointed and frustrated by others, by events.

Is anger, then, ever justified? Of course it is. If someone has knowingly, intentionally, and unnecessarily acted in a hurtful manner, anger then serves to alert and give you the energy to do what you have to do to protect yourself or get what you want. What you do, however, can either be adaptive (problem solving) or maladaptive (self-defeating).

If your child kicks you in the shins, it is appropriate to be angry and impose discipline that says that this is not acceptable and will not be tolerated. It would not, however, be adaptive anger if you kick and beat your child as a way of teaching that aggression is intolerable. It is appropriate to be angry about poverty, ignorance, crime, war, a polluted environment, corruption, cruelty to people and animals. *The important thing is: what do you do with your anger?*

Should children be encouraged to express their anger? Some think so. Analytic psychotherapists warned that anger ''turned inward'' can lead to feelings of depression and guilt, thus they recommended that anger be ventilated (sort of like lancing a boil). The problem is that if you go around venting your anger, others may decide that you're a loony hothead. Life becomes pretty complicated and unpleasant.

Expressing (within limits) can be valuable, however. We do know from research that *unresolved* anger can lead to physical and/or social problems and even violence against self or others. That does not mean, however, that a child should be encouraged to froth and fume and run for a pillow to beat somebody over the head. That could become ''fun,'' and the youngster might learn to enjoy ''laying a trip on others.'' There is also a perverse gratification in sinking teeth into another person's leg. The desire for revenge and the sense of righteousness are very powerful. If you draw up a ''costs-benefit analysis'' sheet, however, you will find that control outweighs rage. What's more, now there is evidence that ventilation may actually *increase* anger, rather than ''release'' it!

Well, Then, How Do I Handle My Own Anger?

If you can't control your own anger, you certainly cannot deal with your child's anger — and uncontrolled anger causes more disruptions in families and relationships than anything else. As noted by philosopher Mortimer Adler, "You don't clear up emotional problems by making yourself more emotional about them...When people can't settle differences by talk, they settle them by force or by fraud..."

Ironically, the explanation for *why* we get angry is quite simple. We tend to become upset any time we interpret something or someone as deliberately threatening our safety, self-esteem, or desires. The process of revving up our anger is also relatively simple, and it starts in our heads. You are always talking to yourself (Thinking is like subvocal speech), and you can build up an incredible rage very easily and efficiently if you fall into one or more of five anger-generating traps: *clairvoyance* ("I know what you're thinking, you brat!"), *overgeneralizing* ("You did not clean up your room and that means you're sloppy and lazy and I'm a rotten mother!"), *magnifying* ("If you don't do the things I tell you to do, it is terrible and I can't *stand* it."), *using the words "should" and "shouldn't* ("You should be grateful and considerate because of all the things I do for you, and you shouldn't *ever* be impolite and sass me back.") and, finally, *deciding that something is unfair and unforgiveable* ("How *dare* you read instead of doing the dishes when I have to work like a dog to put food on the table!") All of this, of course, adds up to being extremely judgemental and irrational (unrealistic as to the way the world works).

Well, if it's so simple, why, then, is it so hard to control anger? First of all, you have to decide that you *want* to control your anger. Then you have to understand how you build your anger through what you are telling yourself. The *hard* part is the practice — working at control; that is a lifetime project for some people. Fortunately, it *does* get easier with practice.

For example, how can you keep yourself from flying through the roof when you have just seen your local disaster area — your daughter's room? She was supposed to have cleaned it before she went off with her friends to play tennis. You want to stay reasonably calm? You want to be rational and problem solving? Here's the way to do it:

...*Don't try to be clairvoyant.* (Other terms for this are "psychoanalyzing" and "mindreading.") You can't know what Tammy was thinking when she left the room in such a mess. If you invent reasons, you'll come up with the worst motives that you can think of. For example, "She takes me for granted. She thinks I'm a fool, her servant, who will pick up after her. I'm nothing to her..." If you want to know why she left the room a mess, *ask* her, then accept her explanation at face value. On second thought, is it really important to know why? The real issue is that she did not clean her room before she left the house.

...*Don't overgeneralize.* Just because someone has done something you disapprove of does not mean that he or she is a totally rotten person. You would be overgeneralizing if you said, "Tammy didn't clean her room because she's sloppy and inconsiderate and will never amount to anything. Oh Lord, where *did* I go wrong!?" She really doesn't deserve every label you can think of. All that happened was that Tammy did not clean her room before...

...*Don't magnify*, that is, don't blow things out of proportion. This is *not* a catastrophe or the end of the world. You need not tell yourself that Tammy's unkempt room and noncompliance are "terrible," "awful," "the worst thing that ever happened" and that you "can't stand it." First of all, it's not all that great, but it's not all that bad either. There *are* worse things that have happened in the world. And, secondly, you *can* stand a great deal. Such exaggerations only fuel the fires and justify your anger. All that happened was that Tammy did not clean her room...

...*Avoid use of the words "should" and "shouldn't."* Those words get *more* people in trouble! You'll only antagonize yourself by telling yourself that your kid *should never* do anything to offend you or that nobody should ever criticize or disagree with or inconvenience you.

"Should" and "should not" are really demands for perfection from others, and usually assume that other people are just around to gratify *your* needs and wishes! In fact, they have as much right as you do to think and do and be what *they* want — as long as they are not physically or verbally abusive. It would have been really nice if Tammy had cleaned her room before she went to play tennis, and she *will* pay the penalty for disobeying you when she comes home — but why upset yourself because she isn't perfect? All that happened was that she did not clean her room...

...*Throw away your mental rule book* of laws of absolute fairness, justice, and universal principles. If Tammy has broken *your* rules of fair play and decency, remember that not everyone has the same concept of what is "just and fair." The criteria of "just and fair" depend on who is doing what to whom. All that happened was that Tammy did not...

Having gone through all of those anger traps, what are you left with? You are left with the real issue: Tammy did not clean her room when told to do so. Everything beyond that is an interpretation that only serves to complicate matters. The real question is: what are the consequences that will help teach Tammy to do what she is told? That should be enough to keep you busy without adding anger to the issue. Isn't it really *her* problem?

Now, wasn't that simple? You really don't have to complicate your life by interpreting and analyzing everything. Remember that life is meant to be enjoyed. Don't bring in unnecessary grief.

What Do I Do When My Child Gets Angry With Me?

When confronted by an angry child — and it's inevitable that you *will* be a target sometimes — your job is to *keep cool*. Easier said than done? That's true, but here are some recommendations:

...*Know your own cues for anger*. Different people have cues that alert them that they are starting to "burn." As soon as you feel *your* cue, start telling yourself: "Keep cool. I'm *not* going to let this get to me." Take a deep breath and tell yourself to relax. Tell yourself "I've handled worse situations than this before. This is Tammy's problem, not mine. I *refuse* to make it mine." Show that you refuse to get upset (defensive) even when Tammy says she hates you and that "other parents know how to treat their kids." Your worth as a person is not at stake no matter *what* Tammy says. Besides, if *you* can't handle peevish, critical reactions, how do you expect *her* to do so? The best way to take charge is not to show that you are upset. Remind yourself that angry Tammy is being extremely judgemental and thinking irrationally that "this is terrible and awful and shouldn't be happening to *me*!" Take a deep breath and try to defuse her anger by agreeing with *something* that she says, no matter how absurd are the charges being made against you. You can say, for example, "I suppose it *does* seem unfair that you've lost telephone privileges for a week because you went to play tennis before cleaning your room."

...*Do not allow yourself to be hurt by the words* which inevitably fly during combat time. You may be disappointed, but you don't have to give power to them by over-reacting and conveying the impression that you are easily intimidated. Remind yourself that *these* words are merely a "clutter of sounds" and you *refuse* to take the insults seriously. Do not counterattack and use hate words or insults in return. Tammy will eventually calm down if *you* don't escalate the anger. Stay task-oriented and ask for clarification of the issue ("What exactly do you want, Tammy?") or state what *you* want firmly and clearly ("I'm sorry that you think that this is unfair, but you are to clean your room now. Because you disobeyed the rule, you have lost telephone privileges until next Friday.")

Do not discourage the angry child or teenager from talking about feelings of anger, but this is not the time for a lengthy discussion. It is usually a good idea to say, "We'll talk about this later when we both feel under control. I don't like being attacked, and I don't want to say anything that might make us both sorry.'' Get busy then with something else. There's no point in prolonging the conflict.

What Do I Do When My Child Comes Home Angry at Someone Else?

...*Be a good listener.* ''Good listeners are in rather short supply and in much demand...'' observed psychologist Bernard G. Guerney. Help your child clarify his or her feelings. Don't rush to make suggestions and give advice on how to solve problems. Ask questions as a way to help your child develop solutions alone.

...*Help your child analyze the situation.* If Billy has been the target of teasing, for example, you might say: ''That boy must feel very small if he has to put others down. Why is his opinion so important to you? Why do you feel that you need to upset yourself over him? How do you want to handle this situation?'' Do *not* solve problems for your child. Ask questions that will help him think things through.

...*Point out that we create our own anger* by what we tell ourselves. It is easier to believe that other people and things *cause* us to behave badly, and therefore, we are not responsible for what we say and do. It takes time and a lot of feedback to learn that frustrations are merely inconveniencing — not devastating — and that no one can *make* anyone feel worthless, or angry.

...*Teach alternative, less volatile language.* The words ''hate'' and ''kill'' are concepts few children fully understand, and they and *all* name calling tend to inflame the situation. Offer words your child can use to express strong negative feelings in less destructive ways. Example: ''Boy, am I *mad!*'' ''I'm so angry I could *spit!*'' ''I feel like hitting *something*.'' (not someone).

The goal is to be able to express feelings appropriately (that is, verbally, not physically, and then to solve the problem, if possible. (See ''Reasoning.'')

Is There Any Way To Avoid Angry Confrontations?

Not if you're alive. It isn't easy to go through life without getting angry or encountering an angry person, but you *can* reduce the number of angry situations in your life by learning as much as you can about anger. At long last, recognition is being granted the truth that anger is a good servant but a bad master.

To learn more about this very important emotion, the following books are recommended: David Burns, *Feeling Good*. New York: Signet, 1980. Carol Tavris, *Anger: The Misunderstood Emotion*. New York: Simon and Schuster, 1983.

A number of recommendations for dealing with the

angry child may be found in the book: *How to Raise an Emotionally Healthy, Happy Child* by Albert Ellis (Institute for Rational Living, 45 E. 65th St., N.Y., N.Y., 1966.) To learn more about control, read *The Assertive Option* by P. Jakubowski and A. Lange (Research Press), 1978. If, however, you're really determined to insist on escalating your anger, read *How to Make Yourself Miserable* by Dan Greenburg, described as the "ultimate in self-demoralizing manuals" (Institute for Rational Living, see address above).

Arguments

WHAT DO I DO WHEN my kid argues and Argues and ARGUES?

"But Mom!...Whaddaya mean clean my room? I gotta go play ball."

"You promised you would do it, so do it now!" (You feel your throat tighten. Here we go again!)

"But the ball game...You know, the guys are counting on me. I got commitments!"

"You have commitments here, too. I don't want to hear another word!"

"It's not fair. You don't make Billy do anything — that kid sits around all day, and you don't say a word. It's okay for little brother to..."

"Billy does too do his jobs. Furthermore, you have responsibilities around here. Your Dad and I..."

Kerplunk! You fell right into the arguing trap again! Doors will be slammed, Johnny will sulk and groan and moan, and the day will be ruined (a couple of hours, anyway). Everyone is in a no-win situation.

It is easy to get trapped. You may feel that "civilized parents" have to "reason" with a child and "justify" their decisions or requests. Or maybe you are insulted when Johnny questions your judgement or motives, and you want him to *admit* that you have a right to demand certain things. You want respect. You want appreciation. That's not unrealistic, but you won't get it by arguing. Arguing is attention, and attention is very rewarding.

Two basic guidelines might help. (It's in print, so you can show these to Johnny!)

...As a parent, you have a right — and responsibility — to make reasonable requests and demands;

...You don't have to justify those requests or demands — or even be right. You are human and sometimes make mistakes. You also pay the bills.

Johnny has a right to disagree with your demand, but expressing that disagreement appropriately is sufficient. You can then either reconsider it (if it really *is* unreasonable) or enforce it. The point is: refuse to argue. If Johnny wants to take it to the Supreme Court, let him!

The Direct Approach for the Child Through Age 12

Here's a familiar scene: Cindy is supposed to take out the garbage before watching TV. You walk into the room, find her engrossed in watching a program, and say: "You didn't take out the garbage. Do it now, please."

"Okay, Dad, I'll take it out during the commercial. This is an educational program. You want me to get educated, don't you? I mean, I've really got to watch this."

Is it important enough to allow an exception to the "garbage-first" rule? (Nine times out of ten it won't be.) If not, go and turn off the TV and say, "I said, do it now. This is a persistent problem." She may continue to argue, calling you unreasonable, unfair, "a pain." Don't debate *any* of that. (You do not have to justify your existence or the state of your personality.) Don't get sidetracked. You merely say, "You're arguing. Take five minutes in Time Out, please." More argument? "Oh, oh, that's another argument and another five minutes. Take ten minutes in Time Out." If Cindy persists, of course, she could earn an hour or more in Time Out. The basic issue is that of compliance with a reasonable request. (Time Out is described in the chapter on "Discipline;" read that section now if you need more help with this issue.)

Adding Power to the Direct Approach

Some children make it tougher on us. They can get into such a bad habit of arguing, they need a more powerful incentive to realize what they are doing. The most extreme case I ever encountered was that of 12-year-old Carl, whose parents were determined to be "reasonable." Throughout the years, they tried to explain absolutely everything that Carl challenged. They finally sought consultation when they found themselves being wakened in the middle of the night (two or four a.m.) by Carl, hovering over their bed and shaking his finger at them saying, "And another point that I want to make about this whole situation is..."

Helping Carl see the error of his arguing ways required the cooperation of his exasperated teachers and parents, who had to learn to refuse to be trapped by his irrational logic. (This kid was an expert!) Ignoring his debates, refusing to be diverted from the task at hand and imposing Time Out were the basic recommendations. This is *not* easy to do!

One of the best ways to start putting a stop to arguing (assuming you are already ignoring and enforcing rules) is to count and tally. Put up a chart on the refrigerator or bulletin board. Tally each time Johnny argues (also impose time out) for the first six or seven days. That gives both of you a visual record of the extent of the problem. If you're lucky, you may not have to go beyond this step; he may argue less and less just to avoid being tallied! If you have 20 arguments on the first day and four on the seventh, you know that something is working. Keep on tallying, adding other procedures if necessary, until you get at least two weeks of only one or two arguments a day.

For stubborn arguers, tallying and Time Out won't do the job. On the eighth day, you can start a "Special Problem Chart" (see page 157) or you may wish to revoke all privileges for the rest of any day Johnny argues more than twice. (Such privileges would include TV, use of telephone, play time, everything and anything except reading and chores.) You would, of course, continue to impose Time Out for arguing in addition to the denial of privileges.

Don't back down; if you say it, do it.

What Do I Do When My Kids Argue with Each Other?

Don't try to be judge and jury and don't wait for fur to fly. Intervene as soon as you notice that they are arguing. Send *both* to Time Out. Don't warn. Say: "You're arguing. Go to Time Out immediately." The timer isn't started until both calm down and are quiet.

Kids need to learn to talk things out, to respect each other's rights, and to cooperate. Don't take on and try to solve *their* problem, but don't tolerate it either. At the end of the Time Out session, ask each if he or she wants to continue arguing. A child who hasn't decided or is non-commital gets another Time Out. They'll learn.

Attention Span

WHAT DO I DO WHEN my 4-year-old won't stick with anything for more than five minutes? She's *always* moving from one thing to another!

Do you sometimes feel that you need a butterfly net to capture the attention of your child who flits from one thing to another? You don't; nor is a lasso necessary. You simply need to understand that most normal preschoolers tend to have, as psychologist Jon E. Rolf puts it, "an overabundance of energy and trouble...in one place for a period of time."

Preschool or school age, however, very active children can have amazingly normal concentration *when they are involved in activities of interest to them!* As observed by Mark Twain, "Work consists of whatever a body is obliged to do. Play consists of whatever a body is not obliged to do." and so-called hyperactive children observe that maxim as well as others.

That such children can attend and concentrate when they feel that it's worth the effort is often demonstrated in my office, to the embarrassment of the mother who has just explained that her 3 or 9-year-old "hasn't been able to sit still since he started crawling." Before God and everybody, the child is sitting as if glued to the chair, staring fixedly at a jar of lollipops on the desk. "So! On top of everything else," says the exasperated mother, "he has to use *this* time to make a liar out of me!!"

What the child is *really* proving is that paying attention doesn't make sense without some goal in sight. Children whose attention is easily diverted are often asked to attend to things that are quite boring to them. If they are going to learn anything, however, particularly in the classroom, they have to pay attention and concentrate on assigned tasks. If you want to increase Albert's attention span, you have to make it worth his while to settle down to something for increasingly longer periods of time.

What is a reasonable expectation? If Albert is four or five, about 30 minutes. (To "be able," of course, does not mean he *will* spend 30 minutes at *every* task!) Now how do you help him to do that?

The procedure is fairly simple but has to be done on a consistent basis. Each day, set aside a special time and place for Albert to work at some assignment — build blocks, draw a picture, color in a coloring book, read. The assignment depends upon his age. At the beginning, set a portable timer for a short time, for example, three to five minutes. You can begin while Albert is a toddler, but it's very important not to ask for too much time too soon. Increasing attention span is a very gradual process.

The only thing you need to do during this "study time" is praise Albert for working so hard. If he has a temper tantrum, use Time Out; then return him to the task for another three to five minutes. As Albert learns that he may as well cooperate during this special time, you can then gradually start increasing the "study time" two or more minutes at a time until he reaches the goal of 30 minutes. Keep a daily record of progress, that is, the number of minutes spent on "study time" and the task assigned. Also, note if he had to go to Time Out.

Do *not* nag or be critical. Praise the child for getting started, for trying, for finishing a task. Time Out is sufficient punishment when needed. After the "study time." be sure to spend five or ten minutes with Albert as a reward for the "study time" — read a book, play a game, have a snack. Do this even though he has had to go to Time Out one or more times. The ultimate goal, of course, is for Albert to learn to enjoy reading and to concentrate. "A journey of 1,000 miles begins with one step."

More serious attention span problems are discussed in the "Hyperactivity" chapter.

Parents who want to learn more about attention span and procedures are referred to *Little People* by E. R. Christophersen and *Effective Parents, Responsible Children* by R. Eimers and R. Aitchison. Both are listed in the "More Resources" section at the back of this book.

Bedtime

WHAT DO I DO WHEN my child refuses to stay in bed or cries after being put to bed?

"Beware the Jabberwock...
The jaws that bite, the claws that catch!
Beware the Jub Jub bird and shun
The frumious Bandersnatch!"
Lewis Carroll

"Nonsense," you say? "I'd rather take them all on at once with one hand tied behind my back than deal with my kids at bedtime!" That's understandable. After a day of trying to cope with trials and tribulations and show the wisdom of Solomon, there's only one logical goal in sight: peace and quiet (translated as *get those kids to bed!*)

Take heart; you *can* get the time that you need for yourself. Here is a straightforward procedure which will within a few days (few weeks at the most) help your kids learn that when you say, "Go to bed," you mean, "*Go to bed!*"

...First of all, decide on a healthy and realistic time for bed. Children of different ages, of course, have different bedtimes. Eight p.m. is too early for the 12-year-old and nine p.m. is too late for the two-year-old. The time, however, is *your* decision, not your child's.

...Explain to Elizabeth that you have a fun new way for her to go to bed, with a special time for stories. Tell her the time you've decided upon (show her on the clock if she is just learning to tell time). Be sure to explain each step clearly so *she* understands; give particular attention to the consequences if she does not get ready on time, or if she gets up. Make it clear to her that you love her very much, but when you say it's bedtime, that's it and that the next steps will be automatic.

...Start "quiet time" about 30 minutes before bedtime. Turn off the TV. No roughhousing. Set the timer. Tell Elizabeth that after she gets ready for bed and goes to the bathroom, she may then call you and you will read or talk until "lights out." Reading bedtime stories or fables provides a wonderful opportunity to enrich the lives of both you and your children. This is also a way of encouraging interest in reading. It has great educational value, not to mention the personal closeness and warmth.

You may have been discouraged from reading before because you've felt tired or feared that the reading sessions would be prolonged. Just make a rule that story time begins only when your child is ready for bed. There is *nothing* that you can give that is more important than these few minutes with you. The timer will give the cue that story time is over. You may elect to be flexible with the time, but remember you're trying to teach that the sooner they're ready for bed, the longer story time will be.

...When the timer rings, tuck your child in bed and say goodnight; tomorrow is another day. Don't spoil this time by mentioning anything unpleasant that may have happened during the day. (You took care of *that* at the time it happened, I trust.) If necessary, leave on a low-power "night light" and the door slightly ajar. Some children feel uncomfortable in the dark; respect their wishes in that regard.

...For the first few nights, be *very* vigilant. You have explained the procedure carefully; now it's time to follow through. If Elizabeth gets out of bed, *do not say a word*; just immediately put her back in bed. If you have to carry her, do so gently, with her back to you. (It's very rewarding to be carried with face close to yours because that implies a hug.) If you must lead her, do so from behind — firmly but gently — with your hands on her shoulders. Place — don't throw — your child down on the bed. Do *not* tuck in or cover. Be as matter-of-fact as possible, say nothing, and walk out quietly. Pretend that you're a friendly robot. This will utterly amaze Elizabeth; she may test you a number of times (be consistent!) until she concludes that you're "no fun anymore," so she might as well go to sleep.

Continue doing this each time Elizabeth gets up — as if you're doing a silent dance routine. You may want to count the number of times she gets up to see if she breaks the record of 72 times! Don't give up and don't get discouraged. It is very normal for a child to test you and the new routine.

...When Elizabeth stays in bed without getting up, be sure to praise her in the morning, and — in her hearing — brag to everyone you know. Kids love the publicity!

Once you leave the room after using the bedtime procedure, do not return or respond to anything that Elizabeth says, although it may be very tempting to do so. She may become enraged or make unique vocal noises or scream loud enough to alert the population in China that it's "nighty-nite" at your house. If you yell, "Be *quiet* in there!" or "All right, already. So write a letter to the editor tomorrow!" that will be music to her ears. *Don't do it.* It won't be easy, but pretend that nothing is happening. So long as you have checked to be sure there is nothing *really* wrong, you know that her efforts are only designed to get your attention so she can stay up longer.

If really determined, a child may cry for one or two hours. (The record is five hours!) If you start feeling guilty and give in, you will create more problems for yourself.

There is no evidence that crying is harmful. It is really good exercise for the lungs!

If you feel that you *must* go into the room to check on Elizabeth, *do not speak*. Check out the situation as quickly as possible. Enter and leave the room without saying a word. You probably have a good idea as to which is the "sick" or "temper" cry. Trust yourself.

It is a good idea to keep a record of the length of time that your child cries each night; you should see a dramatic change within a few nights if you follow the procedure. Don't let relatives convince you that you are "ruining her psyche." *They* don't have to live with the problem. Be sure, though, to praise Elizabeth in the morning for her progress; for example, crying less last night than the night before.

It would be nice if kids dropped off to sleep the moment that lights are turned off, but it doesn't happen that way, and it is even harder when they share a room. The 30-minute quiet time procedure should help unwind them. Tell them that if they have anything to say, they may whisper; but if *you* hear any talking, they will *both* lose some special privilege for the next day. It might be television, for example, or going to bed 15 or 30 minutes earlier the next evening. Be sure that you follow through. It's the follow-through that's critically important — and the most convincing to your kids.

If any of these problems persist beyond two weeks, you may wish to set up the Special Problem Chart system for each child ("Special Problems" chapter).

© Masters Agency, Capitola, CA

"Are you SURE you put her to bed?"

Bedwetting

WHAT DO I DO WHEN my eight-year-old son continues to wet the bed?

> "*PATIENCE n. A minor form of despair, disguised as a virtue.*"
>
> Ambrose Bierce, *The Devil's Dictionary*

You're beginning to lose patience. It's embarrassing when Fido is housebroken and Jerry isn't. Sometimes, given a choice of family secrets, you'd probably prefer to have had an uncle who was hanged as a horse thief!

If it's any consolation, about one in every ten kids at age ten has this problem. The technical term is *enuresis*, and it is generally considered "a problem" for children beyond three or four years of age.

Sometimes kids who have been toilet trained start bedwetting, and there are a number of reasons why that might happen. There may be different reasons for different children. Usually some change or major upheaval in the child's life is involved — moving to a new home, loss of a friend or relative, divorce of parents. When that happens, give time a chance to heal the emotional hurt before intervening more directly. Bedwetting, however, is a problem that needs to be addressed if it persists beyond a week or two.

One approach that can be tried is to restrict the intake of fluids for an hour or two before Jerry goes to bed. Also, a urine-alarm (bell and pad) apparatus can be purchased through mail-order catalogues and large department stores.

See Your Pediatrician

Some kids have smaller functional bladder capacities than others. After a physical examination, your pediatrician may make some recommendations to help increase capacity if that's the problem.

Dietary restrictions are effective in a small number of cases. Sometimes Imipramine (Tofranil) is prescribed and has been effective in 30 to 60 percent of cases and some improvement noted in another 10 to 20 percent. As with most medications, however, the relapse rate is high when the drug is discontinued (about two-thirds of those who stop taking medication).

Your doctor may refer you to a mental health specialist, who will then evaluate Jerry's situation for complicating factors before making specific recommendations. "Traditional" psychotherapy, however, does not seem to be effective, according to the few studies that have been done.

The Special Problem Chart

The Special Problem Chart (see page 157) is often effective when nothing else works. I must admit I don't know why. It may be that if bedwetting does reflect a psychological problem (perhaps Jerry feels neglected or insecure), this chart helps you remember to pay more attention to him in positive ways and stop nagging. If bedwetting represents a power struggle between you and Jerry, this system breaks the need to continue that struggle. When Jerry is involved in the problem solving process, he has a real interest in stopping the bedwetting. (These are only conjectures, of course.)

To use the Special Problem Chart, call a "conference" with Jerry. What would he like to earn? It could be a trip to the zoo, going out on the town for lunch, a game, or toy. This is really gratifying to kids because they are now getting some power to get what they want through their own efforts and don't have to wait for you to feel generous. It's important that you give no special treats (except when designated on the chart) while the contract is in force.

Each morning Jerry has a dry bed, paste a star or sticker with fanfare and plenty of praise on the day block. If there is an "accident," simply express sympathy and say that tomorrow is another day. Jerry must then strip the bed, take the bedclothes to the laundry room, put them through the washer and dryer (if available), and remake the bed. You don't need to "hang him from the yardarm" — undoing the damage is punishment enough. Best to require it be done before going to school; at least *immediately* upon coming home from school, before play or TV.

Exactly what Jerry has to do depends upon his age, of course, More should be required of the nine-year-old than of the six-year-old, who may require help from you to strip and remake the bed.

Don't nag or scold. Jerry is as perplexed and upset about this as you are, poor guy! Talk in terms of "accident" rather than intent. It is a good idea to cover the mattress with a protective cover so that no odor permeates the room. (It is, strangely enough, even possible that the odor may *maintain* the bedwetting!) If nothing else, it is very unpleasant for everyone and a constant reminder that *someone* in this house wets the bed!

It may take four or five days for Jerry to earn stars for the first two blocks on the chart. Don't be discouraging or impatient. Remember, also, to provide a special treat on those days marked "treat" on the chart. It's a good idea to do something that the whole family can enjoy, for example, a favorite cake or pie, a special game or outing. That helps the family get invested in Jerry's progress — sort of like setting up a cheering section for the home team!

Interested in a ''high-tech'' approach? Dr. Kurt Mahoney, a developmental psychologist, has created the ''Wet-Alert System.'' Information: Wet Control Systems, 2600 East Southern Avenue, Suite C-2, Tempe, AZ 85282.

> ***The road to success is always under construction.***

"Bugs Me"

WHAT DO I DO WHEN there are so many problems I don't know where to start?

When problems appear to be overwhelming, and the trials of Job start looking like a piece of cake, one of the ways to start sorting out who is doing what to whom is to use the ''Bugs Me'' Chart, developed at Teaching Research Infant & Child Center in Monmouth, Oregon.

This simple procedure sometimes has ''wondrous'' effects. It helps you focus in on specific problems, and the child gets feedback about his or her behavior in a more palatable way than the customary nagging or screaming.

Most children like this approach and make a point of seeking out the Chart. Some parents continue using this simple feedback system for a while — just to keep *themselves* in line and to remind themselves to appreciate some of the *good* things that their kids do! You may be amazed at how great your children really are!

The "Bugs Me" Chart

This analysis sheet is often used during the initial stage of clinical evaluation of problems, particularly when the parent gives a whole "litany" of complaints. It is useful for any age child, but especially for those who read and are under age 16. A sample chart appears at the end of this chapter.

For a period of 10 to 14 days, list your child's irritating behaviors on the "Bugs Me" side of the page, and check off your responses to those behaviors. It is important that you make notations *at the time of the incident.* Recalling events at the end of the day is *not* acceptable because memories are not reliable.

On the "Pleases Me" side, list those behaviors that are too often ignored, for example, bringing in the groceries, cleaning the bedroom without being asked, not arguing all day. That kid has to do *something* right during the course of the day! Usually, they're the things that you take for granted.

With or without a prior announcement, display the chart on the refrigerator or bulletin board where it is readily available for writing and viewing and see what happens! You may start seeing some changes that you never expected. You may also learn something about yourself. This is one of the best procedures that I have found to help a parent gain some insight into his or her own behavior. Very often, for example, a parent will say: "I hadn't realized how much I nagged!" or "He isn't so bad after all. He pretended that he wasn't interested, but *I* saw him reading the chart." or "Maybe I *did* over-react a little when she spilled the jam. I guess I could have just let her clean up the mess instead of doing it myself and yelling that she was clumsy."

I really don't know why this chart works when it does. One of its great advantages is that it really starts to involve the child in working out problems and becoming more sensitive to what s/he is doing. It also provides visual proof to the child that the parent cares enough to expend the energy to do this task and, further, is willing to be honest about having yelled or screamed. Kids keep a very sharp eye on the "Pleases Me" side and read those notes carefully; so be sure to list as much as you can on *that* side! (It seems that the more you list, the more you get.)

Some parents, however, list four or more "Bugs Me" incidents for each "Pleases Me" event. That is a cue that the situation is more complex than simple mismanagement of the child, and suggests the need for an extensive evaluation of the family, and perhaps some skilled counseling. Those parents who "forget" to list behaviors on the chart also give a strong message that there are other problems on the agenda — marital or personal.

Using the Information From the "Bugs Me" Chart

The purpose of the "Bugs Me" Chart is to start moving the family toward more effective and positive interactions, to give the parents some sense of being in control and some assurance about their child. It may seem to be somewhat simplistic. It is not. When used appropriately, it can have a lot of power.

The chart helps to clarify what behavior(s) appear(s) to be the most troublesome and should be targeted for special attention. For example, it may become the focus of a Special Problem Chart (page 157), or the parent may have to learn new ways to discipline and remember to praise more.

If you're confused about what to do with the information on the chart, consult a mental health specialist, school counselor, or other professional who can help you focus and work out a program (see "More Resources").

Incidentally, although I don't know of any research to support the idea, some families develop a strong "sharing" style by developing a "Bugs Me" chart for the *children* to use in response to *parent* behavior! You might find that fun — and instructive — to try at your house!

"Bugs Me Chart" developed and designed by Dr. Bud Fredericks, Dr. David Grove, Dixie McKinley, and Nancy Johnson of Teaching Research Infant & Child Center, Monmouth, Oregon 97361.

CHILD'S NAME: ____________ WEEK OF: ____________

WHAT PLEASES ME	DAYS	WHAT BUGS ME	WHAT I DID: IGNORED	SHOUTED	SENT OUT OF ROOM	PUNISHED	OTHER (DESCRIBE)
	MON						
	TUES						
	WED						
	THURS						
	FRI						
	SAT						
	SUN						

Teaching Research, Monmouth, Oregon

Cars and Kids

WHAT DO I DO WHEN my children misbehave while riding in the car?

"Insanity is hereditary," warned Sam Levenson. "You can get it from your children," He might have added, "particularly when they are the passengers and you are the driver!"

For a while, perhaps, the "vanilla wafer" approach seems to work. With a box of cookies as standard equipment in the glove compartment, when Henrietta whines, you stuff a cookie in her mouth. Blessed silence then reigns during the chomping time — but, alas, it's all too brief. You now have a *fat,* whiney kid!

Problems are then compounded when there's more than one child in the car. It's really easy, then, to become distracted and angry when Henry joins Henrietta to fuss, cry, scream, kick, argue, fight, stand, or climb around. This is not your idea of a Sunday drive? It's really more serious than that, of course. You have to bring this situation under control; automobile related accidents are a leading cause of death and serious injury and disability in young children.

Start Early!

Start training for car riding when you have a newborn. One of the best investments you can make is to purchase an approved infant carrier, *which should be used in bringing your infant home from the hospital.* Holding the baby in your arms is extremely risky, and is against the law in most states. In a 30 mph crash, your child can be thrown forward with a force equal to 30 times the child's own weight. If you are wearing a safety belt, your child can be torn from your arms and hurled into the dash or windshield. If you are *not* wearing a restraint, both of you may be thrust forward, and your child may be crushed between you and the dash or steering wheel. Those are the grim facts.

If you're fortunate, you may live in one of the 41 states that *requires* restraints for child passengers. A child who grows up using a safety seat accepts it as normal — especially if the parent is wearing a seat belt — and behavioral problems in the car are avoided to a great extent, in addition to protecting the child's life.

Some infant carriers can be converted to child safety seats that can be used by toddlers until they're old enough to wear regular safety belts. Lap belts can be introduced when Henrietta is four or five and weighs about 40 pounds. A car bed, hook-type seat, or light weight plastic child feeder seat used in the home are *not* adequate protection. Look for the label "dynamically tested" before making a purchase.

Some communities have rental or recycling programs where you can rent an infant or child safety seat for a short period of time, instead of buying one. Contact your local highway safety or health department to learn if such a program exists in your area.

The stakes are high. Without a restraint, a child traffic victim may suffer severe head and abdominal injuries and broken bones. Hospital emergency staff witness all too many cases in which children are stabbed by door handles, heads are smashed against windows, and small bodies are hurled around inside cars or thrown from cars like missiles.

What If My Child Resists Using a Safety Seat or Lap Belt?

How Henrietta responds will depend a lot on your approach. Be matter-of-fact when you are introducing a car seat or lap belt for the first time. Do not imply that she has a choice, for example, by asking, "Don't you think that it'll be fun to sit in this?" Simply state that this will be used from now on and point out some of the features.

Each time, until Henrietta consistently observes the rules, describe how you want her to behave, "I want you to sit and talk quietly and not to annoy anyone with hands or feet." Ask her to repeat back what is expected. For the very young child, keep it simple. You might ask, "How are you supposed to sit?" "What are you to do with your hands and feet?" "What are you to do when you want something?" "If I say, 'no,' what will you do?"

Driving with your child in the car is a great opportunity for conversation, and a good time to help educate her about the world. Point out things that may be very familiar to you but not to Henrietta: the post office, fire hydrants, trees, flowers, the police station. Ask questions to find out what she already knows, "There's a fire hydrant. Why do you think it's there? It's red. Why isn't it blue or yellow?"

If Henrietta even *begins* to try to release the seat belt or climb out of the car seat, immediately and firmly tell her, "No!" and give one (only) gentle-but-firm slap on the hand.

If you have a persistent problem with your child, you might plan to take short training trips.

For longer trips, provide several toys that are associated with quiet play and let Henrietta have only one toy at a time. You might even have special toys that are provided only in the car. Remember that the attention span of young children is very short, and it is difficult for them to remain occupied for more than a few minutes at a time.

Children Over Five

Insist that your children use seat belts and don't turn on the ignition until they do. For a while, until they are consistently good passengers, review the rules for car riding before starting the car. Be very specific. Tell them that they are expected to sit quietly, converse pleasantly, that there will be no hitting, kicking, or arguing, that you will immediately turn the car and go home if there are problems. If returning home is not possible, make certain that any offender pays the Time Out penalty when you *do* get home.

If you have a problem while driving, simply pull the car over to the side of the road and sit quietly until everyone calms down. No lectures or yelling. And no one-handed, one-eyed driving while you administer discipline! Safety first!

Sometimes children get very possessive about sitting in the front seat. Have them take turns. If necessary, provide a card or notebook, so Henry and Henrietta can keep their own record of whose turn it is to sit in the front seat.

Make riding in the car a pleasant experience whether the trip is short or long. Praise your children for behaving nicely, converse with them, expand their horizons, share their fun, and above all *travel safely!*

For more information about safety seats, ask for the pamphlet, "Child Restraint Systems for Your Automobile" (Department of Transportation, National Highway Traffic Safety Administration) from your local highway safety or health department. Some of this material was adapted from the book, *Little People* by E. R. Christophersen.

Child Abuse

WHAT DO I DO WHEN I feel that I am losing my self-control with my children? I have to be very careful because I had been abused. I don't want to give the same kinds of memories to my kids. Sometimes I'm afraid — for myself, for my children.

"Take us the foxes, the little foxes, that spoil the vines; for our vines have tender grapes."
Song of Solomon

It's all too easy to lose control. Given a past that builds anger and feelings of deprivation, you seldom feel really relaxed — at peace with yourself. The lifeline of control is fragile and apt to be easily snapped when frustrations pile up — the children are demanding and unruly; there are financial and marital problems; you feel lonely and isolated. Where can you turn? What can you do? Is there anyone out there?

Your concern for yourself and your children is critically important. That is what can provide the energy and motivation to do what you have to do — seek help. *You* know what's wrong. Why can't you seem to help yourself? You can't because we all have tunnel vision in regard to ourselves and our problems, particularly when our emotions are involved. Unwittingly, you may expect your child to fill the void of loneliness, to satisfy all your unfulfilled needs, to comfort. Children are incapable of doing all of that. Without wanting to, you may unleash your long-smoldering anger against your children.

Those who have suffered abuse or neglect early in their lives carry the scars into adulthood. Too often, they live with distrust, fear of contact with others, inability to enjoy life, self-hatred, depression, unable to love or be loved. If that has been your life, you may feel you are always an observer standing on the sidelines watching the parade go by. If you are not to pass on the heritage of abuse, you must come to terms with what was and what *can* be.

How do you start to set your life in order? How do you take on the little foxes that spoil the tender vines?

...*Seek out a parent group*. Parents Anonymous, for example, was founded by a former abusing mother, Jolly K., who knew the tormented feelings of isolation, anger, and despair. The group provides a safe place for those who have similar problems and feelings to talk about frustrations and how these affect relationships with others, to learn about child rearing and behavior, and how to solve day-to-day problems.

...*Call the local Health Department* and ask what services are available for counseling and if there are Crisis Nurseries and Drop-off Centers to provide 24-hour emergency short-term care. Find out what low-cost centers for child care may be available. You need a break from the task of caring for your children on some kind of regular basis.

...*Don't hesitate to use Hotline Telephone Services* if you need support in a crisis situation or to ask for referral to an agency offering counseling or advice for special kinds of problems.

...*Look for Parent Training groups* to learn about child rearing and what to expect as your children go through various stages of development. Seek information from the school counselor or the local "Y" or community college.

...*Contact the Women's Crisis Service* or the minister of your church or the state Children's Services Division for assistance if you feel fearful and need assistance.

...*Develop special interests* of your own. See if you can make arrangements with friends and neighbors to provide child care for a few hours each week. For example, you can take care of their children for three hours each week, and they take care of your children for the same amount of time. Everyone needs a break from monotonous routines. Everyone needs playtime.

...*Decide not to use force* in your family. Beside finding resources, you must make a conscious decision for yourself and your family that force will not be used in any way against anyone. Once you make it a rule that in *your* family there will be no violence, do not let anyone push anyone around — including you. Unfortunately, a lot of people think that it's okay to lash out and hit someone if the other person is being unreasonable. (Even courts have been known to excuse such behavior, calling the reason for abuse "extenuating circumstances.") There is *no excuse* for physical or verbal abuse. There are other ways to deal with frustrations.

...*Learn to negotiate* when there are problems or conflicts to be handled. It is unrealistic to think that there will be no conflict between husband and wife, parent and child, child and child. Conflicts are a part of family life — just as they are a part of life in general. The point is: how are they settled? Your spouse wants to stay home and watch TV, and you want to go out. Your kids want to play with the same toy at the same time, or one wants to play rock 'n roll and the other wants to play a Bach record. Your husband comes home with a six-pack, and the budget is tight. Resolve those irritations by negotiation. There are things you want, and things others want from you. Learn to make agreements: If I do things that please you, I would like you to do things that please me. Learn to assert yourself; read books, take courses, join groups that will teach you.

...*Talk about what is bugging you*, and encourage the other family members to learn to say what is bugging them. Everybody has gripes and wants to be heard. Once the issues are out in the open so that they can be discussed, you can then try to work things out. You can call it confrontation if you like, but it's confrontation without physical or verbal abuse. Don't harbor grievances and let them fester until you can't stand it any more and explode.

...*Learn constructive methods to discipline* your children. Hitting, spanking, yelling and other harsh disciplines teach children that violence is an acceptable way to deal with problems and frustrations. They also come to believe that those who love bring pain, so pain must, then, be a part of love. ("Why do I think he doesn't love me any more?" says the depressed young woman. "He hasn't beaten me lately!") Plaster your home with signs to remind you that violence in our society begins in the home, and that physical punishment trains the youngster to use violence. That cannot be overemphasized.

...*Decide family roles and responsibilities by competencies* — who knows how to do what — rather than by age or sex. The idea that the man *must* be the "head of the family" who makes all the decisions only serves to promote a master-slave relationship and contributes to incidents of wife battering. A marriage license is a legal and personal commitment. It does not give one person the right to possess, control, or dominate another. That is a cancerous perception that is only too pervasive in our society. A marriage is a *partnership* wherein both adults should have *equal* status and *cooperate* in resolving issues and delegating responsibilities. Some people are more competent at doing some things than are others. If the wife is particularly competent in handling financial matters, she would be the logical person to assume that responsibility; the husband need not feel that his "masculinity," in some strange way, is being threatened.

...*Don't hesitate to seek counseling* if there are differences of opinion that cannot be resolved and arguments and discontents escalate. Go even if your spouse won't go with you. *Someone* has to decide to do the sensible thing. The buck has to stop somewhere.

The unfortunate reality is that we have permitted a violent society to develop. "Violence is...built into the very fabric of American society and into the personal beliefs, values, and behavioral scripts of most of our population," observes sociologist Dr. M. A. Straus.

You *can* help make a difference — in the most important place you know — your family. To understand violence, you must understand that it begins in the home with how we treat our infants and children. It is also modeled by adults in the family and how they treat each other. It has been noted that "violence between members of the same family occurs more often than it does between any other individuals or any other setting except wars and riots.''

Let your family be one step toward changing that terrible statistic.

Chores and Allowance

WHAT DO I DO WHEN my kids won't do their chores?

''Who, me? Take out the garbage? Wash the dishes? Set the table? Clean my room? And why do I have to make my bed? It only gets messed up every night anyway! Nobody ever *sees* it! Seems like an awful waste of energy! *You* didn't want a kid! *You* wanted slave labor!! All I do around here is work, Work, WORK!''

Hah! And yesterday you almost fainted when this complainer actually hung up her jacket after three weeks of your nagging about neatness. Oh, for the good old days when kids knew what it was to work — and mind their folks. Why, when you were her age, you had a paper route and milked the cows before breakfast and *then* walked 10 miles to school! (Well, you would have if you'd had to. *You* can't help it if you grew up in Brooklyn.) All you're asking for is a little cooperation. Is that too much to ask in return for bed and board and the weekly allowance? "Now be honest. Is that unreasonable?!" you ask.

The answer is "No," of course, But it would be unreasonable if you asked your youngster to *whistle* while she worked! That *would* be going a bit too far. There is, however, (forgive me, feline lovers) more than one way to skin a cat. One of the best ways is to develop an incentive system. Make Sue an offer she can't refuse. It can do wonderful things for her and for you.

So, what's the big deal? In a special incentive system, Sue *earns* privileges and/or allowance. It is very specific. There are things that you want done, and there are things that she wants. It is an exchange, similar to labor-management bargaining. So why should you have to do that? You do that because she is *not* doing what you want her to do, and because you're expending too much energy for too little return. Further, this is one of the best ways to teach her to be responsible, independent, self-sufficient, and to cooperate. Try it. You'll like it, if you apply it consistently in the manner described below. (That's an old writer trick to keep you reading!)

First of all, you have to put everything into writing. "But *why?*" you ask. "When I say, 'Do the dishes!' that kid should *know* that means wash, dry, no smudges, scour the pans, stack neatly into cupboard, wipe off the sink, and leave dishrag neatly folded." Sue *may* know it, but if she's not doing it, you can eliminate misunderstanding by writing out a "job description." *Don't assume anything!* Your employer doesn't (or shouldn't). Any good organization develops job descriptions for employees. It's best not to take things for granted.

Make this a cooperative project, incidentally. You and Sue should agree on the reasonableness of the jobs, and on the meaning of terms such as "neat" and "clean." She needs to know exactly what you expect of her.

Does that mean that you have to write out a job description each week? When would you have time for anything else? No, write the description for each job once on a card to be posted where it can be conveniently read when needed: on the door in the bathroom or bedroom, or on the refrigerator or bulletin board in the kitchen. You will also be using a "chore chart," and on that, you can just use a few words to label each job.

Below is an example of a good job description, clear and explicit, so the child knows what is expected (from Hall, et al., 1972):

MAKE BED — Covers straight, neat and smooth. Sheets not visible. Pillows covered, blankets folded, no other items on bed.
CLOTHES HUNG — Clothes hung straight on hangers in closet, no hangers on closet doors.

NEAT ROOM — Top of dresser neat, articles arranged symmetrically, no powder spilled, books on desk, no items on floor.
SWEEP FLOOR — No evidence of dust.
STRAIGHTEN AND DUST LIVING ROOM — Magazines on shelves, table cleaned, books in place, no dust on furniture.
KITCHEN DUTIES — Dry dishes, dishes in cupboard, towel on rack, wipe off counters.
BATHROOM DUTIES — Towel on rack, soap in soap dish, tub and lavatory cleaned with scouring powder and dried.
ODD JOBS — To be assigned as needed, for example, cleaning out car, sweeping off porch, weeding, bringing in and putting away groceries, etc.
IMPORTANT NOTE — Many requests will be made that will earn no points. These will be done because they have to be done. If you want to earn allowances and privileges, you will do them when requested.

Allowances? Who Said Anything About Allowances?

I don't happen to believe a child should be *given* money just for eating and sleeping. Allowances should be earned by completing assigned responsibilities. Every family member earns his/her way.

How much allowance should you pay? That depends on the age of your child and what expenses the allowance is supposed to cover. The 6-year-old, for example, may earn 25 or 50 cents a week. Whatever candy or gum she wants, then, she has to buy for herself. You will not provide that anymore. The 11-year-old may like to go bowling or to the show or to the electronic game arcade. With an earned allowance, he now has to make choices as to how he will spend his well-deserved money. One of the advantages of this system is that you no longer have to make such decisions or give "permission."

This approach can save you money, too. With an earned allowance your child gets *only* what s/he works for. You no longer dole out money for spontaneous requests to go skating or to buy a game or record. If Sue doesn't have the money, there is no decision to make!

Do you mean that I should let my kid squander money? Let *her* make these decisions? Well, that may be difficult, but for maximum learning, Sue should be permitted to spend that hard-earned allowance as she will. Expect splurges for a while; she may not save any part of it and may buy things that you think are a ghastly waste of money. Hold your tongue, and let her learn. If you are critical, she may get defensive, splurging just to *prove* that she has the right to make some decisions for herself. (How else are you going to counter the "I've got to be me" wail?)

Don't use the allowance as a club. Once you make a deal, follow through. Sue must know that she will get what is earned no matter how you feel. After all, how would you like it if your paycheck — or any part of it — depended upon the mood of the payroll clerk or your supervisor?

Points and Chores

You and Sue decided together what chores had to be done and how much allowance could be earned. *Now* you have to assign points to each chore. The amount of allowance she may earn helps determine how many points need to be distributed. To make the system simple, let each penny of allowance represent one point. An allowance of $4 a week would mean that 400 points would be distributed among the chores. How many do you assign to each chore? You will find that Sue will be much more enthusiastic about doing those chores that get the most points, *so* assign the most points to the most disliked chores. The rationale for that is that "a little bit of sugar helps the medicine go down!"

List the chores and assign the points, then transfer these to the chart, as demonstrated in the next column.

Chore	Points	Days	Total Points
Make Bed	5	Mon. thru Sun.	35
Clothes Hung	5	Mon. thru Sun.	35
Neat Room	5	Mon. thru Sun.	35
Clean Living Room	10	Mon. - Wed. - Fri.	30
Kitchen Duties	20	Mon. thru Sun.	140
Clean Bathroom	20	Mon. - Wed. - Fri.	60
Feed Cat	5	Mon. thru Sun.	35
Yardwork	30	Saturday	30
			Total: 400 points ($4)

You're Not Through Yet

If you really want to build more power into this system, save money, and provide more learning for your child, now is the time to negotiate for a fairly long-term goal. You will find that on the "Treasure" and "Target" charts. The allowance is fairly short-term in that it is paid on a weekly basis. (Do *not* plan to pay on a monthly basis even though *you* may get a check only once a month. That is far too long for most kids. To them a week is "forever," and a month is an eternity!)

_______________'S CHART TO TREASURE

JOBS	POINTS	MON.	TUES.	WED.	THUR.	FRI.	SAT.	SUN.	SUB-TOTALS

TOTAL:

SPECIAL TREASURE IS _______________.

COST OF TREASURE IS __________. SO FAR

__________ HAS BEEN EARNED.

NEEDED STILL IS __________.

WHAT DO I DO WHEN...? © 1983 by Juliet V. Allen.
Impact Publishers, P. O. Box 1094, San Luis Obispo, CA 93406.

Most allowances cover basic needs and treats, and children (and teenagers) often ask for other things that they cannot afford to buy or would take forever to save from an allowance.

Instead of buying the toy — or record or book or special shirt or shoes or bicycle or game or trip to the zoo or baseball game — let Sue "earn" the desired object or privilege. You will agree to purchase the item when your budget — and her work performance — allows. The way this works is through negotiation. Sue decides what she wants, a record for example, as the "special treasure." You, then, take a look at your budget and decide when you can afford to purchase that item (or event if it is a trip to the zoo or a special restaurant). That determines the "cost" to Sue.

If you can purchase Sue's special treasure in two weeks, and her maximum possible weekly earnings are 400 points, then her "cost" is 800 points (2 weeks x 400 weekly points). If you can purchase the record in six weeks, the "cost" to her is 2400 points (6 weeks x 400 weekly points). It is to Sue's advantage, then, to do *all* of her jobs to your satisfaction if she wants to earn her "target" within the scheduled time frame. It may take her longer, of course, but that's *her* decision.

Another possibility is that Sue may even want to speed up the process by earning extra points at home on bonus jobs (which can only be earned after the regular jobs are done) or may earn money elsewhere to contribute to the purchase. Many creative possibilities exist with this basically simple system.

With this approach, Sue can earn a weekly allowance and also work for the "wouldn't it be nice to have" things. This is a real cooperative effort, in which Sue has the freedom and privilege of selecting a personal special goal, and consideration is given to the family's budget. She can then work for it at her own pace by completing tasks which need to be done. And Sam can no longer say: "You play favorites! Sue gets everything. I get nothin'!" Everyone gets what he or she is willing to work for, and it's an equal opportunity situation. Sam is fully responsible for achieving his goal himself! If he doesn't work consistently, it may take him eight or ten weeks to earn something that could have been earned in six weeks — that's his choice, not yours.

If the goal is very expensive and may take six months to earn, it is a good idea to break it down into parts. For example, if Sue wants a bicycle in January and can't earn it until June, get a picture of a bicycle and each week paste up a part of the bicycle that has been earned. That's the "jigsaw puzzle" approach.

Incidentally, just as you can change your mind about long-term goals for yourself, always permit your child to

NAME: ______________________ WEEK OF: ______________________

CHORES:	POINTS	SUN	MON	TUES	WED	THURS	FRI	SAT	TOTAL POINTS

TOTAL: ______

TARGET:

COST:

ALMOST ON TARGET

HALF WAY THERE

GOOD START!

BALANCE FROM LAST WEEK: ______

THIS WEEKS EARNINGS: ______

BALANCE: ______

POINTS NEEDED: ______

WHAT DO I DO WHEN...? © 1983 by Juliet V. Allen
Impact Publishers, P. O. Box 1094, San Luis Obispo, CA 93406.

change his/her mind about the special goal. Be willing to renegotiate.

The Follow-Through

Okay, the chart is now made out and posted on the refrigerator or bulletin board. You have also written out the job descriptions, and Sue knows what she has to do to get what she wants.

Your follow-through is critical. It is here that your system will either succeed or fail. Remember that you are not only doing this to help Sue become more cooperative and responsible, but it is also to your advantage to have less work to do and to feel more organized about sharing the household chores.

Most kids like this approach because it feels good to know exactly what you want from them on a daily basis. They can get what they want — allowance, free time — without having to beg or plead for it. It also helps you remember to pay attention to what they *have* done. Your appreciation is really the most important part of all of this. If you "forget" to follow through, they will think that this is not important to you. If you don't care, why should they? Granted, it is inconvenient; and it would be nice if kids just did what they were told to do. Just remember that the chart and your check-up are problem solving approaches that are only temporary.

Establish a check-up time for each job. For example, you may want Sue to make the bed before she has breakfast. Until she gets into the habit of making the bed routinely, *you have to check on a daily basis* before breakfast is served. When she starts doing this satisfactorily for two weeks, for example, you can simply give the points and check the job once or twice a week. Of course, if your child starts slipping on the job, you'll have to go back to the daily check again for awhile.

At the check-up you will either be satisfied that the job has been well done (for example, bed made neatly and clothes picked up as directed) and give the assigned points, or — and this is important — you will immediately call Sue to return to complete the job. (Remember, though, that the 7-year-old won't have the efficiency and expertise of the 13-year-old and may require some help from you. Do not, however, accept a sloppy or half-done job.) Tell her, "Call me when you've finished the job." She has to stay with it until the job is finished. All privileges (telephone, TV, outings, free time) are suspended until you are satisfied. (Again, be sure that your expectations do not exceed your child's abilities. This is not a plan to set her up for failure, but is designed to teach how to be a good worker.)

There's another part to this which should help you remember that you don't have to nag anymore. When you have to call Sue back to do the job satisfactorily, only one-half of the designated points can be earned for this chore today. If you have to recall her a second time because the job *still* is not satisfactory, *no* points are given for the chore. Nevertheless, Sue must stay with it — and can't do anything else — until you are satisfied. You will have to go that extra mile only for the most stubborn child, who may be really testing you and your commitment to this system. Try not to be upset. Remember that it's your child's problem, not yours.

Most kids may slip up for a few days, but if you follow through, they quickly learn that it's less of a hassle to do the job right in the first place. Usually, most kids work like beavers during the first week, and then start testing you during the second or third weeks — so be forewarned!

You can start using a chore chart quite early. Even three and four-year-old children love to earn stars and like to have their own charts, particularly when they see that older brothers and sisters have charts. They would then earn their privileges by doing very simple chores, such as picking up toys or emptying waste baskets. Once they learn the value of money, of course, you can design a point system. Remember, though, that rank has its privileges. The older kids do more, but they also get more.

Will Sue be "on a chart" until she leaves home? No. This is just a way to teach her to be cooperative and self-sufficient. When she is consistently earning at least 80% ($3.20 of a maximum allowance of $4, for example), you can simply start phasing out the chart and paying the regular allowance. If your child gets slack, it's simple enough to re-institute the chart and start again. Some kids need more help than others.

When the family goes on vacation, and your child can't do the chores, pay the allowance for the day or period of time that she is absent. Don't penalize Sue for something that is beyond her control.

To Summarize (Play it again, Sam)

...At a conference with your child or teenager, list the chores. Write the job descriptions as specifically and clearly as you can. Agree on the meaning of each description so the child knows what s/he must do. Post the descriptions in a convenient place.

...Agree upon the payoff. There has to be something in this for both of you, or else why should your child "buy in?" Use stars for young children, a point system later. Children age three to five love to earn stars — until they discover that a star is only a star; then you have to work out a more tangible system. For the older child, decide what allowance is to be paid and allot the points to the various jobs at the rate of one penny a point. Give the most points to the most tedious job. (Why do you think garbage collectors are paid over $20,000 a year?!) If you can't afford to pay an allowance, make daily and weekend privileges (TV, use of telephone, free time, radio, record player) available upon completion of all jobs to your satisfaction. For example, "After you earn your points for doing the dishes and feeding the cat, you may see TV and use the telephone." or "If you earn all of your points for making your bed and doing the dishes for the next five days, you can invite Karen to spend the night Saturday."

...Work out the Special Target (the long term goal) with your child or teenager and figure out the "cost" as described. Try to do this even when you can't afford to pay a weekly allowance. As long as the goal is legal and moral, don't argue with your kid about taste or choice. You may prefer that s/he ask for a recording of Bach Variations rather than the latest form of "rock variations," but s/he'll work a lot harder for something s/he wants.

...Explain the check-up times and points for each job and the penalties for a job half-done or poorly done. For example,

the first call-back earns only one-half of the points.
the second call-back means that no points are earned, nothing else can be done until you are satisfied with the job.

Never take away points already earned. That is disheartening and discouraging.

...Start out by checking the jobs every day until your child is consistent in following through for several weeks, then you can start spot-checking, unless, of course, performance deteriorates. Return, then, to the daily checkup. When your child or teenager is consistently earning 80 percent or more of the total weekly points for a period of about three months, you can phase out the chart, while continuing the allowance, with the understanding that it can always be re-introduced if performance falls below standards.

...At some point (probably the third or fourth week), your child may decide to test the system and your commitment, perhaps by getting lax or pretending that the privileges and allowances are meaningless. When that happens, don't nag. Be patient. Just say, "Well, that's your decision. No chores, no points; no points, no allowance (or privileges)."

The advantage of this system is that you can design it to meet the needs and special situation of your child and family. The key is to be consistent — and *follow through*.

If you do have any problem with the system, check with a behavioral specialist who can help you fine-tune it. One or two conferences should do it, unless there are other problems or complexities in your family situation.

Job description reference:

R. V. Hall, S. Axelrod, L. Tyler, E. Crief, F. C. Jones and R.

Robertson, *Journal of Applied Behavior Analysis*, "Modification of behavior problems in the home with a parent as observer and experimenter." 5:1, 53-64, 1972.

"*I told him I lost the car keys in the grass.*"

© Masters Agency, Capitola, CA

WHAT DO I DO WHEN my baby cries a lot? I know a lot about washing diapers and making formulas, but I feel helpless when she cries. How do I deal with *that*?

The day finally comes. Your bundle of joy arrives. You have decorated the room with blue bunnies on the wallpaper, blue blankets, and blue crib. The baby turns out to be a girl. That's wonderful: the blue matches her eyes! But now you find that the crib is for crying, the blanket is for drooling, there's no end to washing diapers, and you can't remember the last time you had a good night's sleep. "Oh Mary Ann, I love you, but...!"

You were told a lot about how to tend to the physical needs of your infant, but no one told you about the crying. You wouldn't really mind all the other chores — if only you knew what to do when the *crying* goes on and on?

Well, don't start thinking that you have no talent as a parent. And try to remember that Mary Ann is an innocent infant, not a tyrant in baby clothing! You will be able to do something about your baby's crying soon. It is possible to dramatically reduce the amount and intensity of that crying by learning a very simple procedure.

The first hurdle that you have to jump is to accept the fact that babies do cry, and some cry more than others, and there's no point in getting upset over that. Crying is good for them and exercises their lungs, and is their way of letting others know that something is needed — food, a diaper change, to be burped or caressed. There is very little that you can do for the first few weeks because your new infant either sleeps or cries and needs to do both of these. Crying is *not* a devious plot to frustrate parents or a sign of rejection saying that your infant wants to trade you in for a new and different family or that you are a failure as a mother.

You are not completely helpless, however. There is something that you can do starting about the sixth to the eighth week when your infant enters the cooing stage. You will notice a period of transition from sound sleep to crying. Mary Ann awakens, looks around, coos, and *then* starts to cry. Learn to listen for the cooing which is the signal to enter the room. That will teach MaryAnn that you like cooing. Don't wait for the crying to start. If she decides that you make tracks only when she cries, she will probably learn to become an expert at crying. She's only trying to please and is learning what works. This approach won't solve all crying, but will help you bridge those three to four months that it takes Mary Ann to outgrow the need to cry.

Learn to ignore your infant's fussiness when it is time to sleep. Most babies cry themselves to sleep. Just tuck in a soft blanket or furry toy with Mary Ann, assure yourself that nothing is wrong, and then leave her alone because sleep is important. Don't create needless problems by hovering anxiously over the crib. If you use a pacifier, use it only for sleeptime and naps — never during the waking times.

Learn, also, to be very matter-of-fact and ignore crying when you have to bathe or diaper your baby. Let her know that you are not impressed with histrionics by remaining calm and continuing the bathing or diapering. Later, you can give her a rattle or toy if she gets rambunctious during diapering. Bathtime can be playtime. Babies love to splash and have fun. Don't worry about keeping a dry bathroom. She won't be splashing in the tub forever and will stop when she's old enough to clean it herself. Now is the time to learn to enjoy. If not now, when?

Incidentally, *never* ignore your child's cries of hunger or discomfort. You will be able to understand your baby's language by about the second month: from cooing, to playful sounds, to fussing, to angry or tired or hungry crying. Try to anticipate Mary Ann's needs to minimize her crying. If you know she's content to stay in the playpen for about 30 minutes, change her environment before she lets you know with a wail that she's had it. Offer her the breast or bottle as soon as she begins sucking her fist. Your baby needs to know that you (and her world) are safe and caring, and that she can trust her parents.

The crying issue is the first of many booby-traps ahead, and some recommendations are made in the "Growth and Development" chapter for dealing with the infant. Basically, your main concerns will relate to problems of mealtime, dressing, toilet training, temper, and compliance. Just deal with one thing at a time, and the first item on the agenda is to teach your child how to get your attention in appropriate kinds of ways, and that cooing is *very* appropriate!

A valuable resource for parents with very young children and infants is *Little People* by E. R. Christophersen. The book has been mentioned several times because I consider it to be a good source of many things that parents need to know. Also, take another look at the "Growth and Development," "Infant Training" and "Sibling Rivalry" chapters in *this* book.

Another important resource is a series of pamphlets, "Caring About Kids," that is published by the National Institute of Mental Health. You can get these free by writing to: Public Inquiries, National Institute of Mental Health, 5600 Fishers Lane, Rockville, Maryland 20857.

Day Care

WHAT DO I DO WHEN I have to find a daytime baby sitter? I just got a job!

"Hi ho, hi ho.
It's off to work we go.
. . ."

Before you go, hi ho, you'll have to do some tough planning to arrange for your children to be cared for by someone. Your major concerns are: How will little Billie and Mary Ann adjust to the new situation? What will be happening for them while you are at work? What is good day care? How do you find it?

How Will My Children Adjust?

Your kids are accustomed to having you around. They know that you've been worrying about unpaid bills, but don't fully understand what you've meant by "looking for a job." Now the time has come for them to learn; you must go off to their mysterious rival for your attention — "the job."

How are they going to handle it? First maybe you

should ask yourself, "How am I going to handle it?" Kids take their cues from adults. If *you* act fearful and uncertain, they may conclude that something terrible is interfering with family life and may resist adapting to your new life style. If you can act as if you know what you are doing and feel confident of the results, the transition will go easier for everyone. You may be whistling in the dark, but *whistle!* Remember the words of F. P. Jones: "Bravery is being the only one who knows you're afraid."

Kids are like chameleons on a time line — they and their needs change as they grow. Depending on the age of your child, you will have different requirements in making day care arrangements.

Very little is known about the effects on infants of mothers working; however, *we do* know that learning begins as early as six weeks of age — maybe earlier. Infant Ernie needs more than diaper changes and feedings. For intellectual stimulation, a baby needs a few toys to feel, touch, and look at as well as someone who talks, cuddles, sings to, and enjoys him during waking hours. Ernie is also learning what it takes to get attention. If attention is paid only when he cries, he may conclude that crying is the magical cue; and the stage is set.

How do you choose a sitter for your Ernie? The answer is: *carefully!* Visit with any potential sitter at least twice if you don't know her/him already. Notice if the person seems interested in your baby and handles him with confidence. Does the sitter seem to be warm and affectionate? Choose someone with experience, preferably someone who has, or had, an infant of her own. Whether you choose a man or a woman as a sitter (neither sex has a priority on warmth of personality), be sure to check references. Incidentally, don't worry that Ernie will become more attached to the baby sitter than to you. Research suggests that a mother is a mother is a mother — and the bond between mother and child is strong.

There is some evidence to suggest that children under two are better off with a caring sitter *in your own home*, rather than going to a strange environment. Do consider that factor if you possibly can arrange it.

The Toddler and Preschool Child

Toddler Tess, between 12 and 36 months of age, is very active and requires the services of a sitter who has a lot of energy. What is usually described as the time of the "Terrible Twos" is a period of curious exploration and of testing limits. The sitter has to be physically fit! This is a critical time for learning, so the caretaker must be both protective and encouraging and able to set limits without losing "cool."

The preschooler, Peter, is aged three to five years, and needs someone who will talk and play and read. This is an important time to teach school readiness behaviors (see the chapter on that subject). You want someone who would encourage Peter to sit quietly at times during the day, working on puzzles, browsing through picture books, reading if he's ready. It is important not to assume that Peter can "run wild" for the first five years and suddenly learn to concentrate on the first day of school! It doesn't work that way.

When you interview, notice how the sitter responds to Peter. Does she look at and talk to him or only to you? Is she warm and friendly? (You don't want on-the-job training while tending to *your* child!) Check references before making a decision. Be sure to discuss the use of discipline in detail. (Perhaps you could go over key chapters in this book with the person you engage.)

You may save money if you hire a friend or relative, but that's all you may be saving. If Peter or Tess don't get quality care, both the child and you will pay a big price!

If you decide to use a day care center, visit the center before enrolling your child. Watch how the children play together and interact with the adults. Is the environment pleasant and clean? Does it feel like a "loving environment?" How would you be involved or consulted? Do you feel good about what you see? Pay less attention to what you are told than to what you see, hear and feel. And remember to ask for Peter's opinion and feelings, too!

You — or your spouse — may consider involving yourself in a baby-sitting co-op where parents rotate in taking care of each other's children. That may be more trouble than it's worth unless all parents who are involved agree as to what constitutes adequate care.

In a parent co-op pre-school, parents work together in rotation to provide organized day-care in a special setting, for example a rented school building or a church. If your schedule allows you or your spouse to be actively involved, this can be an ideal arrangement.

In *any* setting, however, it is generally agreed that no one adult should be expected to take care of more than eight children.

The best judges of the baby sitter or the day care center are Tess and Peter themselves. Pay attention to what they say and do as time goes on. Drop in unexpectedly sometimes to see how things are going. If your child is unhappy, is not learning anything, and is misbehaving after a reasonable period of time (about six weeks), be prepared to discuss the situation with the sitter or teacher and don't hesitate to make a change if necessary. Trust your child!

The School Age Child

The older child requires the least attention, of course, but does need a home base — someone to keep tabs, to give praise, to show interest and concern, and to set limits.

Although school age Sally can be given more freedom, the sitter should know where she is, doing what, with whom. *Someone* has to supervise Sally's homework, completion of chore assignments, and visiting friends.

Be sure to spell out the ground rules both to the sitter and to Sally. To feel competent, important, and self-sufficient, kids should do chores and know and observe the rules.

Preparing For Change

Once you've made the arrangements, don't spring any surprises on your child. Explain what to expect and answer all questions honestly. Talk about when and for how long s/he will be at the sitter's or center, what will probably be happening there, and when you will pick her/him up to go home. Be sure to introduce the teacher or sitter. Be positive and enthusiastic. This is an adventure! Right?

In spite of all these preparations, don't be surprised if your child may protest and cry when you deposit him or her at the door of the sitter or center. Just ignore it and act as if nothing is happening. That won't be easy, but courage is catching. Later, ask about the *good* things that happened that day and share *your* experiences, too.

A Special Incentive

Some kids may need a special incentive to help them cope with the new situation — some extra support to ease the pain of separation and the inconvenience of leaving home. If, after three or four weeks, your child is having difficulty adapting, consider making a change. Trust your child's response. If you do feel *assured* that s/he is getting good and loving care, you may want to make use of the "Special Problem Chart" on page 157. Consult with the sitter or teacher and decide on the problem of most concern: for example, crying, temper tantrums, hitting others. Remember that a "spoonful of sugar helps the medicine go down!"

For more information, look up E. R. Christophersen's book *Little People* in the "More Resources" section at the back of the book.

Like the turtle, I may have to stick my neck out to make progress.

Death in the Family

WHAT DO I DO WHEN my children ask about their grandmother who is fatally ill — but still lucid — in the hospital? Should they visit her? When she dies, should the children attend the funeral?

Death comes eventually to us all, of course, and brings with it special concerns for children. What each child really knows about death depends on the family and what you have taught. It appears that most children go through certain developmental stages. Preschool children, for example, usually do not see death as being permanent and do not take it personally. This idea is further promoted by watching a cartoon character who is blown apart and then becomes whole again. The realization that death is final and that all living things die gradually emerges between the ages of five and nine. They still cannot understand that there is no escape. Death is for other people, other living things. It is not until the period from age nine or ten through adolescence that children begin to understand fully that death is not reversible and that they, too, will someday die. It is then that they may start developing philosophical views of life and death.

I hope you are able to discuss death with your children and to treat it as a natural part of life. It is not an easy or pleasant topic, but we all must deal with it, and you can help your children do that most naturally and easily if you teach them to talk openly about their fears, and to grieve openly when loved ones (including pets) do die.

Such openness and acceptance of death and the need for grieving will do much to help your children deal with the need to grieve and the fear of death when such a situation comes up.

School-aged children may transfer their unresolved feelings about the death of a grandparent to fear that a parent may die next. You'll observe that children often do not grieve as adults may expect. In fact, they may seem quite callous and be given to emotional outburts: "It's all your fault Granny died!" Their stuffed animals and dolls may be "killed" and temporarily discarded almost indiscriminately. Provide a non-critical, accepting environment to allow your child to vent these concerns. Give the message: "Yes, life is hard to understand sometimes. We do the best we can."

If your children are old enough to understand what is

happening, they should probably be permitted to visit the person who has been important to them, providing that both they and the dying person want that to happen.

Some hospitals do not give visiting privileges to children, but a number of them do. More and more hospital staffs recognize the value of such family visits. Visiting the dying can help a youngster to diminish the mystery of death, open avenues of communication, and reduce the loneliness that is often felt by the dying and those who just stand and wait. A child is given the opportunity to feel useful and less helpless if he or she can show some kind of caring.

Be certain that the child *wants* to visit. Under no circumstances should children be *forced* to visit or made to feel guilty if they choose not to make contact. If it is not possible to make a visit, your child may want to telephone. The sound of a child's voice is often good medicine, but again, calling should be done only if your child wants to call and the patient is well enough to receive the call.

To prepare a child to visit someone who is dying, discuss the situation thoroughly in advance. Describe the condition and appearance of the dying relative and explain any sickroom equipment that will be seen. It may also be a good idea to ease hospital fears by reminding your child that most people who go to hospitals get well (however, if your relative is indeed terminal, do not create false hope).

Should your children attend the funeral? That depends upon the child and the situation. If your child is old enough to understand and wants to participate, attending the funeral may be helpful. This is an important ceremony to help survivors accept the reality of death and cope with the loss, while surrounded by caring friends and relatives.

As with the hospital visit, you should prepare your children for what they will hear and see before, during, and after the services. They need to know that because this is a very sad occasion, people express grief in various ways and that some will cry. If your children do not want to attend the funeral, do not force them to do so or make them feel guilty for not wanting to.

It is good for your children to grieve. Mourning for someone is a natural and healing process. By being open with your sorrow, you are showing your children that it is all right to feel sad and to cry. It is not a sign of weakness. As time goes on, you will also show your children that you can adapt, smile again, and go on with your life even though you will always feel some sense of loss. Courage is contagious.

An excellent pamphlet is ''Talking to Children About Death'' from the *Caring About Kids* series; this information was adapted from that pamphlet. You may get a free copy by writing to: Public Inquiries, National Institute of Mental Health, 5600 Fishers Lane, Rockville, MD 20857.

Death in the Family

Another resource is the pamphlet, "The Dying Person and the Family" by Nancy Doyle. Send 80 cents with a request to Public Affairs Pamphlet No. 485, 381 Park Avenue South, New York, N.Y. 10016.

There are also some excellent books in most libraries for helping children deal with death. Recommended:
Mark and Dan Jury, *Gramp. New York: Penguin, 1978.*
Miska Miles, *Annie and the Old One*. Boston: Atlantic Monthly Press, 1971.
Judith Viorst, *The Tenth Good Thing About Barney*. New York: Atheneum, 1971, 1975.

Discipline

WHAT DO I DO WHEN...my son disobeys or doesn't pay attention when I tell him to do something?

"Listen to this, Alfred," you call to your spouse, looking up from this book. "This child specialist says there's a way to *discipline* James and Susie without spanking them! Now what do you suppose she thinks *will* work?"

"I don't know, Clarisse, but *she* doesn't have to *live* with our kids!"

Alfred is right, of course: I don't have to live with your kids. But you *do*, and that's all the more reason to learn *effective* methods for disciplining them.

What is "discipline" anyway? To begin with, it does *not* mean punishment, or hurting, or putting down. The word *discipline* comes from the Greek, and refers to *following* (as in *disciple*). If you think in terms of *teaching your children to follow your instructions*, you'll be off to a good start!

"But what's wrong with a whack or two?" you ask.

"It's quick, easy, to the point — and certainly gets their attention!" Yes, a whack (or two or ten) is quick, easy, gets their attention — and teaches the wrong thing.

"But it works!" you protest. Does it, really? James may have stopped hitting Susie (while you are watching) or may have dragged himself off to do what you wanted him to do (this time) muttering under his breath. But did anything really change? Does he now play by the household rules? Is he cooperative? Or is James still beating up on other kids and ignoring your first twenty pleas to pick up his toys or do the dishes?

So! What Do I Do? Spare the Rod and Spoil the Child?

No. Just spare the rod and *teach* the child! Nobody said it would be easy, but spanking, yelling, nagging, lecturing, sarcasm, and/or putdowns accomplish nothing — except increasing your own feelings of frustration.

James, for example, has been told that he can ride his tricycle only on the driveway. You watch him from behind the living room curtain and see those awful barbarians across the street calling, "C'mon over and play. *We* gotta new swing set." Will James bite the bait? Not *your* James; surely that's not *your* James who paused for three seconds and is now cycling across the street. *What* can that boy be thinking of!? What he's thinking of is a system called: "Buy now, pay later." The beauty of this system — if he can get away with it — is that he has fun first, spanking later. The spanking, then, relieves him of any need to feel guilty or responsible. Once he has paid the debt, he is free to misbehave again. You, however, end up feeling guilty and remorseful, wondering why that child of yours won't mind.

What has James learned? That he can do what he wants to do as long as he is willing to risk paying the dues. Children who are routinely subjected to physical punishment and verbal abuse frequently experience far more devastating effects. No responsible physician, educator, or child care worker would ever sanction such measures. The rod, indeed, can spoil a child. To avoid the rod, the child learns to lie, sneak, hide, even run away — and to behave aggressively in return. Statistics reveal that 90 per cent of delinquents come from homes where abuse — verbal or physical — is the norm. Those, of course, are homes where little praise is ever heard. Those are the homes that produce the victims that will, someday, victimize others.

Most parents, fortunately, do not carry punishment to those extremes. The point is that kids *do* things that irritate. How are you going to handle that? How are you going to convince James to comply with reasonable requests? If spanking, scolding, or lecturing are not recommended, what is?

Is Permissiveness In and Punishment Out?

No, but the problem is that many parents equate discipline with punishment, and include spanking, slapping, verbal put-downs, and inappropriate power plays. ''Punishment'' implies negative feedback. On the other hand, I'm not advocating permissiveness. You are the parent, and you are in charge. James and every other child needs ''corrective feedback.'' But it does not have to be *painful*. What you are trying to accomplish when you discipline is to teach your child to change his behavior, to be self-controlled, to be responsible, to tolerate frustration. You do not want to erode your child's self-esteem or respect for you. By using the following procedures of the ''zap'' and ''Time Out'' effectively, disciplining your child will become a positive learning process.

The usual scene goes something like this: you tell James to pick up his toys; he refuses to do it, ''forgets'' to do it, delays doing it (''Wait 'til the commercial's on''), or does a slapdash job. You begin to fume to yourself, ''I swear that kid only obeys me once out of 100 times!'' (Actually, research shows that even the worst youngster obeys about four times out of ten!) What do you do now?

First of all, do *not* call from another room or from across the room when you are saying what you want done. If something is important enough to make a request, you have to be willing to come into the room and stand within three to five feet of your child and ask for what you want done. Admittedly, that requires some energy — and may be tiring — but the goal is compliance. The day will come when you won't have to do that, but until your child learns to do what he is told, that day has not yet arrived.

The first time you make the request, say, for example, ''Please pick up your toys.'' Stand and wait, counting silently to fifteen. If nothing happens, you may use a remarkably simple and effective approach which I refer to as the ''zap.''

With this procedure, first described by Eimers and Aitchison as ''mild social punishment,'' you go directly to your child or teenager, and place your hand firmly on a shoulder, look at him directly with a disapproving (but not hateful) expression, and say in a low, intense voice, ''I told you to pick up your toys. Do it now!'' or ''I don't like it when you argue with me. Stop it and go clean your room right now.'' Do not shout, threaten, or hit. You don't have to. With this approach, you say what you want only twice — the first time, then the ''zap.'' There is no third time. You would then impose Time Out (described below), but, believe me, it is very difficult for most children to resist the persuasiveness of the ''zap.'' (What would *your* reaction be if someone zeroed in on you, face to face, in an intense way?) Do not plead, argue with, cajole, or justify your request when James makes excuses or says "Why do I have to do everything around here?" or "Other kids have *decent* parents who don't make them do all this stuff!"

If you learn to make your request in this kind of way: one, zap, and Time Out, you will save a lot of energy. (Did you know, for example that the average parent nags or scolds a pre-school child about 55 times a day? Do you realize how much energy that takes!?) By using the zap, you get to the problem before it gets out of hand. I'm sure you have noticed that misbehavior and emotions usually build in intensity and gather force and energy unless stopped at the early stage!

The beauty of the zap procedure is that there is no wasted movement. You get James' attention by looking square in his eyes. By moving close and touching him firmly on the arm or shaking your finger ominously, you are letting it be known that *you mean business* — and he better believe it! You avoid any possibility of giving a double message by making certain that you frown or look very serious. When you discipline, look like you mean it. You will give a double message if you smile or speak sweetly.

To avoid lecturing or nagging, make only a very brief statement as to what you do or do not want. Talk a lot when you praise — not when you discipline. Kids' hearing is much better when you praise! It is very effective to speak in a low, intense tone. Eimers and Aitchison suggest that if you *really* want to get your kid's attention, try whispering while hovering. If you've been a screamer in the past, this really impresses your child!

Once you become effective in using the zap, the day will come when all you'll have to do is give a disapproving look from across the room to stop a misbehavior or to get compliance to a request. In fact, this procedure is so powerful, be sure you really *want* compliance!

There is one last important step: *show appreciation for obedience!* Be sure to say "thank you" or "I like it when you're helpful, or don't argue, or..."

Use this approach with your child any time that you feel irritated. Don't let him do things that will trigger your dislike. Other people, including teachers, will not be very tolerant of misbehavior, so don't set your child up to be disliked by others.

Nothing Seems to Work! What's This "Time Out"?

"Time Out" is a very simple but effective procedure in which your child is put into a very dull place (Siberia?) for a brief period of time. This is really a time to think. Sending a child to his or her room is a form of Time Out that is very *ineffective*. "Remember when your mother used to say, 'Go to your room — ?" observed comedian Sam Levenson. "This was a terrible penalty. Now when a mother says the same thing, a kid goes to his room. There he's got an air-conditioner, a TV set, an inter-com, a shortwave radio — he's better off than he was in the first place!'' Time Out is really five minutes, or multiples thereof, in a very dull place. It is better to use a brief time out procedure 100 times a day than to use one long time out period. Children learn more and faster when they are given many opportunities to practice behaving.

In Time Out, you sit James in a very uninteresting and unexciting place — for example, a kitchen corner — facing the wall for a specific period of time to think about what he has done. Just sitting quietly is sufficient. *Do not* try anything exotic, for example, making him put his nose to the wall. Never, *ever*, use a closet, bathroom, or other dark or dangerous place. Just find a very dull place.

Time Out is recommended for use with children 18 months through 12 years. (Other procedures, such as ''costs'' and withdrawal of free time or privileges, are more appropriate for teenagers.) This is the most effective and efficient way yet devised to teach your child to behave appropriately. It is a disciplinary approach that permits you to let off steam in a constructive way.

For the very young child, the Time Out place can be the crib, high chair, or play pen (without toys or mobiles), where the toddler is placed immediately after misbehaving and ignored for a brief period of time. The length of Time Out is calculated by the age of your child, that is, one minute for each year of age (two minutes for a two-year-old, three minutes for a three-year-old) until the age of five. From that point on, five minutes and multiples thereof are used. It is very important to use a timer so that your child is assured that you won't forget him or her, and the procedure appears to be ''fair.''

Discuss this procedure with James *before* you use it. Tell him that you're tired of yelling, spanking, and wasting your time nagging. Most kids will be pleased to hear that and will then watch to see if you follow through.

The Time Out Procedure

After the second time you have asked your child to do something as in the zap procedure, or *immediately* if your child has hit someone or has been verbally abusive, say ''You are not picking up your toys as I told you. Take five minutes Time Out right now'' or ''You hit your brother. Go to Time Out please. Right now.''

(Note: The only time you use the zap procedure is in regard to a request. Time Out is imposed immediately if you see your children hitting or hear them arguing. Don't wait for things to escalate. Send both children to Time Out. Don't try to be judge or jury. They'll learn to work things out once they learn that they both have to pay the penalty!)

If your child delays or dawdles on the way to Time Out,

walk up behind him, place your hands on his shoulders firmly but not harshly and march him there. If you have to carry a toddler to the chair, hold him facing away from you so that a trip to Time Out isn't confused with a hug.

When your child is quiet (or when all are quiet if two or more children are involved), set the timer for the appropriate number of minutes. (Extensive research has shown that five minutes are as effective as 30 minutes, so don't get carried away!) This is "silent time." No one is to speak to the offender during Time Out, including *you*!

If your child makes noises, screams, or cries in the middle of Time Out, reset the timer for another five minutes. If he gets off the chair before the timer rings, give one firm-but-not-hard spank on the bottom, and return your child to the chair. Reset the timer. If your child is really determined to test your commitment and fortitude, he could spend several hours on the Time Out chair. Remember that's your child's decision, not yours. You reviewed the rules with him *before* you started using Time Out.

When the timer rings, go directly to your child and ask if he is now ready to do what he was told to do in the case of noncompliance, or if he is willing to be more pleasant and polite, in the case of hitting or arguing.

If your child refuses to answer or just grunts, impose another five minutes in Time Out. He has to learn to be courteous no matter how he feels, and courtesy starts at home with you. Besides, a child who is still angry will end up back in Time Out anyway within a few minutes and may as well spend more time cooling off instead.

When you go to reset the timer, your child may decide to change his mind and say, "No, I'll be good. I don't need more time." Do *not* fall for that. He has to learn not to play games with words, that you will take the first response seriously. This is a very important point. Many people say "no" when they mean "yes" and vice versa. Time Out is a good opportunity to train your child not to do that.

After Time Out has been served, your child starts with a clean slate. The penalty has been paid. Do not lecture or nag. You have already said what he did wrong. He may, of course, repeat the misbehavior again and again — some children take longer to learn than others. There is nothing wrong with that, if you consistently impose Time Out.

There is one more part to the procedure. Within five minutes or ten minutes after your child leaves Time Out, find something that you can praise. For example, you might say, "Thank you. You did a good job of picking up your toys" or "I really like it when you play nicely with your brother" or "You're really being a help."

Incidentally, if your child (seven years and up) refuses to cooperate with Time Out in the beginning, take away a privilege such as TV until he agrees to abide by the rules (see box below). After a week or two of Time Out used correctly, even the most recalcitrant little tyrant will realize that Time Out is fair, effective, and better than Mom or Dad yelling, spanking or nagging endlessly.

Time Out Rules for Kids

1. Understand that one minute is served for each year of age, up to five, then the minimum time served is five minutes.

2. When told to go to Time Out, don't argue. Just go. Each argument will cost you another five minutes. (If you're not careful, you could pile up 10 or 20 minutes before even sitting down.)

3. The timer starts when you are quiet, and only your parent can start the timer. If you talk or make noises or leave the Time Out chair, the timer will be set for another five minutes.

4. If your brother or sister tease, laugh at, or talk to you while you're in Time Out, you will then be excused from Time Out and he or she will serve your time. (The same thing, of course, works if *you* tease or bother your brother or sister who may be in Time Out.)

Time Out Rules for Parents

1. Be sure that the Time Out corner is in a very dull place where you can keep an eye on your child. *Never* use a dark or dangerous place such as a closet or bathroom.

2. If you threaten, scream, or nag, you can't use Time Out. That's called "double jeopardy." There's no need to "hang, draw, or quarter" your child!

3. The portable timer is a big help. Purchase one just for this purpose. Use it rather than relying on your memory so that your child is assured that you won't forget or be unfair.

4. Remain quiet while your child is in Time Out — even if he or she is being testy. Time Out is quiet time. Do not nag, scold, or lecture after time has been served. Let Time Out, imposed again and again, do the job.

5. For any act of aggression (hitting, sarcasm, arguing), use Time Out *immediately*. Do not warn. Simply tell your child why he or she is going to Time Out.

How Do I Impose Time Out When We Have Guests, Go Visiting, or Have to Leave For An Appointment?

Although you may find that James will test you at critical times, you will also discover that he can be very reasonable if you don't spring surprises.

If you know that guests are coming to visit, tell James ahead of time and discuss what kind of behaviors you expect. For example, "Our friends, Bill and Jackie, are coming over tonight to play cards. I want you to come and say hello to them, take their coats to the closet, and answer their questions if they ask any. Later, I'll tell you to go to your room to play quietly until bedtime, and I expect you to go without arguing. If you cause any trouble, you'll have to go to Time Out." James has to know that your top priority is that of being a parent, not a host or hostess, and that guests in the house offer no escape from Time Out.

Be sure to ask James to repeat your advance instructions back to you, to make certain he understands them. After the guests leave, praise him for what he did well.

If you are going to visit someone, again tell James what kind of behavior you expect of him. Ask him to repeat what you've said. If he misbehaves and you can impose Time Out at your friend's home, do so; otherwise, when you take him home, impose Time Out at home. Again, let James know that being out doesn't remove the consequences of misbehavior.

If you have an appointment, and James has earned Time Out but you don't have an opportunity to impose it, then he owes the Time Out. *As soon as you return home*, impose Time Out. This should not really be a problem, however, if you have been using the procedure over a period of several weeks.

Try not to spring surprises. If you state your expectations clearly and briefly and ask that they be repeated, most children will try to oblige. Anticipate the best, not the worst. Children usually live up to our expectations of them!

How Can I Impose Time Out When I'm On the Telephone?

Tell James that you expect him to play quietly and not interrupt when you are on the telephone. Work with him to develop some interesting activities he can engage in when you are talking on the phone. Ask that he write a letter and deliver it to you after your phone conversation is over. Or, if he is younger, have crayons or paints or a game handy to occupy him. Practice with him if needed. If he does interrupt, just tell the other party on the phone that you have pressing business and will need to excuse yourself for a few moments, or perhaps call back later. Put the phone down, or if necessary, hang up, and impose Time Out. If the problem persists, you may want to use the Special Problem Chart as well as Time Out.

Warning: At some point, James may announce to you that he really likes Time Out and may even sit with arms folded and a smug smile on his face — even offering to go to Time Out. The little dear is just trying to psych you out! Just say, "That's nice" and keep right on imposing Time Out. Feel assured that you have a very clever child — but you're smarter!

References:
R. Eimers and H. Aitchison, *Effective Parents, Responsible Children*, McGraw-Hill, 1977.
E. R. Christophersen, *Little People*, H & H Enterprises, Inc., 1977.

Dishonesty

WHAT DO I DO WHEN I catch my daughter telling a lie?

"I am different from Washington," said Mark Twain. "I have a higher, grander standard of principle. Washington could not lie. I *can* lie, but I won't!"

What a low blow! Cleo stands in front of you telling a bald-faced lie, and she doesn't even have the grace to blush. "Who, me? Eat the cake you were saving for dinner? (Break the vase? Cut class? Take the coins on the table? Hit my brother?) How *could* you accuse me of such a thing? Don't you *trust* me? What kind of parents won't trust their own kid!" A Shakespearean actor emoting in Act III, Scene IV would be envious of the performance. You are probably thinking that your family is doomed. Where *have* you gone wrong?! How *could* this happen?

She seems to be so hurt. Have you injured her psyche? Could you *possibly* be wrong? The answers: no, it takes a lot more to "hurt a kid's psyche" than confronting her about something; and, of course, you could be wrong, but probably are not.

How Can It Happen?

Kids learn to lie for several reasons. It may be a desperate, last-ditch attempt to avoid punishment (after all, sometimes it works). Cleo may feel that lying is the only way to get what she wants. It's a calculated risk that may or may not work, and it's your job to make certain that it *doesn't* work. You just have to be smarter than your child.

So How Do You Handle It?

First of all, don't fall apart and don't get taken in. Lying *is* a serious offense, and you have to address the issue. This relates to the issue of trust, and if you can't trust your kid, it's all downhill from there. She has to learn that it's *her* problem, not yours, and you refuse to accept it. How do you do that?

Do not come across like the King when he accused the Mad Hatter of stealing tarts: "Give your evidence," said the King: "and don't be nervous or I'll have you executed on the spot!" You're in charge. Just state your case.

Never ask a question when you know the answer. That's "entrapment," a real set up, almost challenging your child to lie. Remember that your kid is *not* George Washington (the story of the cherry tree isn't true anyway).

For example, Billy is crying, and you *know* that his older brother, Jimmy, hit him. This isn't the first time this has happened. Don't dash into the room like an avenging angel and ask: "Did *you* hit Billy?" (What would you do if he said, "Yes, I cannot tell a lie. I did it with my little fist"?) All you have to do is come into the room and say firmly: "You hit Billy. Take 5 minutes Time Out *right now*." If Jimmy protests or argues, you add, "You're arguing. That's another 5 minutes." (Of course, if they both were fighting or arguing they *both* go to Time Out.)
OR

You find that your precious 16th century Ching vase is broken. There's no point in asking Ivan if he did it. There is no one else in the house! Simply *tell* Ivan that he broke the vase, and ask him how he's going to replace it. (Of course, if it's *really* a 16th century vase, it could take him years! Be fair.) If he debates or argues, send him to Time Out until he finally works out restitution with you.
OR (and this is the toughest one of all)

You find money missing from your purse, and you've suspected that Jackie has been pilfering coins from her sisters and brother for several weeks now. Don't ask: "Who took the money?" Go directly to Jackie and say, "I have been concerned for some time now that you have been taking money. There's change missing from my purse. I believe that you took it, and I'm going to ask you to replace it." Trust your judgement. No one knows your kids better than you do. You don't have to prove your charge. If Jackie has an allowance, make certain that she pays you one-half of her allowance each week until the money is paid. Keep a record. You may even have to set up extra jobs for her to do to earn the money to repay you. (Note: If you take *all* of your child's allowance, you will create resentment and discouragement. Always leave something. You want to teach responsibility; don't overdo it!)

Do not argue with the child. "Give a child enough rope, and he will trip you up," cautions L. J. Peter. You don't have to justify your suspicion or present your evidence like a prosecuting attorney. You may not be right in every instance. Your child, not you, created this lack of trust by doing certain things in the past, and it is the child's responsibility to establish credibility — not yours. It's a hard lesson to learn: trust is a precious commodity — easy to lose, and difficult to regain.

Remember, also, not to call your child names or predict doom. "If you have the name, you may as well play the game."

Work out how amends will be made. There has to be a real cost for lying. Just promising never to lie again just won't do. If something has been taken, restitution must be made — or if the cake was eaten, your kid may have to bake another and buy the ingredients besides! *But* the issue of lying remains. The cost for that might be loss of bike privilege or even all privileges (TV, telephone, play time, free time, special activities) for two or three days or more.

Let's run it by once more:

...Do not entrap your child by asking leading questions. Just state your suspicions or evidence in a direct way.

...Do not argue. (It won't get either of you anywhere.)

...Work out how amends must be made. Paying restitution is a powerful teacher.

...*Don't back down!*

If another incident of lying occurs, however, then you will want to seek help from a counselor or mental health specialist as soon as possible. We can't always solve our own problems. It's impossible to be entirely objective.

Finally, remember to notice and praise when your children do show themselves to be trustworthy. Give lots of attention and warmth in response to *honesty*.

Honesty is the easiest position to defend.

Dressing

WHAT DO I DO WHEN my son persists in dawdling while dressing, and my 3-year-old is having a hard time learning to dress herself?

"She makes me wash, they comb me all to thunder...The widder eats by a bell; she goes to bed by a bell; she gits up by a bell — everything's so awful reg'lar a body can't stand it," lamented Huckleberry Finn. Mark Twain's "widder" knew that the best way to provide a stable environment and feeling of security for a child is to set up expectancies and a routine. (Psychology books were not available in his day, so he dispensed wisdom in 19th century popular language.)

Morning dressing problems tend to wear out a day before it even begins. Set up a system to teach your youngsters how to dress and to dress promptly with a minimum of fuss. With a little know-how and expenditure of energy, you'll find that you'll have time for an extra cup of coffee in the morning. *And* you can teach your kids to be more independent in the bargain.

Learning to Dress

Kids are smart. They quickly learn that if they *pretend* that they can't do something, or wait long enough, they get a lot of service. What they're banking on is *your* impatience, so don't get trapped. If Patty has once put on a shirt or pair of socks, you know that she *can* do it again. From that point on, she stays in the bedroom until she does what she knows how to do.

At the very beginning, however, you will have to plan to set aside enough time to help each child learn how to dress. Talk a lot while you're putting the child's clothes on and explain what you're doing, for example, "Here's the tag. It's always found on the back, so put your shirt on so that the tag is on your back." Ask her questions: "How do you know which is the right and left shoe? Is there a right and left sock?" Be sure to praise any attempts she makes to help herself — even when it's wrong — then show the correct way. "Hey! You tried. *Very* good, but it'll work better if you put the blouse on with the buttons in the front."

The trick of teaching this basic skill: talk a lot about what you are doing and why; dress Patty up to the last step; let *her* complete the job. For example, on the first day, put on her T-shirt, draw her arms through the sleeves, and then ask her to pull the shirt down over her head. On the second day, go through the procedure up to where *she* has to put one arm through the sleeve and pull the shirt down. Each day, you do less and less and she does more and more. Finally, all you'll have to do is lay out the clothes, and she can take it from there.

Be sure to praise a lot. If there are any tantrums, just use Time Out and go on from there in a matter-of-fact way.

Shoe tieing is more difficult because it requires well-developed manual dexterity, so expect that you'll have to help her tie the laces. The day will come when she'll want to do it herself — particularly if you're lavish with praise. Use the same technique of completing all of the tieing up to the last step which *she* will do. Each day, ask her to complete more and more of the steps involved. Before you know it, she'll be tieing her own shoes (probably some time after age four).

Dawdling While Dressing

Sometimes dawdling can be resolved almost magically just by using a portable timer. It is not unknown for kids to take anywhere from 65 minutes to four hours to get dressed in the morning. In the case of the girl who took four hours to get dressed, all it took was a little ingenuity and she was dressing herself in 20 minutes within two weeks. What was the solution?

She had to stay in her room until she was dressed.

The portable timer was set for 20 minutes, and she was told that she could have her choice of breakfast and see TV for 30 minutes *if* she "beat the bell." If she did not, she simply got cereal and *no* TV.

That's all there was to it. But, you say, you have a tight time schedule? You have to get to work, and your kid has to get to school? Don't fret. There's more you can do.

Set the timer for 20 or 30 minutes, and tell your kids that they must dress in their room. No TV or breakfast until completely dressed. Breakfast is served when the bell rings.

If Patty is not dressed by the time the bell rings, go into her room and dress her but do *not* talk except to give *very brief instructions*. No nagging or lecturing and, of course, no TV. She may then have a very simple breakfast before going to school or day care.

In addition to this procedure, you can also set up a star-earning system on the Special Problem Chart (see page 157). Try the regular procedure, though, for a period of two weeks before introducing the chart. You don't want to use a cannon if a fly swatter will do!

The situation is very different if Patty is nine or older and still dawdles and refuses to cooperate. You can still start out by using the procedure and chart, but if neither of these work, I suggest you consult with a counselor. The situation at that age may be somewhat more complex.

Family Conferences

WHAT DO I DO WHEN the family conference ends up in a free-for-all? Isn't this supposed to be a way to resolve problems — not create them?

Who and where is that wretch who recommended having family conferences? You had one last night, and now nobody's talking to anybody! Well, don't despair; you can learn about some of the pitfalls of family conferences and how to avoid them.

Family conferences are a very important and meaningful family activity. Just as business firms have staff meetings to plan and coordinate efforts, a weekly session can help work out some of the trials and tribulations that inevitably crop up in family living.

Much depends upon how you go about it. Talking about problems *can* do more harm than good! It is not enough to "talk things out." As a matter of fact, families who are asked to repeatedly discuss their problems become more hostile and less apt to solve their problems. Does that mean that the solution is *not* to talk about troublesome things? Just ignore them? No, it means that you have to know what you want to accomplish and how to do it. The power of the family conference is in the process, and the process can be taught. You don't have to be an expert. You just have to know the rules of problem solving.

Before you start, though, know that there are limitations, and family conferences cannot solve every problem. For example, those relating to serious psychiatric problems (psychoses), addictions (alcohol or other drugs), medical or congenital disabilities, or crises and severe personality disturbances that lead to abuse require help from specialized counselors.

Your family problems, however, are typical of most if they revolve around issues of trust (the most important), chores, choice of friends, dress, money, independence, discipline, appreciation and love, boy-girl matters, problems with authority, and sibling rivalry. It may seem that a lot of things have changed in our society, but these kinds of problems are not very different from those 10, 20, or more years ago.

What are the advantages of having family conferences on a regular, weekly basis? For one thing, they help keep these problems from getting out of hand. Family conflicts can be reduced and positive relationships developed when

A Contract for Family Problem Solving

Date: ______________________

Addressed to: ______________________

THE PROBLEM: ______________________

How often it happens: ______________________

When it happens: ______________________

Where it happens: ______________________

PLEASE:

Do this instead: ______________________

When: ______________________

How often: ______________________

IN EXCHANGE:

I will: ______________________

When: ______________________

Who will keep track of the Please Request: ______________________

Agreed to by: ______________________

and ______________________

parents and kids learn how to solve problems together. Also, this is a way of giving your school-age children and adolescents some power whereby they know that they can do something that will make a difference, and that they will be heard. They are also getting important experience in problem solving and dealing constructively and creatively with each other.

I recommend a straightforward process of family negotiation. You may feel that anything that simple just can't be effective. Admittedly, it is plain, not fancy; but it has very specific rules to help avoid the pitfalls. As a first step, give everybody a plain 3'' x 5'' or 5'' x 7'' card. (''A card! What kind of conference *is* this? Don't we *talk*?'' This is an *organized* conference, and the purpose is to *solve* problems!)

Each person is allowed 15 minutes (no more) and may discuss only one problem which has come up with someone else in the family. Someone should be a time keeper. The person who raises the problem should make notes on the card to keep track of the problem solving process. Here's one sample format which describes the *problem*, a ''please-do-this-instead'' *alternative*, and an offer to do something favorable in *exchange*:

One of the pitfalls of family conferences is that problems often are not stated specifically, and tend to be vague or accusatory. It really helps to state the problem so that it can be observed and counted. Saying, ''You are very stupid and insulting'' just won't do it. It is much better to say, ''When I try to tell Mom and Dad something at dinner time, you correct and contradict me.''

Another useful problem solving approach is to say exactly what you want. ''You never let me see the TV program I want'' is not helpful. Instead, say ''I want to see the science program 'Nova' at 7 o'clock on Tuesday nights.''

Choose some behavior that happens fairly frequently, not something that happens once in a blue moon. For example, saying ''You always forget to give me anything on Valentine's Day'' is not helpful. Instead, focus on recurring complaints, ''You were late for dinner three times last week.''

The same rules of thumb apply to asking for what you want: be specific; ask for exactly what you want; ask for something that happens fairly often. Rather than ''Stop leaving a mess in the kitchen when you take a snack,'' say, ''Put away everything you pull out and clean off the counter by 4 p.m. and again before you go to bed.'' It is not helpful to say, ''Busy yourself with *something* while I'm on the telephone and don't interrupt.'' Instead, say, ''When I'm on the telephone, *write me a letter* and give it to me when I hang up.''

Family conferences sometimes break down when

someone is told about a complaint, and, instead of listening, interrupts, denies, or counterattacks with insults, criticisms, and countercomplaints. Agree in advance that such defensiveness will not be permitted, and include some penalty for doing that. (It might be a small fine for each offense or perhaps a special chore.)

Any *legal* contract requires something from both parties. The family member who is describing the problem must offer something in exchange; for example, "If you wear your own clothes instead of taking mine without asking, I will let you borrow my blue sweater on Saturdays." If agreement is reached, both parties sign the contract, and arrange for someone (usually the person who made the complaint) to keep track, through tally or notes, whether the contract was kept. The situation should then be reviewed at the next family conference, and renegotiated if necessary.

When families are in conflict or when problems have to be solved, a contract is a very direct and practical way to translate negative emotions and attitudes into specific, more positive behaviors.

Similar steps may be applied to solving more general family problems, planning for upcoming activities, sharing household chores. Following an organized negotiation process will minimize conflict and feelings of unfair treatment all around.

Finally, remember that a family conference is also a great time to be very lavish in sharing positive feelings, perceptions and attitudes. You can never say too much about what you like about someone else!

References:

C. Moore, "Fortifying family ties," and E. Corfman, "Games that help solve life problems." Both in E. Corfman (ed.) *Families Today — A Research Sampler on Families and Children*. NIMH Science Monograph 1. DHEW Publication No. (ADM) 79-815. Washington, D. C.: Superintendent of Documents, U.S. Government Printing Office, 1979.

A mistake is just a road sign which says, "Try something different."

Freedom

WHAT DO I DO WHEN my daughter tells me that she needs freedom to be herself and that rules will stifle her creativity?

> *"There's no use trying," she (Alice) said: "one can't believe impossible things."*
> *"I daresay you haven't had much practice," said the Queen. "When I was your age, I always did it for half-an-hour a day. Why, sometimes I've believed as many as six impossible things before breakfast."*
> Lewis Carroll

And, of course, one of the impossible beliefs is that "freedom" means license to do and say whatever one wants without sensitivity, guidelines, or cost. Another is that "creativity" is some kind of magical quality that does not require self-discipline.

The reality is that freedom imposes many responsibilities, particularly in regard to decision making. It can be very frightening to feel really "free." Without guidelines or touchstones to help them feel "focused," some young people latch on to gurus or sects as a way of feeling secure and less aimless. Erich Fromm, the psychoanalyst, identified the panic which accompanies such "freedom" in his book *Escape from Freedom*.

Freedom is "nothing else but a chance to do better," suggested philosopher Albert Camus. You are introducing freedom to your child each time you give him or her opportunities to learn and to behave in effective ways. No one can possibly be "free" who behaves in self-defeating ways. Nor is there freedom if one is very limited in terms of alternatives. We are really only as free as the number of alternatives that we can choose. The child who does not know how to read or write or reason or be self-controlled is at a great disadvantage, a victim and permanent prisoner of such limitations.

Again and again, research shows that when you, as a parent, set limits, clearly state what you do and do not want, and show appreciation for things well done, you are providing the best environment to help your child feel secure and self-assured. When children are not given such guidelines, they then have to learn through trial and error; and that can be very costly. They become self-confident when they know what is expected of them and when those expectations are reasonable and contribute to the quality of life. The truly creative person is self-disciplined, not self-indulgent.

Some years ago, a "Memorandum from a Child" was published. If your child knew how, this is what s/he'd tell you.

1. Don't spoil me. I know quite well that I ought not to have all I ask for. I'm only testing you.

2. Don't be afraid to be firm with me. I prefer it. It lets me know where I stand.

3. Don't use force with me. It teaches me that power is all that counts. I will respond more readily to being led.

4. Don't be inconsistent. That confuses me and makes me try harder to get away with everything that I can.

5. Don't make promises. You may not be able to keep them, and that will discourage my trust in you.

6. Don't fall for my provocations when I say and do things just to upset you. Then I'll try for more such "Victories".

7. Don't be too upset when I say "I hate you." I don't mean it, but I want you to feel sorry for what I think you have done to me.

8. Don't make me feel smaller than I am. I will make up for it by behaving like a "big shot".

9. Don't do things for me that I can do for myself. It makes me feel like a baby, and I may continue to put you in my service.

10. Don't let my "bad habits" get me a lot of your attention. It only encourages me to continue them.

11. Don't correct me in front of people. I'll take much more notice if you talk with me in private.

12. Don't try to discuss my behavior in the heat of a conflict. For some reason my hearing is not very good at that time and my cooperation is even worse. It is all right to take the action required, but let's not talk about it until later.

13. Don't try to preach to me. You'd be surprised how well I know what's right and wrong.

14. Don't make me feel that my mistakes are sins. I have to learn to make mistakes without feeling that I'm no good.

15. Don't nag. If you do, I'll have to protect myself by appearing deaf.

16. Don't demand explanations for my wrong behavior. I really don't know why I did it.

17. Don't tax my honesty too much. I am easily frightened into telling lies. When you know I did it, tell me. It's hard to live up to George Washington and the cherry tree.

18. Don't forget that I love to experiment. I need to learn, so don't belittle my ideas.

19. Don't protect me from consequences. I need to learn from experience.

20. Don't take too much notice of my small ailments. I may learn to enjoy poor health if it gets me much attention.

21. Don't put me off when I ask HONEST questions. If you do, I'll stop asking and seek my information elsewhere.

22. Don't answer "silly" or meaningless questions. I just want your attention.

23. Don't ever think that it's beneath your dignity to apologize to me. An honest apology makes me feel really warm toward you.

24. Don't ever suggest that you are perfect or infallible. I won't believe you, and I can't "live up" to perfection anyway.

25. Don't worry about the little amount of time we spend together. It's HOW we spend it that counts.

26. Don't let my fears arouse your anxiety. Then I will become more afraid. Show me courage.

27. Don't forget that I can't thrive without lots of understanding and encouragement, but I don't need to tell you that, do I?

Remember, I learn more from a model than a critic.

From: International Study Group Newsletter, Chicago Community Child Guidance Centers, Inc., November, 1963.

Growth and Development

WHAT DO I DO WHEN my child is still crawling and my neighbor's child, who is the same age, is now walking? Don't all children go through the same stages of development?

"Training is everything," said Mark Twain. "The peach was once a bitter almond; cauliflower is nothing but cabbage with a college education."

It would be very convenient — but dull — if children were programmed to develop physically and mentally on a fixed time schedule. Then, you would be justified in being concerned if Evan lags behind another of the same age. However, children are highly individualistic — each has his or her own rate of development. They do not walk, talk, or become toilet trained at the same time. (Einstein, for example, did not talk until he was four years old!)

It is a good idea to know something about child development; children *do* go through certain general stages. It is important to learn to respond differently as Evan matures. You don't want to treat your 9-year-old as you would your 5-year-old. Each has different perceptions, abilities, and needs. Remember, though, that developmental stages are simply guidelines — not laws. And remember too, that Evan needs just as much love and understanding from you at *every* stage!

The Early Years — Infancy Through Age Five

Try not to get nervous, but the first three years of Evan's life are considered to be the most important. That is when the foundations are laid for language, curiosity, ability to relate to others, and intelligence — all of which are necessary to competency. Let's take a close look at that period.

For the first few weeks, infants sleep and cry a lot, but their five senses are fairly acute. Newborns can focus their eyes and follow bright moving objects. They hear sounds and can distinguish between pitches. They like to hear a voice in the normal range, and research suggests that arm and leg movements are actually muscular responses to changes in the mother's speech. It is believed that these responses may somehow be part of earliest speech development. The sense of taste is well developed at birth. From the beginning, Evan can taste the difference between milk, water, and other liquids and will show a preference by sucking longer and harder when pleased.

The language-learning starts with babbling at about eight months, in which speech is imitated. Most children start using words after the first year. The period from six or eight months to two years is considered to be *particularly critical* because this is when infants start moving about, understanding language, and relating to others. This is a period of emerging self awareness, and Evan starts thinking of himself as a person with a separate identity.

"Between eight months and 24 months or so, one of the most gorgeous experiences you will ever see takes place," says psychologist Burton White. "Children establish a relationship, usually with the mother. They learn thousands of things about what they can and cannot do in their home, what they can and cannot do in interactions with the...caretaker, about how to read the primary caretaker's different mood states, and an incredible number of other things."

"Fantastic," you say. "Isn't this also the time when the terrible twos begin?" Yes, you will probably notice negativism starting between the 14th and 24th months. This is a normal part of development — not some terrible plot directed against you! Evan will start asserting himself, reject any suggestions you have to make, ignore your commands, test the limits, and, in general, flex muscles. This is a period when Evan will dig in his heels and try to assert new-found powers, thus announcing to the world that he is no longer a dependent baby. This is probably the most difficult period that you will endure — particularly when you see your child deliberately defying you. The good news is that if you use firm discipline appropriately and consistently (and hang on to your sense of humor!), the period will end in about six or seven months, and parenting will become relatively easier and increasingly more enjoyable during the next few years.

By age three, Evan should be able to get and maintain adult attention in socially acceptable ways, ask for what he wants, express both affection and anger, take pride in and brag about something he has done. He'll both lead and follow peers and be able to compete with them, as well as express anger and affection toward them.

Fours and fives tend to be concerned with order and ritual. They will do certain activities over and over again and establish certain rules for girls and boys ("This is the way you should behave and what you should do.") What they don't know, they invent. Gradually, they become more selective in choosing playmates, and their play becomes more complex. At five, Evan tends to be individualistic and likes to play with friends, but may also decide to play alone and/or observe others at play sometimes.

The task seems monumental, you say? How can you help during these critical years? What can you do to give Evan the best possible start in life? Fortunately, you don't have to take 20 courses in Child Psychology or be rich or brilliant. Caring about your child is critically important, although caring alone is not enough. Psychologist Burton L. White, who has spent years studying what early experiences contribute most to the development of *competent* youngsters, suggests three key elements:

First of all, to protect and encourage curiosity and intelligence (problem solving), *child-proof your home*. Make it safe as possible, and arrange it so that Evan can explore without being constantly confronted by "no's." Place your priceless objects out of reach — not on the coffee table. (Why complicate your life and his?) There will, of course, be forbidden cabinet doors and drawers. It's best to provide a place in your kitchen cabinets where you can keep special pots and pans and other objects for Evan to bang around.

Second, to develop language and social skills (relating to others) — as well as curiosity and intelligence — *put interesting things around* the crib, carriage, or room. Hang colorful pictures on the walls or paste decals on the crib or hang mobiles from the ceiling. Enrich Evan's infant world. Talk a *lot* to him. Talking, holding, singing, and rocking are the earliest forms of stimulation that are important to development. As noted in the "Infant Training" chapter, you are also beginning to train Evan as early as the sixth week when you learn to listen and attend to him during the cooing (rather than the crying) stage.

As Evan becomes a toddler, start listening to and responding to his questions and concerns. Play with and read to him. Get enthusiastic about things that he is discovering, for example, that the light switch has magical effects or that a flower has petals. Praise a *lot* — even simply for shutting a cabinet door when told to do so or picking up a piece of paper from the floor. *Never* talk baby talk. Ask a lot of questions. Satisfy your child's curiosity by explaining in simple terms and identifying objects. None of this will take hours of your time — two minutes here, 30 seconds there, five minutes somewhere else is sufficient. Be available. You're the most fantastic person in your child's world! Provide stimulating games and toys — pots and pans, empty spools, pieces of cloth, scraps of lumber, books, music boxes, blocks, jig saw puzzles. Turn off the TV, turn on the record player, read to him.

During these early years if you are asked the following questions, what would your answers be? Are there books in your home? Do you use the library? Is there story time at your house? Do you take your child to the zoo, the museum, and other places? Do you correct your child when he or she uses incorrect language? If you can answer "Yes," you are providing important stimulation that helps make the difference between less and more competent children.

Finally, to begin young Evan's "socialization" (learning about how the real world works), *be loving and encouraging and lavish with praise, but set clear limits* right from the time he starts crawling and exploring. Research shows again and again that there's a strong link between consistent discipline and competent children.

You have to use different kinds of discipline at different stages, of course. Distraction tactics work very well for children up to 13 months ("No, no, don't play with daddy's hi-fi. Here are your blocks. See how pretty they look stacked up?") From 13 to 18 months, children require distraction *and* physical removal. After 18 months, children require distraction, verbal instruction ("Now play nicely with Sandi in the sand box"), and the use of Time Out ("You hit Sandi. That hurt poor Sandi. Come to Time Out. Right now.").

The Older Child

By the time Evan is six, in addition to the social skills already described for the 3-year-old, he should be able to speak well and be sensitive to the reactions of others; anticipate consequences ("If I eat this candy, mother is going to get angry"); be able to deal with abstractions of numbers, letters, and rules; plan and execute activities, such as games and chores; and concentrate on a task at hand. These are the fruits of your training during the first few years.

From ages six through eleven, children's physical development slackens; and they are now concentrating on learning to think and analyze situations. They tend to be judgmental and have definite opinions on what is fair, how things work, how parents and others should behave. They take what they see and hear very seriously and tend to be opinionated and become impatient with anyone who attempts to reason with them. What they see on television tends to have serious impact on their perceptions. (Monitor that box well, mom and dad!)

Other people — peers, teachers — become increasingly important and influential to Evan now. He is spending more time away from home. More demands are made upon him, and he must make on-the-spot decisions as to what he will or will not do when tempted by others. He will make mistakes; but if he also reaps the consequences, he will learn from them. He wants explanations for rules and may argue about these, often with exquisite irrational logic. He prefers written lists, a schedule of chores, and a clear understanding of penalties and rewards rather than sermons and nagging. (Does *anyone* like sermons and nagging?)

Evan is now developing a value system, and your guidance and discipline, wherein certain behaviors lead to certain consequences (both good and bad), are particularly important. Respect your youngster's right to have a different opinion but be firm about setting limits. "But suppose I make a mistake in judgement?" you ask. Well, there's no law that says that you have to be right *all* the time! Learning that adults are fallible is valuable information, too. There's no point in expecting perfection from a highly imperfect world, and you might want to remember Mark Twain's observation: "When I was a boy of fourteen, my father was so ignorant I could hardly stand to have the old man around. But when I got to be twenty-one, I was astonished at how much he had learned in seven years."

The coming years are tough for you and for Evan. Prepare yourself for a shock when your child goes through ages 12 through 15. You may find yourself asking, "*What did we do wrong?!*" Entry into the 7th grade tends to be a critical time when all the learning that has gone before either pays off or seems to have been forgotten. As during the period of the "terrible two's," your authority as a parent may again be challenged; and your mild-mannered Evan may seem to become a stranger. Even though you still control allowances, privileges, and the emotional climate of the home, you may find that your teenager has the power to create chaos. He can punish you in ways that would impress the leaders of the Spanish Inquisition. Observed psychologist Robert Aitchison, "Living with a teenager is usually nobody's bargain!"

Your control and authority will now start shifting. You have to set limits, but you also have to "let go." Evan the teenager is exposed to many temptations and has critical decisions to make, and trust is now critically at issue. All the training of the past — or lack of it — now comes into play. You best serve by letting him accept the responsibility for and consequences of those decisions. That is the only way your son can learn to function independently and discriminatively. You have a right — and responsibility — to clearly specify where he may go, when to come home, and what is expected in terms of household chores and school responsibilities. That is how "freedom" is earned, and freedom is very important to the teenager. (To all of us for that matter!)

When problems arise, both you and Evan benefit when opinions are expressed openly and honestly. If you disapprove of his choice of friends, don't be reluctant to say so with very specific reasons for your judgement. Don't, however, attempt to intimidate or induce guilt. Simply add: "It's your decision. I can't control what you do, but this is how I see it." If you *forbid* your teenager to do anything, you have simply presented a challenge that he *must* meet to prove that he — not you — is in control of his life.

Some parents try to make friends of their teenagers at any cost — or perhaps try to live vicariously through them. They permit beer or pot parties at home, or sit with the young people to view X-rated TV movies. Their usual explanation is: "Better at home than somewhere else." Don't do it unless you are prepared to give the message that you really have no values or limits of your own.

You will best survive these teenage years by not over-reacting and taking personally the brashness, criticism, and insensitivity that may be heaped upon you. Set limits but be yourself. Your worth as a person — or parent — is not dependent upon the whim of anyone (including your teenager!). You have a right to your opinions and feelings. Evan will be more impressed if you give him the right to have opinions and feelings as well, even though you may disagree.

The Young Adult

The end of your guidance and training starts when Evan enters the period from 16 to 20 years of age. Now is the time that this young man will prepare to leave home and become self-reliant. Trying to "wing it" may lead to some traumatic experiences as the young adult experiments with decisions about intimate relationships, sex, drinking, drugs, career, life-style, education, values. Be morally supportive but don't move into the "rescuer" role. Rules of conduct within the home should be continued but don't change your personal life style just to accommodate him. Cooperation and responsible sharing between family members is the name of the game.

It is tempting — but useless — to give advice during these years unless asked. You may have nurtured this person, but you don't *own* him. As with anyone, you have a right to make observations, for example, "This is how I see it, but it's *your* decision. It's *your* life." Clarifications should be made about continued financial support — the amount, time span, and purpose. That is the *adult* way of doing things and strengthens the family relationship while fostering independence.

At all stages of development, we all — children and adults — need lots of love and a sense of the emotional support of the family. The process of growing up is one of gradually increasing independence. You offer the best atmosphere for that growth by showing love, consistency, and high standards, and by encouraging your youngster's growing *independence* and *integrity*.

For excellent information about child rearing, write for copies of "Caring About Kids" to Public Inquiries, National Institute of Mental Health, 5600 Fishers Lane, Rockville, Maryland 20857. Ask for "Stimulating Baby Senses", "The Importance of Play", and "Cognitive Development", and others of the series. (They are free as we go to press.)

More references:
Families Today: A Research Sampler on Families and Children. Ira Gordon, "Improving Parent Skills," and Burton White, "Developing a Sense of Competence in Children" (with Herbert Yahraes). National Institute of Mental Health, 5600 Fishers Lane, Rockville, MD 20857.

© Masters Agency, Capitola, CA

"Where did we go wrong?"

Guilt

WHAT DO I DO WHEN my kids don't show appreciation for what I give them and do for them? I feel guilty for being resentful, but I also feel that I'm being taken for granted.

In days of yore, the appropriate garb for repentance and guilt was to wear a hair shirt and beat oneself with barbed branches. This is now frowned upon, and it is more socially acceptable to *brood* — especially while sitting on a hard chair at the kitchen table, sipping a cup of cold, black coffee (particularly if you like sugar and cream).

There is another alternative. You can heat up the coffee, throw in sugar and cream, refuse to be a "love junkie" and give up the guilt. "Ridiculous!" you say. "Did you ever see a tear-stained face? A disappointed child? And know that *you* are responsible? How can you be so cold-hearted?!! For shame!! What do you mean — love junkie?"

If you feel that you should give and give to your kids, and not expect anything (including reasonable cooperation and courtesy) in return, you qualify for the label, "love junkie." Further, if you believe that you are a "rotten" parent unless your children are happy, always love you, and never experience frustration, you have fallen into the "good parent trap." Do you feel that it is your fault if your children get upset about anything? Do you say "yes" when you should say "no?" Do you simply threaten instead of following through on discipline, then say, "Well, I'll forgive you *this* time?" Are you always the giver and never the taker? If your answers are "yes," you have definitely earned the right to feel exploited.

Why are you doing these things? This usually happens if you are hungry for love and approval. Not knowing how to get love any other way, you may try to buy it and ask for nothing in return. That is a disservice to you and to your kids, who then learn to have unrealistic expectations of the world and may even become sophisticated manipulators.

All children — and immature adults — want what they want when they want it. They believe, irrationally, that others must never disappoint, criticize, or frustrate them. They often learn to pout and act unhappy to get what they want. Indulged children get unearned privileges and material goods (a bedroom furnished with all that modern technology has to offer, a car on their 16th birthday, expensive clothes, lavish allowances). The cost, however, of this indulgence can be "learned helplessness." This phenomenon, first described by psychologist Martin

Seligman, suggests that when children are *always* indulged or *always* deprived, no matter what they do, they experience feelings of depression and hopelessness. They conclude that nothing that *they* do makes a difference. They feel contempt for themselves and for others who, they conclude, have no standards or expectations.

If you want your children to develop independent social skills, integrity, and responsibility, you must teach them that what they do *does* make a difference — that privileges and penalties depend upon what *they* do and not upon how you happen to feel at the time. You must also teach them to learn to cope with disappointments and frustrations. They don't have to get emotionally upset just because they don't get what they want when they want it.

It is better that *you* teach those lessons rather than that they learn from uncaring strangers in an indifferent world.

How Can You Escape the Good Parent Trap?

Your self-worth does not depend upon your child's evaluation. You don't need a stamp of approval from anyone but yourself. If you feel assured about what you are doing and why, you are then less likely to submit to the guilt feelings which may result when your children charge: "You don't love me" or "I hate you." (You rotten parent, you!) Very young children say those words without knowing any meaning other than "You aren't giving me what I want!" Older children use them if they have worked with you before!

Think of your role as being an "effective" parent rather than as a "good" or "bad" parent. You will then do what is necessary to train your child in those skills that will help him or her survive in a difficult world. You will be less likely to give in to childish demands. You will understand why it is necessary for your child to *earn* both privileges and penalties.

To be effective, you will be very specific in setting up rules and making requests. You'll be sure your children understand what is expected of them. You won't accept a sloppy job or put up with irritating behavior, because that is not in the best interest of your child. You won't be reluctant to impose penalties or praise a lot when either is earned. (Parents who only praise, or only punish are *very* ineffective.)

You will not be apologetic when your children upset themselves about your rules or about being denied something. You may be sympathetic, but you will also tell them the facts of life, that is, that *they* earned the penalty or the rule — not you. Remind them, too, that they have a choice as to how they will feel about something. You might say, for example, "You knew that you could not go to Little League if you did not finish your homework. Getting upset won't change a thing. I'm sorry that you're angry, and I hope that you won't upset yourself any more than you want to. It's your choice. You may either pout in your room or finish your homework and join the family this evening."

Effectively raising kids is difficult but not impossible. It may help to remember an observation made by psychiatrist Maxie Maultsby: "The only thing I know that comes quick and easy is trouble. Everything else takes time and effort." There's no point in complicating that effort with *your* feelings of guilt!

Some ideas from: *Interaction*, Rational Behavior Therapy Center, Dec. 1979. Author: Linda Carpenter.

How to avoid criticism:
say nothing, do nothing, be nothing.

Homework

WHAT DO I DO WHEN my child won't do his homework or class work?

'And he was as intelligent as other people, his soul was pure and clear as crystal; he was noble and affectionate — and yet he did nothing!'
'But why? What was the reason?'
'The reason...what reason was there? Oblomovism!'

"Oh, no! You mean that my child has caught *oblomovisim*? Is it fatal? That poor child! And all this time I thought he was just lazy! How embarrassing!" No, oblomovism has nothing to do with it (that was just a way of getting your attention). There are a number of reasons why your child is not doing his work. The important thing is to get to the problem as soon as possible — it can snowball. Learning is built upon learning, so you don't want your child to get behind; that places him or her at a great disadvantage. Feelings of failure can even lead to dropping out.

How do you start? Ask for a conference with the teacher and perhaps include the school counselor. Discuss whether your child *can't* or *won't* do the work. A psychological evaluation may be recommended by the counselor, and you may also need to arrange a checkup for vision and hearing or an exam to rule out other physical disabilities.

If the evaluation suggests that learning disabilities are involved, the school staff can develop an individual program for your child to help correct the problems and provide special learning aids. Insist upon an Individualized Educational Plan (IEP) if your child is legally classified as handicapped; federal law requires the school to provide it.

But how do you get Howie to do his homework? Well, you can't make him *want* to do anything, but you *can* arrange some incentives. Trying to "force" him to study is not going to work. If you say, for example, "You *will* study one hour every night," Howie may decide to reject studying and learning forever. You certainly don't want *that* to happen.

"What do you *mean* I should set up an incentive system!? Howie should study because it's an opportunity. He should do the right thing without any kind of rewards!" Well, that's the goal. Ideally, a child should learn just for the joy of learning. The problem is that Howie may not yet have discovered the "joy." You can lead him to that discovery by setting up some obvious payoffs for learning. We have to work with "what is," not "what ought or should be." There is no point lecturing about the merits of education and how Lincoln studied by candle light, in a cabin, snuggled in a blanket to ward off the cold...and, further, walked 20 miles to borrow a text book. That will make no impression whatsoever. You have to be more clever than that. Howie wants something, and you want homework done. You simply set up doing homework as a way for him to get what he wants.

How do you do that? Well, one way to motivate your child to do school and homework is to set up a home-school card system as discussed in the "School Behavior" chapter. That system, of course, has to be worked out with the teacher and counselor.

If you can afford a home computer, that is an excellent study aid. Special learning programs are being developed, and kids love to work with a machine that gives immediate feedback and never, ever gets impatient or irritated or critical. Another advantage is that you can set up a system whereby Howie can earn 30 minutes of "game time" for every 30 minutes of study time. Remember, though, it's study time first, *then* play time.

A home computer can be a powerful advantage in another way as well. You can set up a system whereby the only way Howie can earn extra game-playing time each evening (for example, an extra 30 minutes) is to hand in all class work. That requires that you contact the teacher on a daily basis. You can either call or ask her to send home a daily report. (Warning! Follow through to the letter whatever system you set up. Trust your child, but remove temptation. If Howie says that he lost the report, no game time. That's the same as "work not done." Kids are not stupid. They will find a weak spot of it exists!)

Incidentally, calculators and computers are wonderful tools for learning, but remember that Howie will need some basic skills when the machines are not handy. Be sure he learns to spell, add, subtract, multiply, and divide on his own!

You may have tried to motivate your child by promising to pay $1 for every A, 75 cents for B's, or other amounts or rewards for report card grades. You found, then, that this did not work. Why? The reason is that it is a long time between report cards! Most kids need more frequent feedback, and that's the advantage of a daily report system.

Children have to be taught good work habits. Nine-year-old Eddie often daydreamed through his class and homework assignments. Tired of the teacher's complaints, his mother finally told him that, from now on, he would be given 30 minutes each day to do his homework. (Eddie, his mother, and teacher agreed that was enough time if he stayed on the job.) When asked when he preferred to study, Eddie decided that seven p.m., after he had cleared off the dinner dishes, would be a good time. The kitchen table had good lighting, and was a place where his mother could keep a friendly, supervisory eye on him. With the timer set for 30 minutes, he could earn a maximum of 20 cents at each study session. If he had ten arithmetic problems, he received two cents for each correct answer *at the end of the session.* On the other hand, if he had 20 reading questions to answer, he earned one cent for each correct answer. If he did not complete his homework by the time the bell rang, he got what he had earned but had to stay and finish his homework without further compensation. He received 20 cents automatically if the teacher sent home word that he had completed his assignments at school.

If you decide to use this procedure, it is easy to set up a very simple daily feedback system with Howie's teacher. It is also a good idea to check in with the teacher once a week, for example, every Friday, to be assured that the system is working — and to help keep your child honest — until he gets into the habit of doing school and homework.

Direct payment in cash, of course, is not the only immediate reward system, or even the "best." The point-earning chore chart (see page 41) could be used, with points earned for correct homework answers and bonuses earned for "no homework days because work was done at school.'' The Special Problems Chart (page 157) is often useful as a fairly long-term payoff system. You can negotiate as to what your child would like to earn: game, record, time at the video arcade game, special privilege. Your child can earn a star or points for each day that all homework is completed within the 30 minutes and after any errors were corrected. *Two* stars or double points could be earned for each day that Howie did not have to bring work home because it was finished at school.

Keep the program simple. Make it clear. Follow through.

It is worth extra effort to resolve the school work problem before your children become teenagers because then the situation becomes more complex. Usually, the only control you then have is ''free time.'' Even that is manageable if you are willing to keep in close contact with the school and follow through. Don't hesitate to consult with the school counselor or another specialist in behavioral contracting if problems emerge with your teenager.

A useful reference for parents of adolescents is *How to Deal with Your Acting-Up Teenager — Practical Self-Help for Desperate Parents,* by R. T. Bayard and J. Bayard, San Jose, CA: The Accord Press, 1981.

''Oblomovism'' was coined by Ivan Goncharov in his essay, *Oblomov*, published in 1859.

© Masters Agency, Capitola, CA

''I've got to hang up now; I promised Dad I'd help him with my homework.''

Hyperactivity

WHAT DO I DO WHEN I think my child is "hyperactive?" I think he'll do okay, but how do I survive?

"All around the mulberry bush
the monkey chased the weasel.
The monkey thought 'twas all in fun;
Pop! goes the weasel."

"At Last!" reads the headline, "Perpetual Motion Discovered." In *your* house? It's your child!

Anyway it seems that way with some youngsters. Don't be too quick to attach the label "hyperactive," however. It's a "buzzword" which can *cause* trouble that isn't there.

Only a *very* small percentage of children are actually "hyper" active. The term "hyperactive" is simply a way of saying that a child is "really a handful" (restless and distractible). Unfortunately, some parents and teachers treat it as a disease. It is not. Why are some kids very active? There is no one reason.

As a parent of a very active youngster, you will have to learn to cope — for your own benefit and that of your child. There is no magic that will transform little Hermione or Herman into the little dreamboat that you wanted. Read special books and articles on the subject; bring yourself up-to-date on such factors as poor diet, lack of stimulation, and inconsistent parental standards.

Meanwhile, *how* do you cope? First of all, don't feel guilty. You are not a great sinner. Herman's behavior is not "punishment" for your behavior! Your child may require some special consideration but he does *not* have a disease. He is simply very active. And don't take Hermione's behavior *personally*. Sometimes it may seem so, but she is not deliberately going out of her way to make *you* miserable (even though the trials of Job may seem to be overstated in comparison!) She'll act pretty much the same active way with anyone.

The big problem of living with hyperactive children is all the energy it takes to socialize them. You have to monitor behavior far more frequently than with "average" children. You have to check up on behavior every few minutes, and may have to impose Time Out again and again and again. Whereas the "average" child may learn what is not acceptable after 20 Time Outs, Herman may require 95 or 200 Time Outs. But don't despair. He'll learn eventually. Teaching very active children to think before they act is *very* important. (See "Reasoning.")

Basic guidelines for dealing with Herman and

Hermione are the same as those for any child — set limits, impose consequences, praise. Some other guidelines:

...*Be slow to "pigeon hole"* your child. Labels such as "hyperactive" do not explain anything, may not be accurate, and tend to *create* problems. Treat Hermione as a human being with special needs.

...Learn to *give simple instructions* and to break up chores into small assignments. Remember that Herman's attention span is limited, and he is easily distracted. Learn to give many cues, for example, to remind him that it is 15 (10) (5) minutes before dinner or before a chore must be done.

...*Be realistic.* Do not expect to eliminate hyperactivity, just try to keep it under reasonable control by setting limits. Just because Hermione is very active does not mean that she should be excused for jumping up and down on the sofa.

...*Provide a place* where Herman can run and be boistrous. A fenced yard helps. In bad weather, a safe recreation room or garage where he can let off some energy without criticism should be available. He needs to learn where it is *okay* to "let go," and where more sedate behavior is expected.

...*Set routines.* A time for meals and sleep should be established and consistently followed. Active children feel most comfortable when there is a time and place for things. They like their lives to be well-ordered and predictable.

...*Set limits*. Do not permit Hermione to "get out of hand," to harm herself or others, including animals. Use Time Out consistently. It works as well with such kids as with less active children. Do not roughhouse with Herman or permit siblings to do so, especially in the evening. The active child has difficulty calming down once he has been overstimulated.

...Find time to *read stories* to Herman (especially calm and peaceful stories), and teach him quiet games of increasing difficulty; start with building blocks and eventually progress to card and board games. Herman is as able as others to concentrate when involved in situations that are new and intriguing. Electronic games and teaching programs should be a great help if you can afford them.

...*Provide safe and unbreakable toys.* Do *not* give Herman a lot of toys at once. That will only confuse and overstimulate him.

...*Gradually introduce the social world* (church, restaurants, gatherings). At first, the visits should be brief (about 10 minutes) and always tell your child ahead of time what is expected of her. Give a lot of praise when she behaves well, but don't hesitate to gently impose Time Out or remove her entirely from the situation if you have to. Don't feel apologetic or embarrassed. Other people will simply have to understand.

...*Don't compare any child* with "model" children. Active children especially will suffer from comparison because they are tougher on parents. Herman is a special child and always will be. Don't expect friends and neighbors to appreciate all that you have to do to socialize your child, who will probably make many mistakes. Hang in there. He'll learn. Any you'll both be better off if you remember that *every* child is unique and special. Don't compare 'em!

...Last but not least, *make time for yourself.* Plan to take an afternoon a week and an occasional evening out. You deserve it. You need it. Enrolling Hermione in a preschool nursery or Head Start class is also helpful. If you need guidance and moral support, don't hesitate to consult with a mental health specialist.

What Causes Hyperactivity?

According to Oregon psychiatrist Dr. Clement Vickery, many children develop hyperactive symptoms when feeling depressed, anxious, or otherwise troubled. With others, the cortex may have been injured at birth. Neurological or genetic factors may be involved. Although the evidence is mixed, diet may be a contributor, especially excessive sugar and/or artificial coloring (i.e. "junk foods" are not recommended). Some youngsters are "hyperactive" in school when they become bored by repetition, dull lessons, or distraction by other children.

Symptoms of chemical/genetic hyperactivity are evident by the age of two; even earlier an infant may be noticed to be tense or jittery, and to be erratic in establishing feeding and sleeping patterns. It is very hard to know what to expect. *Do not create problems where none exist, however, by assuming your "fussy" baby will be a "hyperactive" child!*

One interesting finding about highly active children is that their speech development appears to be different from that of other children. A Russian scientist, Dr. A. Luria, found that most children go through three stages while acquiring speech. At first, the infant is nonverbal and responsive to simple, directive speech. During the second stage, from two to four years, the child starts to talk to him or herself while playing. (We adults usually do that — particularly when we are learning something new or reviewing a mental check of things to do. We call it "thinking out loud.") During the third stage, the child stops talking aloud, and speech "goes underground" (becomes subvocal).

Apparently, very active kids do not go through the second stage of self-directive talk. That may be one of the reasons that they have impulse control problems. They do not learn to think things through before acting on them. Instead, they tend to react with the first idea that occurs to them without considering the consequences of the act. As a result, they have to be taught to learn to reason (to think before they act).

How Do Active Children Differ From Others?

If your Herman or Hermione is a very active child, you will probably experience one or more of three major complaints. Teachers will probably complain that your child is inattentive (easily distracted, doesn't seem to listen), impulsive (acts before thinking, needs a lot of supervision), and highly active (always "on the go"). Dr. Vickery notes that the attention-span deficit appears to be of most concern. You won't be surprised to be told that your active child has difficulty concentrating on most things for very long and is unusually adept at creating chaos in the classroom. You've seen the same at home. As a result, your child may have learning problems at school.

You may also notice that your child tends to be overfriendly ("never knows a stranger"), and you have to give very special training to teach him or her to be reserved and discriminating in regard to others.

Families that include a very active child experience unusual stress, notes Dr. Vickery. In addition to the more obvious behavioral problems, such a child can be the source of family arguments and disrupted relationships because of problems of discipline. The child has a remarkable capacity to be persistently demanding, which usually exhausts the patience of parents and teachers — who must be equally persistent in being firm and consistent. Because of the child's persistence, it is difficult for adults to be consistent! Too often, the child may be spanked one day, ignored the next, and even indulged on the following day — all for essentially the same behavior.

Do Drugs or Diet Help?

The results in regard to drugs or diet are inconclusive — even controversial.

"Medication is too often used to alleviate hyperactive symptoms," says Dr. Vickery. "It is a form of instant panacea that is presumed to have a magical quality. It is a 'band-aid approach' and not a real treatment modality. The danger is that the parent and child may rely on medication to keep peace in the household. Without teaching the child appropriate social behaviors and some retraining of all concerned, the family is totally dependent on the doctor and his prescription pad."

Medication can sometimes help, notes Dr. Vickery, but "it should be used discriminately. Some children are so active and so easily distracted by any stimulus that impinges on them, they cannot pay attention to limitations for more than very short periods of time. Medication, then, serves as a simple survival measure for the child and those around him until his behavior is brought under control through a behavioral program using rewards and Time Out consistently."

Medication, such as Ritalin, may lead to some side reactions, but these are relatively minor and usually not significant in the doctor's decision to prescribe medication, says Dr. Vickery.

Many subtleties are involved in determining whether medication is effective, for example, the expectations of the child, the family, and the doctor. Even the home setting, the moods and personalities of the persons involved help determine effects, observed Dr. Vickery. *For real behavior change, it is the wish for change, the integrity and commitment of the parents that determines whether a treatment will — or will not — be successful.* It is preferable, he thinks, to *try other approaches before resorting to medication.* The guidelines above are a good place to begin.

As a final note, be sure to also read the chapter "Attention Span," which has a number of ideas you'll find helpful.

Infant Training

WHAT DO I DO WHEN my baby is brand new? When do I start training my infant?

Tis education forms the common mind:
As the twig is bent, the tree's inclined.

Alexander Pope

Get ready! Get set! Go!...on one of the most wonderful adventures you will ever experience; that is, to help and watch your infant slowly change from a small, helpless being to a purposeful personaltiy. When do you start training (teaching)? You start the day that you bring infant Rosemary home from the hospital. Don't press the panic button. It is not all that complex, and some guidelines are provided here to help you give your child a good start in one the the most important years of her life.

Tending to Rosemary's physical needs is only part of the job. To help in the bonding process (that is her relationship with you), that, in turn, affects how she will relate to others, you need to understand how to deal with crying as well as how to show your love. To help her develop some feeling of competency even at this early age, you need to provide a stimulating environment and understand some things about temperamental differences in children.

Science has finally substantiated what most mothers have known for thousands of years — that babies are born with different temperaments. Some move all over the crib. Others never seem to move from one spot. Some are easily distracted, others are more persistent. Some resent change in routine, and others are always ready to party.

If you're lucky, Rosemary will be an "easy child" — regular in habits, quick to enjoy new situations and people, generally cheerful. This is known as the "parents' delight." You don't have to hesitate to waken this child to show off to relatives because she'll glow in the limelight. Don't take too much credit for training this gem — the genes had a lot to do with her disposition.

The "difficult" infant is irregular in eating, sleeping, and eliminating right from the beginning. She tends to protest vigorously when exposed to new situations and seems to be related to the Grinch who stole Christmas. This child expresses disappointment "not with a whimper but with a bang," and her temper tantrums are wondrous scenes to behold. This is *not* the infant you would waken out of a sound sleep to show off to Aunt Mable — unless, of course, you want to cut her visit off short.

Then there is the shy or "slow to warm up" infant, who adapts very slowly and tends to withdraw from new situations rather than to fuss and fume. This child lets new food just dribble out of her mouth. Later, in nursery school, she is likely to stand on the sidelines and have to be pushed into activities. If you have a "shy" infant, warn Aunt Mable that she needs time to warm up and not to indulge her with attention and affection until she does so.

The type of child you have is what you've got, and there's no point in bemoaning your fate. Understanding just means that you have to learn how to deal with your ingenious and unique child. The recommended techniques are appropriate for most children, but you will have to use more energy to train some than others.

...*Establish routines very early.* Don't expect Rosemary to put herself on a schedule. She will feel safer and more secure if you use the same place to diaper, same time and place to feed and bathe so that she learns what to expect. Your baby, however, will signal you when she is ready to eat or sleep less. Don't compare your infant with others. If you are concerned, consult with your pediatrician. Your baby is unique and has her own developmental schedule and needs.

...*Providing stimulation is critically important* to help any child feel wanted and loved and to energize and sensitize intellectual development (to make smart). You do that best through your attention. Any time you respond to your baby — pick up, talk to, feed, hug, sing to, diaper — you are stimulating the growth and development of sensory organs and the brain structures that make them work.

...*Talk to your baby a lot. No baby talk* because you are setting the stage for language development, and you don't want to start any bad habits. Talk about anything. Your baby loves to hear your voice when you talk in natural and soothing tones. Recite poems, talk about your day, discuss the weather, read the newspaper or bedtime stories.

...*Sing to your baby.* That old rocking chair is still a great invention — hard to beat for singing to and rocking baby. A papoose-carrier is highly recommended as a way to give Mary Ann a sense of motion and close body contact while permitting you to go about your errands.

...*Turn off the TV* and play records. Babies who are subjected to the continual blaring of the TV vocalize less and talk later than do other children.

...*Cuddle and touch your baby.* When you bathe, diaper, or hold your child, gently rub fingers and toes, stroke hair, massage your infant's body soothingly. Don't worry about spoiling him or her by giving too much love and attention. You are building a relationship with a small person. By the tone of your voice, facial expression, and gentle handling, you are conveying the message, "You're a lovely baby. A real joy. We like having you around and will help all we can." Through frowns and jerky, irritated movements, another, less happy, message can be conveyed that says, "You're a bother and a pest, and life was better when you weren't around." Each message sets up certain expectations. You can bring out the best or the worst in your infant by the message you give. Also, the way you handle your baby during bathing and diaper changing, tells your infant how you feel about bodies, including sexual organs. Matter-of-fact and gentle handling gives one message. Expressions of shame or disgust give another message.

...*Provide toys and stimulating objects* right from the start. New born infants can focus their eyes and follow bright moving objects with them. At first, hang mobiles from the ceiling and toys from the crib or carriage. Put colorful pictures on the walls and paste decals on the crib at baby's eye level. Later, she'll be intrigued with measuring cups and spoons, boxes and plastic bottles, soft scraps of fabric. Rotate toys and do not put more than five in the crib or play pen at a time.

Babies love to swing and sway in wind-up canvas swings, some of which have built-in music boxes. Later, they enjoy bouncing up and down in canvas "jumpers" and to rock on rocking horses.

...*Don't confine your infant for long periods*. Do not

expect your baby to stay in a crib, play pen, high chair, or swing for hours at a time. When Rosemary starts moving about, do not limit her to a play pen for more than 30 minutes at a time. That provides time for play and learning to focus and develop attention span; however, your child also needs the opportunity to move about and explore the place she calls home. It's a good idea to schedule 30 minutes in a confined area (play pen or swing) and 30 minutes to explore freely.

...Be sure to *childproof your home*, and do not place your infant near electrical outlets, hot radiators, or fans. Ask yourself, "Can this hurt her:" or "Would I be upset if she broke that?" Infants love to tear papers. You can fill a bottom drawer full of old newspapers, but place unread, favorite magazines out of reach. Provide a special cabinet in your kitchen to house pots and pans that baby can play with, but make certain that it's not near the stove. Find an out-of-reach place for poisons and cleansers. You have to protect your child, but you don't want to discourage curiosity and exploration. Don't worry that your house won't qualify for a feature article in *Better Homes and Gardens!* There's plenty of time to make an impression later. Now, you want to keep your home clean and safe.

...*Get into the habit of monitoring* (checking up on) your infant often to make certain that she is okay and not getting into unexpected mischief. This will become increasingly important at the two- and three-year-old stage.

...*Don't attempt to discipline your infant.* Divert instead. When your baby gets into forbidden things, simply say "no" gently but firmly, pick her up, and move her to something she *can* play with. Always say "No" to what you don't want or like and provide a distraction. If you have a fretful, crying baby, seek help from others. *You* need "Time Out!" Dr. E. Christophersen suggests that even an infant can be placed in a crib or play pen after a misbehavior and then released from Time Out after five seconds of quiet; but don't expect too much too early! The toddler from 15 to 36 months can be placed in a chair or other room and released after three minutes of quiet. (See "Discipline.")

...*Introduce other trusted adults* to your baby and let them play with and care for her from time to time before she gets to the period when she is able to discriminate between those she knows (Mom and Dad) and other people. That occurs between six and nine months. Your baby, however, does not need playmates and may or may not be interested in watching other children play. Her own company and the attention of her family and other significant adults are quite sufficient.

Your child's first year is very important and only a few guidelines are provided here. Don't be afraid to seek assistance when, and if, you feel you need it. Don't wait to feel desperate before you consult with your pediatrician or child specialist. Look for parent training groups to learn about child development and to get support from others who also sometimes feel frustrated, harried, and wondering what to do when. Be sure, also, to find a trusted baby sitter whom you can call on because you need time out for yourself.

For more information about teaching and learning about your infant, the following are recommended:

Your First Months With Your First Baby by A. Barman can be ordered for 25 cents by writing to Public Affairs Pamphlets, 381 Park Ave., South, New York 10016.
Successful Parenthood: How to teach your child values, competence, and responsibility, by W. C. Becker and J. W. Becker, Follett Publishing Co., 1974.
T. Berry Brazelton, M. D. *Infants & Mothers,* Dell Publishing Co., 1979.
Working with Parents and Infants: An Interactional Approach, by R. Bromwich, Baltimore, University Park Press, 1981.
Frank Caplan, Princeton Center for Infancy & Early Childhood, *The First 12 Months of Life*, Bantam Books, 1973.
Little People by E. R. Christophersen, H & H Enterprises, Inc. 1977.
Ira J. Gordon, *Baby Learning Through Baby Play*, St. Martin's Press, New York: 1970.
Stimulating Baby Senses and *The Importance of Play* of the Caring About Kids series, published by the National Institute of Mental Health. Single free copies can be received by writing to: Public Inquiries, National Institute of Mental Health, 5600 Fishers Lane, Rockville, Maryland 20857.

Life is a do-it-yourself job.

Lecturing

WHAT DO I DO WHEN my daughter won't listen to reason? I've told her a hundred times...!

You are talking "reason." To you, your words are clear, distinct, and logical as you explain why honesty is the best policy or why cooperation is important. If you were on the stage or an attorney in a courtroom, the applause would be deafening. You are in fine form — the best ever! But what is Eloise doing? Is she impressed? No! You can almost "see" your pearls of wisdom drift in one ear and out the other while she stands attentively (well, upright anyway) with eyes glazed over. You may as well be reciting Lewis Carroll's classic poem:

"Twas brillig and the slithy toves
Did gyre and gymble in the wabe:
All mimsy were the borogoves
And the mome raths outgrabe."

Now *that* is frustrating! How can you convince this child that civilized people "listen to reason" and then do the proper thing? *She*, unfortunately, calls it "Lecturing" (a form of persecution designed to keep her from doing something she wants to do). Given the opportunity, Eloise would probably debate your basic premise: the virtues and power of reasoning in the history of humankind. (Give the kid credit. At least she knows when to keep still!)

Why doesn't lecturing work? Because children, along with almost everyone else, are more readily persuaded by consequences than by logic. (Think of all the money and energy that could be saved if we didn't have to have traffic lights, policemen, and laws! All we would need would be a lecture or two about good citizenship and safety.)

There are other reasons why you might want to get off the lecture circuit. Any discussion longer than three sentences tends to be rewarding to a child, according to psychological research. Thus, your lectures may actually be *rewarding* your daughter (though not if she's a teenager!) with attention for the very behavior that you want to eliminate! Eloise may not hear a word you say, but think how intrigued she must be to see you (a grown person) talk on and on and on, seriously and intensely. Why, attention like this just can't be bought anyplace! *So*, the moral to that is: talk a *lot* when Eloise does something that pleases you. You will find that her hearing and attention will improve miraculously; you will be considered to be a marvelous wit! You will also get a lot more of the behavior that brought on the "I Approve" talk.

Another problem with lecturing, especially as Eloise gets a little older, is that she may conclude such reasoning represents a form of parent weakness, signalling indecision and uncertainty. ("If you're so sure about what you want, why do you have to explain it so much?") Another unwanted side effect is that she may learn to become a "Philadelphia lawyer" — expert at debating, arguing, or devising ingenious excuses and accusations designed to inspire your guilt. Some children become so skillful that they build an incredible record when they enter school, putting an army of teachers on the defensive. It is very difficult to break the "debate habit" once it is developed.

Resist that urge to "talk her out of" misbehavior. Restrain yourself and be very brief and direct when you are correcting her. Use consequences, not lectures, as a way of helping Eloise learn to think things through. Refer to and use the procedures described in the "Discipline" and "Reasoning" chapters. You will then have more time to share your perceptions, experiences, and values during *pleasant* conversations involving give and take with your child.

The real key to lecturing is...don't!

Matches and Fire

WHAT DO I DO WHEN I find that my son has been playing with matches?

Hard to believe isn't it? *Your* child play with matches? You thought that he had more sense than to do that? After all you told him! It must be the influence of Beelzebub, that kid down the block whose parents just let him run wild!

It *is* frightening to find that your child has been playing with matches. But some kids *do* experiment, and you're fortunate if you discover that before there's real trouble. You have to react, of course, but how? What kind of consequence can you impose that will help Freddy remember that matches are not playthings? Lecturing or threats won't help. Taking him to the fire department, or asking a fireman to come to the house to talk about the hazards of fire *could* be exciting and rewarding instead of punishment. However, if your local fire department has an active fire safety/prevention program, talk with them and see if they may be of help.

I recommend that you have a *serious conference* with

Freddy. Tell him that you are disappointed in this behavior, that playing with matches can cause death or injury. He should arrange to pay for any damages, and lose a treasured privilege, for example, a favorite TV show, his bike, or playtime with friends, for a period of two weeks (yes, *this* time!). Ask Freddy to repeat back to you what is going to happen and why. (In that way, you will know that he understood what you said.) Each day, then, for the following 14 days, ask him to explain — once or twice a day — why he is being restricted. "Because I played with matches." You then ask, "What's the rule?" It's sufficient for him to respond, "I am not to play with matches."

At the end of the two weeks, you have to teach Freddy when matches *may* be used. It's unrealistic to tell him that he "must NEVER, EVER touch another match again." That's not true, for one thing, because fire and matches are a part of our lives; everyone has to learn how to use these safely. The day has to come — around five or six years — when you have to *teach* Freddy how to use matches, otherwise he *will* probably experiment. (Don't we all tend to become intrigued with what is novel and forbidden?) If Freddy views matches as a household item that has to be used carefully, he will probably think that Beelzebub down the block is weird and boring for being fascinated with matches.

To remove the mystery of fire and the challenge of the unlit match, you need to permit Freddy to light a match *under your supervision* as a part of some assigned chore. One of the best ways to do that is to start using candles at the dinner table (it's important to make a ritual out of dinner time anyway.) Older children can learn to light fireplace and/or barbeque fires. Tell Freddy that he will be assigned the job of lighting the candles (or fire), but *only* when Mom or Dad is watching to see that the job is done properly. Be sure, then, that he tells *you* when he may light a match, and the answer must be, "When told to, and *only when Mom or Dad is watching*."

Training kids about matches begins very early, usually when your toddler starts to bring small, "found" items — a toy, flower, stone, or other discovery to you. It's important to pay attention and praise that little ritual. Matches are likely to be among the things Freddy finds occasionally. Keep them in a special place and don't make them too readily available. Freddy will pick up the cue from you that matches are special and need to be handled carefully. Sometimes, you may hear him exclaim, "Oh, oh!" when he finds a forbidden object, such as a book of matches, and brings it to you. Be sure to praise and make a big deal out of that!

If, in spite of these efforts, you have more than one incident of playing with matches, I suggest you consult with a counselor and/or fire prevention professional. The situation may be more complex than childish curiosity. *Fire setting* is a different, more deliberate act than playing with matches. If *that* happens, run, don't walk, for professional help.

Mealtimes

WHAT DO I DO WHEN my kids misbehave at the dinner table and in the restaurant?

"A child should always say what's true
And speak when he is spoken to,
And behave mannerly at the table,
At least as far as he is able."

Robert L. Stevenson

It's really difficult to have candlelight dinners and scintillating conversation when bread is flying across the table and kids are nudging each other, there're fingerprints in the butter, and charges and countercharges of "You did!" "I didn't!" and "Ma, look what she's *doing*!"

You could, of course, send them all off to camp, but that ends up being costly (and very difficult to find in the winter). There's another solution. You can *train* them to have company manners at home, which takes care of problems at the restaurant.

You've thought of that, of course, but how to do it? The procedure is simple; following it may not be. Read the instructions below, then follow them carefully *and* consistently! There's no promise that you'll end up feeling like you're having dinner at the Ritz, but things will be a lot more peaceful in a very short time.

Start with a "proclamation" to the family (writing it in calligraphy is impressive but not necessary):

...Dinner will be served at a regular time for the whole family. No TV, no phone calls (friends can be told of the agreed hour; other callers can be called back later).

...*Everyone* is to remain seated until excused from the table.

...Teasing, hair-pulling, grabbing, arguing, or interrupting when someone is talking are all off-limits.

...Small portions will be served (second helpings are always available), and must be eaten before dessert will be offered. *"Now hear this!"* Anyone who does not eat his or her dinner or is excused from the table for misbehavior, will not eat *anything* until the next meal. (Water, of course, is always available.) No one has ever starved to death in three or 12 hours — even three days!

...Each person will be encouraged to contribute some conversation about the most interesting things that happened during the day. (No blood and gore stories. Nobody is interested in who beat up whom at school.) No nagging or complaining at the table — and that includes Mom and Dad.

...The emphasis will be on positive, sharing communication, building "family spirit."

"Okay, Mom," says your eight-year-old, "Can I turn on the TV now?" *"After* I'm through talking, dear, and after you've picked up your toys in the living room. You need to know that when any rule is broken — if you hit or annoy or interrupt even once — you will be told to go to Time Out. I will not warn you. I will simply *tell* you, and I will do so without guilt, pity, or remorse. You may then return to the dinner table when the buzzer rings."

"Good Heavens!" you say, "At that rate, dinner could last all night!!" No, because (and this is the *piece de resistance*) each child is permitted only two Time Outs. The third time means that the meal is over for him or her. There are, then, no snacks, *nothing*, until the next meal.

It's amazing how quickly this works. And this is only the beginning. Just wait until your kids hear about the assigning of chores — table setting, clearing, and doing dishes — after dinnertime problems have gotten under control. When can you start this? From age three on up to college.

But What Do I Do When We Go to a Restaurant?

Be sure to tell your kids, from age three on, exactly how you want them to behave when they go to the restaurant. You want them to sit quietly, not to rough house, and not to leave the table without permission, It's also a good idea to tell them ahead of time what they may or may not order. (Some kids may have steak appetites on a hamburger budget! It's better to disillusion them at home than in the restaurant.) Help them to understand that their restaurant behavior affects not only the family but also the other people who have come to enjoy the meal. They need to be even quieter than you require at home. Ask each child to repeat back to you what you have said. Remember that they may not be hearing everything you're saying, but you won't know that until they've told you what they heard.

Also, tell your kids that anyone who misbehaves will be taken to the lobby or car — under supervision — "to cool off" for a few minutes. (*Never* leave a child under 12 alone in a car without adult supervision.) If there is more than one "cooling off" period, that child will be left home the *next* time the family goes to the restaurant.

If you have a lot of problems with a very young child, for example, under age five, you may have to plan some "practice trips" whereby you take your child out for a coke or ice cream. When he or she starts behaving well, then you can plan a mealtime visit. Start small. Fast food restaurants are better places to practice than dark, intimate dining rooms! Be sure to praise your kids a lot when they are behaving well. Nagging and lecturing just won't do the job.

Dinnertime is one of the most important rituals that involves the family. It represents one of the few times, in this crazy age, that most family members actually meet together in the same room and can converse and share experiences with each other. It is a daily opportunity to nurture good relationships; make the most of it!

Every pearl is the result of an oyster's victory over an irritation.

Praise

WHAT DO I DO WHEN my nine-year-old daughter over-reacts to criticism? She can't seem to understand that if we didn't love her, we would not take the time and trouble to point out her failings.

"A baby is fed on milk and praise."
Charles Lamb

If you want your child to do something, praise a lot. Don't wait for big successes. Praise the small attempts, the little victories. When your child brings home an arithmetic test paper, make a point of being impressed that six problems were right and only four problems were wrong, and isn't that great! If your son washes the dishes and some have to be rewashed, say, "The plates are so clean they sparkle! You did a *good* job on those. The pots and pans need a bit more work, though."

The secret of success in the parenting job is to find what's right — to "accentuate the positive and eliminate the negative." You may have to look long and hard, but I guarantee that you'll be amazed at the results.

"But," you protest, "Isn't there such a thing as constructive criticism?" That depends upon how "constructive" and how "critical." Can it be constructive to be fault-finding and highly judgemental — to whittle away at feelings of self-confidence and competency? If, as the Chinese proverb says, "Words are the voice of the heart," what message do words of criticism convey?

"Do you mean," you may persist, "that a child should be permitted to do anything s/he wants and never be criticized?!" Of course not. We all have to have feedback to correct our mistakes. Correction, however, implies *teaching*, and the opportunity to improve performance with encouragement. It is directed toward the *behavior*, not toward the *person*. You won't get very far if you tell Melinda, for example, "Look at the mess your room is in! How can you be so lazy and sloppy? How are you ever going to amount to anything? What did I do to deserve a kid like you?" You *will* get the cooperation you're after if you say instead, "You did a really nice job of making your bed, and I see that you dusted that corner of the desk so it shines. You can go bike riding after you finish the job list: polish the desk, put the clothes in the hamper, tuck the socks into the drawers, and hang up your jacket in the closet."

Love is best expressed and positive attitudes and behavior are built through praise for what Melinda does

99 Ways to Say "Very Good!"

1 You're on the right track now!
2 You're doing a good job!
3 You did a lot of work today!
4 Now you've figured it out.
5 That's RIGHT!!!
6 Now you have the hang of it!
7 That's the way!
8 You're really going to town!
9 You're doing fine!
10 Now you have it!
11 Nice going.
12 That's coming along nicely.
13 That's great!
14 You did it that time!
15 GREAT!
16 FANTASTIC!
17 TERRIFIC!
18 Good for you!
19 GOOD WORK!
20 That's better.
21 EXCELLENT!
22 Good job.
23 You outdid yourself today!
24 Well done!
25 That's the best you have ever done.
26 Good going!
27 Keep it up!
28 That's really nice.
29 WOW!
30 Keep up the good work.
31 Much better!
32 Good for you!
33 That's very much better!
34 Good thinking!
35 Exactly right!
36 SUPER!
37 Nice going.
38 You make it look easy.
39 I've never seen anyone do it better.
40 You are doing that much better today.
41 Way to go!
42 Not bad.
43 Superb!
44 You're getting better every day.
45 WONDERFUL!
46 I knew you could do it.
47 Keep working on it, you're getting better.
48 You're doing beautifully.
49 You're really working hard today.

50 That's the way to do it!
51 Keep on trying!
52 That's it!
53 Nothing can stop you now!
54 You've got it made.
55 You are very good at that.
56 You are learning fast.
57 I'm very proud of you.
58 You certainly did well today.
59 You've just about got it.
60 That's good.
61 I'm proud of the way you worked today.
62 I'm happy to see you working like that.
63 That's the right way to do it.
64 You are really learning a lot.
65 That's better than ever.
66 That's quite an improvement.
67 That kind of work makes me very happy.
68 MARVELOUS!
69 Now you've figured it out.
70 PERFECT!
71 That's not half bad!
72 FINE!
73 You've got your brain in gear today.
74 That's IT!
75 You figured that out fast.
76 You remembered!
77 You're really improving.
78 I think you've got it now.
79 Well look at you go!
80 You've got that down pat.
81 TREMENDOUS!
82 OUTSTANDING!
83 I like that.
84 Couldn't have done it better myself.
85 Now that's what I call a fine job.
86 You did that very well.
87 Congratulations!
88 That was first class work.
89 Right on!
90 SENSATIONAL!
91 That's the best ever.
92 Good remembering!
93 You haven't missed a thing.
94 It's a pleasure to teach when you work like that.
95 You really make my job fun.
96 You must have been practicing.
97 You've just about mastered that!
98 One more time and you'll have it.
99 Congratulations, you got that right!

well or tries to do and helping her correct what she needs to learn to do or to do better. Put downs, criticisms, and sarcasms are corrosive and coercive. They are the bricks that build walls between you and your child. The child who seldom or never hears a word of praise becomes an easy mark for sympathetic exploiters later in her life.

"Isn't there such a thing as too much praise?" you ask. "Won't that ruin my child and make her conceited?" Conceit (defined as "an exaggerated estimate of one's own ability and importance") *is* undesireable. To be praised and *never* corrected is as unrealistic as always being corrected and never praised is defeating and demeaning. "Be virtuous; not too much; just what's correct," advised Jacques Monvel, "Excess in anything is a defect."

The important thing is to strike a balance, but tip the scales toward praise. At a minimum, find something to praise for each correction you make. The ideal ratio is three or more praises for each correction; then watch Melinda's spirit thrive and glow. You'll be amazed at the cooperation you'll get.

Some youngsters are so starved for praise that when parents start being more positive, they complain, "Raymond wants praise for everything! I'm exhausted saying 'good' and 'very good.'" So what's wrong with that? Raymond is also doing a lot more than he ever did before; he may even seem to be a new, different kid!

It may be an old cliche, but it's nonetheless true: A family with a million dollars is still impoverished if there is no affection and praise in the home. A family without a red cent, little to eat, few toys, no privacy, but with warmth and a show of caring, is wealthy. "Love is not to be purchased and affection has no price," observed St. Jerome.

Maternity wards, along with the formula prescription and care instructions, should give every parent a copy of "99 Ways to Say Very Good." Praising is an art that most of us have to learn more about. On the "family world market," it has had a history of being in short supply. A lot of talk about love, and very little practice! Eliza Doolittle, in *My Fair Lady* said it simply: "Show Me!" Most of us have been trained to be critics; we need much more skill in expressing love and praise.

The most explicit instructions for effective praising that I have found were described by psychologists Dr. Robert Eimers and Dr. Robert Aitchison. They recommend that you go directly to your child. Coming close gives a powerful sense of intimacy and warmth. Putting your hand on your child's arm or giving a hug conveys the message that this is important, and you mean every word. Be sure to smile. (A smile is *always* rewarding whether from near or far.) Say something like, "That's *all right!* I'm impressed. You *really* tried" or "Thank you. You helped a lot." Praise right away. Don't give a monthly progress report or wait until Friday to praise something done on Monday. Get excited about little things. Remembering to shut the screen door happens a lot more frequently than being elected class valedictorian.

If you haven't praised in the past — or exercised this talent frequently, it won't be easy, but remember that practice makes perfect. It's a good habit to develop, is inexpensive, can be used everywhere with everyone, and has an excellent return yield. You will find that praise can do what criticism can never do — build the desire to please.

Have you praised your child today?

© Masters Agency, Capitola, CA

"No, this is not the Sleepy-Hollow Rest Home. You're not even close."

Prejudice

WHAT DO I DO WHEN my seven-year-old comes home talking about the "niggers" and "greasers" he has trouble with at school? I've always tried to teach my kids to respect others, regardless of race or sex or religion or whatever.

"I am free of all prejudices. I hate everyone equally," said W. C. Fields. That approach is as unrealistic as "loving everyone equally." Both reveal equally poor judgement. It is preferable, I think, to err on the side of acceptance rather than rejection; however, there *is* a middle road. One can try to respond to every individual on the basis of his or her behavior, not because of some preconceived notion about race, religion, color or sex. Now how do you convince a child of that when other forces — experiences, peers — are beginning to impinge and scar? A seven-year-old will not understand — not yet — but there is a way to start.

As a toddler, your child has no concept of stereotyping or differences, unless, of course, *you* have pointed out certain members of the human race as not acceptable.

Prejudice — an unfavorable opinion formed beforehand and without consideration for the unique qualities of each person — is learned. If you conclude, for example, that blondes are dumb, Poles are ignorant, Blacks are inferior, Cubans are lazy, mothers on Welfare have loose morals, the impoverished lack ability and talent, Indians are the white man's burden — you will likely convey those stereotypes to your child. Children readily pick up such cues through "jokes," comments (slurs), or more subtle frowns, raised eyebrows, and avoidance of contact.

Prejudice can also develop through experience, and impressions are then generalized. If your child is offended or hurt by another child who obviously represents some racial or ethnic group, he or she may jump to the conclusion that *all* members of that group are lazy or aggressive or ignorant. Your child may then start looking for the evidence to justify that conclusion and treat those who do not fit into the stereotype as exceptions to the rule. You have to point out again and again that everyone has a right to be judged as an individual.

Your child, perhaps encouraged by peers, says, "That stupid nigger (or honky, or greaser, or...)." You could say, "Hey, wait a minute. That person has a name. What is the name of the kid who did what you didn't like?" Explain that *your* family doesn't use such words as "nigger" or ''greaser,'' and point out that such labels are degrading and unfair. Your child may be upset with one person — or even a small group — and has a right to reject that person or group, but that doesn't mean that *all* members of that race/sex/group are no good.

Just as you do when you discipline, try to help your child separate the person from the offensive behavior. Often, we can bring out the best or worst in each other by our ''self-fulfilling prophecies.'' It is best to act *as if* each person means well and is doing the best he or she can — unless, of course, that person proves differently.

In addition to specific experiences, early learning in the home is critically important in developing personalities that are more or less likely to be prejudiced. Prejudice is very complicated, and the causes for being prejudiced differ from one person to another. Children who have poor self-esteem are more likely to be prejudiced and look for those they can look down upon as a way of feeling better about themselves. Those who feel insecure have difficulty tolerating frustration and lash out at anyone they think stands in their way. They want certainties and cannot tolerate ambiguities in a highly ambiguous world.

The home environment most likely to produce the prejudiced personality is harsh and punitive. The child is severely punished and subjected to rigid rules. The parents are intolerant and disapproving and seldom, if ever, show warmth or understanding. On the other hand, children are more likely to be tolerant and accepting of others if they grow up in a home atmosphere where they feel loved and encouraged and rules are reasonable, where parents teach democratic values and individual responsibility rather than dividing the world up into ''right'' and ''wrong.'' In short, acceptance breeds acceptance.

As your child grows, make it clear that some language and behaviors are not acceptable because they are put-downs. It is very difficult to completely avoid stereotyping others; that is one way we have of ordering our world. However, we must allow for individual differences. We invite the labels ''good,'' ''bad,'' and ''indifferent'' based on how we act. Everyone has the right not to be prejudged on the basis of skin color, gender, ethnic background, religion, age or handicap. Everyone has the right to be judged by behavior.

There is yet another side of the coin. Why not take pride in being different? In being a part of a different culture with different customs? Do we really want to have a ''melting pot?'' A sense of identity by affiliation with a certain culture can be a valuable source of self-esteem. It would be very boring if everyone were the same. No one should apologize for being a representative of a certain group. The only important requirements are to be yourself and to be considerate toward others. Take pride in who you are. Give others the right to do the same. Let's celebrate our differences!

I recall that when I entered high school, someone came up to me and said, "Hey, Bohack."

"What?" (I had grown up in a neighborhood of Czechs, Poles, and Italians, and had no idea that anyone else existed. I met my first WASP when I went to college, but entering a high school of over 4,000 students introduced me to the polarization of the different groups.)

"You're a Bohack, y'know — a Bohunk. Who needs 'em?"

"Are you implying that I'm someone of Czech descent?"

"Yeh."

"Am I supposed to be worried about that?"

I was quite sincere, (a very serious child) and remember that my antagonist never bothered me again. There was no point to it. I was pleased to be what I was, but I was also fortunate in that I was white and bright and did not experience the prejudices and discrimination directed toward members of other minority groups. It was only as an adult woman that I experienced discrimination; I received half the salary of my male associates in some jobs.

As individuals we can be fair — give others a right to be accepted or rejected as individuals and not to condemn a whole race or other group because of one or two bad examples. And we can teach our children the same sense of fairness. We teach them best by our own example, of course. Do you have friends of different races, sexes, ages, religions? Do you read books, watch TV shows, go to movies which treat all groups fairly? Do you support civil rights organizations? The ERA? Do the sex roles in your home represent a fair distribution of the chores to be done? Is your language free of put-down expressions and ethnic jokes? Fairness from the system is far more complex. We should insist that our government, our laws, our legal system give equal opportunity to all to succeed or fail on their merits. No favors. Just fair treatment. Educational and employment opportunities are critical.

"I have always believed," said Paul Krasner, "that to have true justice we must have equal harrassment under the law."

Profanity

WHAT DO I DO WHEN I overhear my 13-year-old daughter using foul language in conversations with her friends? She tells me that everybody does it and that I'm "not cool" to be concerned.

"What else could I do?" said the father, while 11-year-old Brian sat sullen out in the reception room. "He called his brother a 'bastard.' I washed his mouth out with soap."

"What was that supposed to teach him?"

"Not to swear, of course," he said impatiently.

"Did it work?"

"No. He's worse than he was before. That's why I'm here." He paused. "I'm worried. Brian's my son. I want things to be right between us."

"What did you expect? That he would thank you? Want to please you? Love his brother? That's asking a lot from a bar of soap, isn't it?"

"Well, you just can't let a kid say those things. Y'gotta do *something!*"

That's right. "Y'gotta do something." Swearing is a cue that should not be ignored. The very young child may pick up street language and bring it home to see what happens. Using Time Out at that age is an effective way to teach Joel or Mary Beth that profanity is not acceptable at *your* house. (See "Discipline") Of course, if Mom and/or Dad salt their conversations with lots of four-letter words, they need not be surprised if their offspring do the same. They'll have to change their own speech habits as a way of setting an example.

With older children, obscenities may simply be bad habit or may be symptomatic of more serious issues — chronic anger, poor self-concept, feelings of neglect, cultural deprivation, or depression.

What *can* Brian's father do with his 11-year-old son? In this actual case, the profanity was a symptom of anger and depression, of feeling neglected and often criticized. Physical retaliation — washing out the mouth with soap or putting pepper on the tongue — only serves to reinforce the feeling of helplessness and inadequacy. When aggression meets aggression, it *feeds* aggression. Too often, the youngster begins to plot revenge, and retaliation becomes full-blown during the teen years, if not before. Brian's words *were* aggressive and provoking. They were *meant* to be. The boy did not know how to ask for what he wanted — consideration, affection, respect. At least, the words courted — and got — attention; and *any* attention is better than none. When children (or adults) feel desperate, they do desperate things.

The incident that brought the family into the agency for counseling was not their first, of course. It was simply the "last straw." Prior to that time, the parents had told themselves, "Brian should be appreciative and shape up. We give him a roof over his head, food on the table. He should show respect. Do what he's told to do. What's the matter with this crazy kid?!"

Everyone in the family was angry. They needed to cool off, to change some perceptions, to assert themselves rather than get aggressive, to negotiate with each other. Finally, they had to learn how to express appreciation for each other.

The first step in this journey may seem rather basic, but nothing else would be successful without it: an allowance-and-privilege-earning contract (as discussed in the "Chores and Allowance" chapter) was negotiated between the parents and Brian. This served two purposes: to begin by giving something to everyone; and to evaluate if the parents really were motivated to *follow through* on recommendations and make some changes. Fortunately, they were, and that opened the door to further improvement in the family situation. Six months later, the family had made enough gains that counseling was reduced to an "as needed" basis.

Brian's family had little time to lose. When a youngster enters the teen years, the problems become more complex. Peers become extremely influential, and parents may become targets of vengeance; *that* means grief for everyone concerned. In other instances, the use of obscenities may simply be a bad habit or a means of peer acceptance. Mary Beth may try to convince you that everybody's "loose in language." Admittedly, there's little verbal grace or wit to be found in most communication — including the media — these days. No matter; somewhere, standards must be set. Where else but in the home?

There is no point in giving inspirational lectures, or suggesting that Mary Beth read Shakespeare (who brought insult and profanity to an elegant form of art), or making her write "I will not say !/†=#&*!" 500 times. There are other ways to make an impression and encourage change more quickly and effectively. Try these:

...be sure you have defined "unacceptable language."

...post signs ("Keep a good tongue in your head." "A foul mouth is not cool." "Think first, then speak.") over the telephone and other places as needed.

...set up a contract (see "Special Problems").

...advise Mary Beth that each obscenity will earn 30 minutes of yard work (or similar chores).

...withdraw all privileges — TV, telephone ("*Mother*!

You wouldn't!!" "Oh, yes, I would!!") , record player, radio, and so forth — if other penalties are ineffective or ignored.

...follow through to the letter.

If nothing else works, consult with a counselor. "Speech is a mirror of the soul," said Publius Syrus, the ancient. "As a man speaks, so is he." You must convince Mary Beth of the importance of what she says. She needs to take seriously the impression that she conveys to others. Help her communicate that she thinks well of herself.

Mistakes are great learning tools, if I work with them.

Reasoning

WHAT DO I DO WHEN my child seems determined to act without thinking? She gets into more trouble than I ever thought was possible because she simply doesn't stop and reason things out!

"Too often we give children answers to remember rather than problems to solve."

— Roger Lewin

Sometimes children *do* behave as if they were related to the Scarecrow of Oz! (Let's face it: some *adults* seem filled with straw at times!) No one can blame a parent for hoping that girl someday will find the Wizard, who will magically endow her with wisdom!

Guess who has been nominated? That's right: *You are the Wizard!* Neither magic nor a trip to Oz is required to help you *teach* your child how to reason, which is really a skill and not an inborn gift.

"The difference between blind obedience and reasoned action is in the ability to anticipate possible consequences,'' observed psychologist Dr. J. D. Krumboltz. To help your child make good choices and avoid a lot of problems, *you* have to teach how to make informed decisions. It helps to start early because the process takes a lot of practice, spread over a number of years.

Much evidence now suggests that parents can provide a solid foundation for reasoning beginning with the infant. Mobiles, colorful beads, pictures near the crib are visually stimulating and enrich the environment. Remember, however, that *you* are the best source of stimulation. Talk a *lot* to your infant. (See ''Infant Training''). As your child grows, she will learn fastest from exposure to a variety of new experiences, such as contact with other children and adults, travel, games, books. Most valuable are activities which allow or require your child to do some problem solving and/or to practice visual, hearing, movement, and, later, reading skills. Permit her to experiment and make mistakes. If you have to show her how something works, explain what you are doing and why. As her intellectual capacity expands, be sure to point out — repeatedly — the relationship between behavior and its consequences.

''Reasoning'' (thinking) is learning to talk to ourselves in our heads in problem solving ways. That is, you reason by considering the available alternatives and the possible consequences: ''If I do this, that may happen — or if I do that, this may happen. What do I *want* to have happen?''

Thinking is tricky business. Some children learn more readily than others to relate causes with consequences. Others require more training because they tend to be more impulsive, are less introspective and analytical and do not think things through. Still others create problems for themselves when they think, but then draw the wrong (irrational) conclusions.

Dr. Albert Ellis, a psychologist who espouses rational thinking, cautions that, for many children and adults, ''reasoning'' often results in anxiety. These are the people who concentrate on the worst (catastrophic) consequences. In effect, they cross bridges before they come to them and feel defeated before they even decide to take action on anything.

No matter how hard she studies, Grace concludes she will probably fail an exam or won't be chosen for the team or will ''fall on her face'' when she goes to recite before class. There's no point in telling her that these things never happen — they sometimes *do* — nor can you simply tell her not to think about such things. The point is to say, ''Okay, so what if you *do* fail the exam or don't get chosen for the team, how are you going to handle that?'' If she's not going to find a hole and crawl into it, she has to decide to *risk* failure and rejection. She has to learn to ask, also, ''What is the *best* thing that could happen if I do this (or that)?'' She can then decide if the risks are worth the possible gain. (''I may *not* fall on my face when I recite before the class.'' ''*If* I recite, I won't have to write a term paper.'')

All of this may sound simple enough, but you say that you haven't the foggiest notion how to go about *teaching* that sort of self-talk? One child therapist who has written a great deal about teaching children to reason is Dr. Rudolf Dreikurs. He emphasizes ''the natural consequences'' of behavior, and points out that children learn more readily if parents relate the *consequences* to the child's *behavior*. Restricting a child for three weeks because he broke a window is not a natural consequence. Having to earn money to replace the window *is* a natural consequence that teaches destruction of anything has the cost of replacement.

Other helpful suggestions have been made by Dr. Wesley C. Becker of the University of Kansas, who suggests that you always *tell* your child what he did that earned a reward or penalty. You may think that Billy should automatically *know* that hitting brother led to Time Out or that the reason he can't see TV tonight is because he came home late from school. You may be surprised to learn that some kids may conclude that you're just being mean and unfair. It is also important to *tell why* he is being given some special privilege or treat, for example, ''Because you ate your dinner, you can have dessert'' or ''Because you were so helpful today, you can see an extra 30 minutes of TV.'' In that way, Greta learns what to do to get what she wants and how to avoid what she doesn't want, and that your *mood* has nothing to do with it. (Keep Dreikurs' ''natural consequences'' in mind to make this job easier.)

Learn to *ask* why Greta thinks that she earned a reward or penalty. This is one of the very best ways to get her to start reasoning, so do this a *lot*. For example, ask, ''Why do you think I baked your favorite cake for dinner tonight?'' or ''Why do you think you can't go to gymnastics practice tonight? What was the deal that we made about homework and practice?'' What a child *says* seems to become more imprinted on the mind than what she *hears* — which, as you know — can go ''in one ear and out the other.'' Think out loud with Greta. This is also an opportunity to correct her perception that she could not go to gymnastics because you hate her or she's just a bad kid who will never amount to anything.

As occasions arise, work on general rules for living which can serve as guidelines when problems come up and you're not around. For example, you might say, ''You did a good job of cleaning your room and can take in that show you wanted to see tonight. Good things often happen when you work hard, don't they?'' or ''I noticed that you shared your toys with Billy today. He shared, too. It's really nice when people cooperate with each other, isn't it?'' or ''I was really proud to see how well you handled the situation when Jenny was chosen for the team, not you. I know how disappointed you must be, but that was a very professional way of handling the situation. That's the way the pros do things."

Any time your child has a problem and starts discussing it with you, that's an excellent opportunity to try to help her think it through. (If you hear about a problem through someone else, for example, the teacher, don't *you* hesitate to bring it up.) Again, be sure to ask questions rather than to make suggestions.

David is angry because a classmate spent the day teasing him. David's "solution" is to beat up the classmate.

Mother: Well, what's the Golden Rule?

David: Don't do to others what you don't want them to do to you — but Eugene's doing *plenty* to me. It's not fair.

Mother: Maybe not, but what will happen if you hit him?

David: I guess he'll hit me back.

Mother: Will that stop his teasing? Haven't others tried that with him?

David: Yeh.

Mother: Did that stop him?

David: Nope.

Mother: I wonder what you can do that will let Eugene know that you don't care what he says? What do I do that really irritates you sometimes?

David: Well, sometimes you don't pay any attention to me.

Mother: Right. Sometimes I get really busy with things and don't hear you. And sometimes I don't *want* to pay attention, such as when you interrupt. I wonder what would happen if you did that same thing to Eugene?

David: He'd get mad, I bet! But maybe he'd stop it if he knew it didn't get me!

Using these ideas for a week or two won't work miracles. You have to go over these things again and again and again. Gradually — and to your great relief — David and Greta *will* learn to reason. Reasoning will even become "automatic" — and increasingly painless — as a result of the repeated practice.

The point is to get David and Greta to start thinking about the different things that they can do to get what they want from life events. Of course, there may be nothing that can be done about some situations. Reasoning that out may help make the situation more tolerable until something better comes along.

Finally, with reasoning as with most other areas of your child's growth, *you* are the most important "model" of how it's done. If you demonstrate and explain aloud your own reasoning process as you solve problems, your child will develop the same invaluable skill.

Want to read more about it? Try these books:

W. C. Becker, *Parents Are Teachers*, Research Press, 1971.

A. Ellis, S. Mosely and J. L. Wolfe, *How to Raise an Emotionally Healthy, Happy Child*, Wilshire Book Co., 1966.

J. D. Krumboltz and H. R. Krumboltz, *Changing Children's Behavior*, Prentice-Hall, Inc., 1972.

Rules

WHAT DO I DO WHEN my kids constantly break the rules I make for them?

"To promise not to do a thing is the surest way in the world to make a body want to go and do that very thing," observed Mark Twain.

How many rules do you have at your house? Really? *That* many?! You're worn out nagging at your kids because they don't seem to understand that a rule is a rule is a...? No *wonder* you feel frazzled; however, the good news is that you can relax and enjoy life if you will learn a few simple rules for making rules.

A rule is a stated expectancy that certain things will be done at certain times, for example, "You are to clean your room every Saturday morning;" "...practice the piano 30 minutes each day before you go out to play;" "...be home at 11 p.m. on Friday nights;" "...wash the dishes before you see TV." Some families even put these into writing. Other parents believe that their children should *know* what the rules are without being told (probably through a process called "osmosis") and then wonder why they feel as if they're in charge of a zoo. Whether you write out the rules or just state them, you need to know that each rule must meet three standards if it is going to produce the results you want and be manageable. It must be (1) reasonable; (2) specific; and (3) enforceable.

...*Rules must be reasonable.* That means that your request should relate to something that is necessary and practical to do, and something that your child *can* do. A rule that requires every family member to contribute to keep the house up is worthwhile. However, it would be unreasonable to ask your two-year-old to wash the dishes! Your toddler, however, *can* fetch a wastebasket or pick up toys.

Don't ask Jimmy to hang up a coat because it's the "decent thing to do," but because it helps clear up clutter — and the coat lasts longer. It's easier to find things when they are in their place, and that's one more way he can obey the house rule that "everybody helps."

Don't ask Mary Ann to clean her room because you can't *stand* to see an untidy room. Admittedly, no one is thrilled about housing a disaster area, but that's not the issue! Room cleaning teaches her to take care of her clothes and other possessions and helps her find her rubber boots the next time it rains.

It is certainly reasonable — and thoughtful — to require everyone (adults included) to call if they'll be late.

An example of an unreasonable rule is demanding that Jimmy must "eat everything on his plate" at dinner every night. Why bother? If he does not eat his dinner, he loses the dessert and snack privilege until the next meal. Making him sit at the dinner table until he cleans off his plate is coercive and may lead to a power struggle. He learns easier and faster if he knows the consequences (no dessert or snacks). The decision — and problem — is *his*, then, not yours. Why create unnecessary hassles for yourself?

...*Rules should be specific.* All that means is: say exactly what you want done. Don't assume that Jimmy knows what you mean, for example, when you say, "Please clean up the kitchen," particularly if he has never done it before. Do you mean "put the food away," or "wash, dry, and put away the dishes," or just *what*?

Examples of poorly defined rules: "I expect you to come home at a *reasonable* hour." "When people come over, you might, at least, act *decent*." What time is "reasonable?" What is "decent" behavior? Be specific. Don't expect Mary Ann to be clairvoyant.

"Whatever happened to common sense?" you ask, "After all, haven't I set an example for years?" There's no point in upsetting yourself with those assumptions. If your youngster is not doing what you want in the way that you want, don't take it as a personal insult. You're not a failure, and your child is not stupid. It just means that you need to make your expectations clear by being more specific.

...*Rules must be enforceable*, or as old Mr. Dooley aptly put it, "Thrust ivrybody, but cut th' ca-ards." The way you "cut the cards" is to make certain that Jimmy has done what he has been told to do. You *must* monitor the follow-through. Yes, that is time-consuming and inconvenient, but it is critically important. If the cat's away, the mice *will* play, you know.

Why can't you just *trust* Jimmy to do what he is told to do? You will eventually, once you have established your authority and integrity as a parent who *really* follows through. Kids are like anyone else. They'll test the limits. (Why do drivers, for example, tend to drive more cautiously through some towns than others? You guessed it. Enforcement *varies* from town to town!)

The point is that if you can't *enforce* the rule, you can't *make* the rule. That may not be joyous news, but it does have its bright side. That saves your energy. If you're not willing to follow through and enforce the rule or if you can't enforce it (even though you want to), you won't be making too many unnecessary rules — and that is healthy for everyone!

Because you must enforce your rules, you cannot demand that Jimmy must empty the trash every day "by four p.m." unless you are at home to monitor the time. You *can* say that you want the trash to be emptied by the time you get home at five or six p.m., *if* you are willing to check and to tell him to stop everything and do the job if it has not been done.

You cannot make a rule that Mary Ann may not wear lipstick until she is 16, or that she cannot associate with certain people, because you cannot enforce such rules (unless, of course, you're willing to become her shadow — and that's not advised.)

You may want to, but you cannot even make a rule that your teenager may not smoke or use drugs. You may say that such behaviors are not permitted in your home, provide guidance regarding the consequences, and *request* that s/he think very carefully when tempted by others. This is one of the reasons that establishing a good and positive relationship with your child is critically important. At some point, your teachings will be challenged by your child's peers. You must establish standards of conduct. But you must do so in a way that will avoid a power struggle, in which your child feels the need to *prove* to you that s/he will do something in spite of you — or to spite you. Any time you say, "you can't" or "I forbid," you've entered a power struggle. All enforcement of rules is a form of power struggle. Don't enter a struggle you can't win. Everyone, then, is a "loser."

Rules

Unless you plan to break your child's spirit, at some point you must give the message that you have confidence in your child's ability to make good decisions. Mistakes will be made, but rest assured that it's better to make mistakes at age 12 than at age 16. Each mistake can be a learning experience, if you *help* your child learn from it by not nagging or criticizing.

"Hey, look! I found a loophole!"

© Masters Agency, Capitola, CA

Some parents feel guilty when they establish rules for their children to do chores around the house, or anything else that is time consuming or unpleasant. As the old Proverb says: "Hard work is respectable but not popular." But don't fret, Folks. Kids who come from homes where limits are set and they have specific responsibilities feel a lot better about themselves than those who don't. Rules and guidelines provide orderliness and predictability to life. They are like roadmaps and guardrails on a hazardous road. If everyone knows what is expected, no one, including you, has to assume the full burden for maintaining a pleasant and neat home. By setting up rules, you help your children develop the competencies necessary for self-assurance and the desirable habits needed for social relationships. Eventually, your children will learn to make rules and set up expectancies and limits for themselves. And that's what self-discipline is all about.

When expectations, rules, limits and consequences are clear and predictable, children feel a sense of security. Home becomes a refuge from a highly unpredictable world, but also serves as a safe place to learn that society makes demands and imposes severe consequences when those demands are not met. If you only give and ask for nothing in return, you do a disservice to yourself and your children.

You may have noticed that not all families inevitably go through a period of adolescent rebellion by their teenagers. What makes the difference between those who feel compelled to rebel and those who do not initiate a power struggle? A major factor appears to be that the rebellious kids were subjected to years of fuzzy rules and inconsistent enforcement of those rules by their parents. It was like playing Russian roulette. They never knew when their parents would ignore or give in or bear down hard!

"But isn't there such a thing as too many rules? I don't want to become an authoritarian parent!" There's really no danger of that *if* you follow the simple rules for making rules — that they be reasonable, specific, and enforceable.

As you have probably guessed, it takes a lot of caring to enforce rules. It can be very difficult to deny Jimmy a very special privilege when a rule has been broken. It is hard to say: "Sorry, you can't go to Little League because you didn't cut the grass. You know the rule, Son: you must finish all your chores *before* you go to play ball." The stakes are high and involve his perception of you as one who is reliable and has integrity. Do you care enough to say, "No?"

School Behavior

WHAT DO I DO WHEN the teacher complains that my son is disruptive in the classroom and won't do his work?

Bang the drum slowly. You are off to see the teacher again to learn what Harold has done *now* to set himself up as a good example of a bad example! The litany of his offenses may be painful — running, hitting, pushing, sassing back. This time, he pushed some little girl on the playground and stomped on her new little red hat. Well, what are you going to do about it? He may be a problem, but he's *yours*! You have talked to him, warned, threatened, restricted, pleaded, stormed, taken things away. What more is there?

Well, have you tried setting a mouse trap? ("Please. This is serious. My kid is in big trouble and you're talking about *mouse traps*!") It's a figure of speech, of course, but how *do* you catch a mouse? By baiting the trap. Well, you want your mouse to learn to think of the consequences before he acts and annoys others, and you also want him to do his classwork. The secret of success is the saying, "In baiting a mousetrap with cheese, always leave room for the mouse." There are things that your child will do a lot to get — even study and behave himself. ("You mean *bribe* him!?") No, there's nothing illegal about this kind of bait. The point is that Harold is getting a lot of attention for misbehaving. You can turn that around, but it will take a plan, cooperation between you and the school, follow-through, time, and patience. Eventually, your mouse will nibble at the bait.

Where Do I Start?

Ideally, the time to start is the first time the teacher calls you to say that Harold is a problem. Don't wait for the parent-teacher conference or the report card to discover that he is a classroom disaster.

As a matter of fact, if you have had a history of complaints from teachers about Harold, you may wish to check with the teacher several weeks after the school year starts. Don't just cross your fingers and hope for the best. This is a problem that you want to zero in on before he establishes a reputation of being a trouble maker. Don't sound the alarm, however. Just inquire as an interested parent. If the teacher has no complaints, there is no point in alerting her to the fact that his last teacher's hair turned grey before the year was over. You don't want to set him up. You just want to alert him and the school that you're interested.

Meanwhile, do not encourage Harold if he complains that the teacher is unfair and hates him and that other kids "make" him mad and get him into trouble. He must learn that there are all kinds of people in the world, and that he is responsible for what *he* does no matter *what* others do. Nobody can make him behave badly. That's *his* choice.

If you learn of a classroom behavior problem, assure the teacher that you want to cooperate with her and the school to help work out the solution. Be sure, though, to ask the teacher to be specific about what Harold is doing. Saying that he has a "bad attitude" is *not* specific. Is he teasing, hitting, arguing? What is he doing and how often? Every day? Once a week? Nobody's perfect, and the teacher may be upset with him for reasons beyond his control. He needs your support as well as your interest. And he needs your help in learning to deal with difficult situations; the world is not always *fair*! (And teachers are not always right!)

If you are assured that Harold is *causing* problems at school, it is important that both you and the teacher refuse to get upset about his behavior. Both of you may be inconvenienced, but he has to get the message that *the problem is his*, and that you and the teacher will work together to help him decide to behave in more socially acceptable ways, and to do his work. No need to dump a load of guilt on him, however. He's really not a candidate for juvenile hall. Just let him know that he has a problem, and you are going to work with him to solve it.

As soon as possible, meet with the teacher and the counselor and whoever else may be involved in planning the special program for Harold. Ideally, he should be included in the planning sessions as a way of convincing him that people in his world are pulling together. Also, since he's the problem, he should be a part of the solution. The problem has to be given to *him* and not assumed by the concerned adults. After all, if everyone else will take care of him, why should he worry?

Most classroom behavior problems can be solved through this cooperative child-parent-teacher effort. However, the school staff *may* decide that Harold needs testing for special learning problems. Although no single test is likely to give all the answers, a comprehensive evaluation may show such learning barriers as visual or hearing impairment or basic skill deficiencies.

Whether an evaluation is recommended or not, the next step is to decide what behaviors are currently of most concern. Be specific, and do not list more than three behaviors. Mark Twain had the right idea when he said, "Habit is habit, and not to be flung out of the window by any man, but coaxed downstairs a step at a time." The point is that expecting Harold to become a model child overnight is unrealistic; therefore, completing and handing in his work would be one behavior. The other two, for example, teasing and hitting, could be the social behaviors targeted for change.

(The original complaint should also be addressed, for example, that Harold pushed a girl and stomped on her hat. Make certain that he apologizes to the girl for hurting and embarrassing her. Also, if her hat needs to be replaced, set up some household jobs, so that he can earn the money for the replacement.)

Having targeted the behaviors of concern (work, teasing, hitting), the next step is to set up a daily feedback system whereby Harold gets a daily rating by each teacher for his social and academic behavior. Those ratings, then, determine what privileges Harold has earned at home — all, some, or none. *Follow-through is critically important.* The privileges are the bait, and the follow-through is the trap.

The rating is admittedly subjective, but most teachers are fair and can justify their decisions, especially if the standards for Harold's behavior are spelled out in advance.

Cards, similar to the sample shown here, are provided to Harold by the counselor or parent. (Decide at the conference who will prepare the cards.) It is Harold's responsibility, then, to remember to take the card to school, get the rating and signature from each teacher at the end of each hour (if he has more than one teacher), or at the end of the day (if he has only one teacher). He also must remember to bring the card home. After all, it's *his* privileges that are at stake. The number of privileges are determined by the number of points earned at school.

Keep the card simple:

NAME ______________________ **Week of or Day** ______________________

TARGET BEHAVIORS: Complete and hand in classwork, discontinue teasing and hitting.

DAYS or TEACHERS						
WORK						
SOCIAL BEHAVIOR						
TEACHER'S INITIAL						

0 - Did not complete work, or poor classroom behavior.
1 - Some improvement noted.
3 - Average. Not perfect, but improved work or behavior.
4 - Better than average.
5 - Great day! Work or behavior.

Thus, Harold may earn up to ten points a day from each teacher (five points for his work and five for his behavior). With five teachers, he *could* earn 50 points a day. Realistically, it is best not to expect a perfect performance. Goals should be set up with some likelihood of success. Make adjustments according to Harold's ability and progress. Here is a sample schedule:

8 points or more (out of 10) -	all privileges are earned. For example, TV, use of telephone, radio, bike, record player, free time for play.
7 points -	TV privilege is lost. Retains other privileges noted above.
6 points -	TV and bike privileges are lost. Retains other privileges.
5 points -	TV, use of telephone and bike, and record player are lost. Retains free time and radio privilege.
4 points or less -	Loses all privileges and goes to bed 30 minutes earlier. May read and must do chores as usual.

Admittedly, this is ''playing hard ball'' with Harold, but there's a lot at stake for him. With ten points for each class/teacher, he would have to earn an average of eight points per class (a total of 40 points if he has five teachers) to earn all privileges under this system. If he has only one teacher, he would have to earn 8 points to keep all privileges. No more freebees!

Other Fine Points You Need to Know

If Harold has to stay home because he's ill, he loses all privileges, since they are earned only through school attendance and performance. Is that fair? Do you want him to learn to become a ''sick kid?'' What happens if *you* run out of sick leave days on *your* job?

If Harold ''loses'' or ''forgets'' his card, he automatically loses all privileges for the day. If, heaven forbid, he forges the teacher's signature and rates himself, he loses all privileges for the day and for the following weekend. (Why doesn't he lose privileges for the rest of the school week? Because he has nothing to lose, then, by misbehaving and refusing to work.)

Build in some very special privilege for the weekend if he averages seven or more points for the week (out of ten) for the first four weeks of the program. Then increase the requirement to eight out of ten until he is phased out of the program. The special privilege could be going to a ball game with Dad, having lunch at his favorite restaurant, going fishing, being able to see an extra hour or two of TV, or even being taken to the video game arcade! You may not approve of what he enjoys and chooses to do, but as long as it's legal, at least *accept* it! Remember that he's working hard to earn that special privilege.

Follow this system for three weeks, including regular conversations with Harold about his progress, and occasional direct contact with his teacher(s). If you do not see any improvement, consult with a counselor who is a specialist in contracting and negotiations. Ask for help in "fine-tuning" the program and/or analyzing other issues which may be interfering with its success.

Will Harold be on This Program Forever?

If you and the teachers follow through on a well designed system, the daily feedback card can be highly effective within a short time. This approach, incidentally, is effective for children six through thirteen (sometimes even older).

Harold's progress will determine when he can be phased out of the program. If he decides to dig in his heels and test everyone's commitment, it will take him longer. If he *does* start testing, don't give in and don't get upset. Remember that it's *his* problem, not yours.

When he is consistently earning seven points a day or more (depending upon your/his goals) and the teacher(s) feel(s) pleased about his progress, you can then discontinue the card system. The understanding, however, must be that the first time you get a teacher complaint will again make him a candidate for the card system!

If I worry about appearing stupid, I probably won't ask the important questions.

School Readiness

WHAT DO I DO WHEN it's time to start getting my child ready for her first year at school?

You thought that day would never come, but here it is — time for your youngster to start fending for herself in that big world out there. Talk about mixed feelings! It's not easy to feel glad, sad, and little scared at the same time — but you can handle it, and so will your Erica.

You cannot really prepare your child for school the day before — or even the month before. "School readiness" means that your child has learned certain skills (competencies) necessary to feel self-confident and independent. You started the training long ago. There are a few things that you can do shortly before school starts to provide assurance and to ease the transition from home to the school world.

Specifically, What Does Your Child Need to Know?

Erica should be able to take care of herself and know what to do with buttons, zippers, and other fasteners. That will make the teacher glad to have her in class. What will make teacher even happier is that she knows how and when to use the bathroom, a handkerchief, and the water faucet!

Erica also needs to know how to use pencils, crayons, scissors, games, and how to care for books. She should be acquainted with colors and different shapes and sizes. (That's one of the reasons you spent time earlier playing and answering and asking thousands of questions.)

Getting along with the teacher and other kids will be made easier if Erica knows how: to ask politely for what she wants instead of pulling, pushing, or hitting; to play cooperatively; to share toys. (See "Social Skills" and "Aggression" chapters.)

If Erica is going to learn anything in the classroom, she has to be able to listen to instructions and follow through. If your child is not reasonably compliant, you can expect to have a *lot* of teacher conferences within the very near future. However, she should also know the difference between those requests which *must* be obeyed and those about which judgements must be made (see the chapter "Sexual Abuse").

Being able to sit and concentrate on one activity for a minimum of 15 minutes is helpful in school. Nobody can learn anything if always on the run or easily distracted (see "Attention Span").

All those add up to the personal and social skills that you have taught during the preschool years. *Now* comes the big day. How do you deal with *that*?

Preparation for the First Day of School

No doubt about it: This is a major event. Children are very sensitive to subtle cues, so if *you* act nervous and anxious, Erica may decide that this is a scary situation. Don't expect *her* to reassure *you*. There won't be any "Don't worry, Mom, (Dad) I'm a big girl now" speeches. (Those will probably come much later about entirely different issues!)

Here are some tips for smoothing the transition from home to school:

...*Show enthusiasm for your child's new experience*. Talk about it ahead of time. Explain what to expect and answer all questions honestly. Kids like to know the number of days and length of time they will be in school as well as how they will get there and back. If you're a working parent, clarify what arrangements have been made for before and after-school care. It helps to ask the child to repeat back what you have said, so that you know that she has fully understood.

...*Be sure that your child knows your work and home telephone numbers*. (Tattooing these on arms, incidentally, is frowned upon. You *could* print them in a shoe, though.)

...*Make transportation plans clear*. If Erica will walk to school, take the route together a few times, both before and after school starts. If there are other children of the same age in your neighborhood, try to arrange for her to walk with them.

If Erica must go by bus, make certain that she can identify the vehicle. Encourage the older kids to watch over younger ones. Once the bus arrives, look calm and matter-of-fact even though you may feel queazy. (You are not *really* throwing her to the lions! This is the wonderful moment. Remember?) Say good-bye and allow her to board alone. Try not to feel disappointed if she bounces up and into the bus without a backward look; but if she *does* look tearful or cries, ignore it. Wave and say, "You'll do great! *That*'s my big girl." You can then go home and cry, too, if you want to! Remember that the show of courage is catching. Also, Erica does *not* have a choice about going to school.

(You might encourage the school district to set strict rules for behavior of children on the school bus and to enforce those rules — even though it may mean that your own child may be expelled from the bus one day. It is especially important that older kids not be allowed to intimidate or harm younger ones.)

...*Ask your child about the school day*. Be a good listener. Set aside 10 or 15 minutes of listening time, if you can, shortly after your child comes home. Give Erica talking time at the dinner table. Concentrate on the *good*, happy things that happened.

...*Get to know your child's teacher*(s). Volunteer your services, or check out ways you can help improve school conditions, especially if you are unhappy with them.

...*If your child claims to be ill, take a temperature and put her to bed until the next morning.* Do not permit Erica to stay home if there is no rise in temperature, but do not expose other children if she is genuinely ill. If she is *really* too ill to go to school, she is also too ill to see TV or play with friends and has to remain in bed until the next day. Teach that privileges are earned through school attendance.

...*Let your child settle quarrels or difficulties with friends* unless physical harm is involved. Help Erica think things through but don't interfere. Don't encourage fighting as a way to resolve problems. Aggressive kids lose friends very quickly and present a real problem to teachers, other children, and themselves. Fighting is a danger signal, and you may have to see a counselor if this becomes a common complaint.

...*Do not be overprotective*. Erica must learn about the world and how to cope with all kinds of experiences. The more she does for herself, the more competent your child will feel. Be available, though, to give support and guidance.

...*Avoid comparing your child's* school experiences with how brothers or sisters or neighbors did when *they* began school. That will not be appreciated. Erica, and every other child, is unique and has a right to be different.

Self Esteem

WHAT DO I DO WHEN my son seems to lack self-confidence? The teacher tells me he has "low self-esteem." What is self-esteem? How do you get it?

...Everybody's got something to sing about...

Self-esteem, also often referred to as "self-concept," is the psychologist's label for the way a person feels about himself or herself. High self-esteem, or good self-concept is another way of saying "I like myself," or "I consider myself a worthwhile and competent person."

Your son's self-esteem began the moment he was born. Your smiles, your words were the first messages of endearment and of saying "Howdy! How *nice* to have you around!!" Children learn to value themselves to the degree that they have been valued. There are several specific ways parents can help their children develop healthy self-esteem. Here is a difficult-but-possible starter list of self-esteem builders you can give your child: *love and commitment, trust, focused attention, empathy,* and *competence in basic skills*. These all add up to one word: love!

...Your "no strings" *love and commitment* will help maximize your child's sense of security. Your son needs to know that you will *never* abandon him and will love him no matter what. In disciplining make it clear to your child that it is his *behavior* — not *him* — that you are unhappy with at the moment. The Time Out procedure ("Discipline") shows you how to do that. Some parents even threaten to send their children to relatives, boarding school, or foster homes if they don't "shape up." Worse yet, some actually do. Such a child then feels like a "piece of luggage" rather than like someone of worth. Your child is not a little adult, and your expectations of his behavior should be realistic. He will then be willing to make the mistakes necessary for learning to take place because he will know that it's okay to be imperfect — and that and the development of skills leads to self-confidence.

Because you love your child, you will praise more than you criticize and will never withhold your affection or approval because your child doesn't "measure up" to all of your expectations. Look for what's right, not what's wrong. To eliminate the negative, "you gotta accentuate the positive!" That will help your child conclude: "Yeh, I make mistakes, but I'm competent at a lot of things. Hey, World, look me over — I'm a loveable kid! Look, Ma, I'm dancin'!"

Because you love your child, you will discipline and set limits. (You have to really *love* your child to do that because it's easier to ignore or give in.) No matter how many mistakes your child makes, give the message that he *always* has worth as a person and will always be given a chance (or two or three — or a million) to do better.

...*Trust* and have faith in your child's ability to learn from experience. Children will make mistakes, be imperfect — even obnoxious — many times. Learning is a lifetime project. The message that you want to give is one of confident expectation that your child can be relied upon to come sunnyside up. "You will make many mistakes, my child," the French writer Colette said to her daughter, "But do so with enthusiasm."

...*Focused attention* means that you will be willing to forego all the busy things in your schedule to spend time with your child. You don't have to do anything special — just a smile or a pat on the back — a minute here, a moment there. Plan to do things together. Remember, always, that touch speaks louder than words! Remember Liza Doolittle's sage advice in "My Fair Lady" — "Don't speak to me — *show me*!!"

Be lavish with love and praise and be stingy with criticism. "I much prefer a compliment, insincere or not, to sincere criticism," observed the ancient Greek, Plautus.

...*Empathy* helps build self-esteem, and you show empathy when you *listen* to your child. That's more important than giving advice. Don't be afraid to say, "I think I understand," "I'm sorry that you feel bad," or "I'm so happy for you..." Your listening is comforting. Lecturing is a "turn-off." If you don't know what else to say, you can always ask, "Is there something I can do — or say — to help?" The message that you want to give is: "I'm on your team."

...*Competence in basic skills* develops with each new step and each small success. "A journey of 1,000 miles is traveled one step at a time." To help your child gain competence, praise a lot! Find *at least* one thing to praise for each thing that you find to criticize. When was the last time you heard that some poor child wasted away from too much praise?! And if you've forgotten how to praise, or never learned how, read the chapter on that subject.

Help your child become competent and self-confident by praising his or her persistence and small victories. Find what's right — not what's wrong. Competence is a long-term project. The more your child knows about getting along with others, taking care of himself, solving problems, reading, playing games — the higher his self-esteem will become. Remember always to consider your child's developmental level in setting goals and making requests. Your four-year-old is not as skilled as your eight-year-old, so don't set yourself and your child up for disappointment.

Trying and *persistence* are what count.

And *never* compare your child with that fantastic kid down the block who is neat, clean, and upright all the time or even mention how great *you* were at his or her age. "Few things are harder to put up with," said Mark Twain, than the annoyance of a good example."

The bottom line — after all is said — is: set up standards of conduct, be encouraging, and have fun. You will add much to your own life by learning to get excited about little things. Don't wait for your child to be elected governor of the state before you say something nice! Remember, also, that if you show appreciation for what your child does, he or she will learn to return the favor. Fun and affection are highly contagious.

People who complain that there is no communication in their families are usually saying that all they hear are complaints, that the many little favors and good deeds are ignored. Along with personal commitment, that's what love is all about — recognizing and communicating your appreciation for the other person.

Everybody's got something to sing about. And you can help the members of your family find the melody and the words! They'll do the same for you.

One problem with the term "self-esteem" is that it is often used as a grab-bag to "explain" why Jack can't read or Jill is selfish and won't share her toys or Wanda sucks her thumb. The implication is that if you can somehow infuse your child with a dose of improved self-esteem — or find someone who has the expertise to do so — voila! Jack will become literate, Jill will become generous, Wanda will take up a new hobby. The problem is: the cart is placed before the horse. Basic skills must be taught — by example, explanation, and practice.

It is not a one-way street, however. Studies show that the single most critical factor in school achievement for young children is not "I.Q.," or reading ability, or verbal skills, but high self-esteem — the child's perception: "I can do it, and a mistake is only a mistake — not the end of the world." By praising and encouraging your child, you can build the bridge between self-concept and basic skills competence.

A child who is often criticized or ignored and seldom, if ever, praised soon begins to feel inadequate and helpless. It is very difficult to go out and conquer the world if you feel like a reject. Those feelings were vividly described by the late Charles McCabe, long-time columnist for the San Francisco *Chronicle* in his column several years ago. I am grateful to the *Chronicle* for permission to reprint it here:

"I don't know about you, man, but I was brought up to feel unworthy. Maybe worthless. At home I would do this, that or the other thing, or be thought to be doing this, that or the other thing (which was equally bad) and my mother would make her usual statement. It was generally toneless and without emphasis, because it had been repeated so often and because it had the ring of revealed wisdom: 'You'll end up in Sing-Sing'...

"I wasn't worth a nickel and I knew it. How I would ever fit into that great grown-up world where people wrote books and built homes and repaired plumbing and sailed boats and planted trees, I could never figure out. I had daily assurance that I was a misfit...

"I know that I am anything but unique in having this kind of training...If there's any point to life at all, it is that it should be embraced joyously. And the task of education, at home and abroad, should be to persuade the child of his eminent fitness for joyous embracement...The slogans might be: 'You will end up in the White House, my boy,' or, 'you will end up on the board of overseers at Harvard.'...We are, to an unfortunate degree, what we are told we are. If we are assured, unremittingly, that we are budding felons, then felony will have an irrational lure for us.

"Life is to be lived. The essential ingredient for this great adventure is confidence that it can be lived, and well. The job of instilling that confidence in a child is perhaps a parent's most important function. If it is not performed, the parents are guilty of cheating the child out of his most important heritage: the relishing of his years."

I need acceptance only from those I love — not from everybody.

Selfishness

WHAT DO I DO WHEN my nine-year-old feels that he has to win at any cost — even a game of checkers, and my four-year-old refuses to share her toys? I want my children to behave in unselfish and cooperative ways!

You thought it would be easy, didn't you? You would set the example, and like flowers gradually unfolding, your children would demonstrate the values that you hold dear — honesty, cleanliness (which is next to Godliness), good citizenship, patriotism, good scholarship, and a love for opera, ballet, Shakespeare, and Bach. And what have you got!? Kids who would sell their souls for bubblegum, rock 'n roll, computer games, and a talent for saying, "If you touch that, I'll hit you with a stick! It's *mine*!"

It's confusing when your child looks at you "With affection beaming in one eye, and calculation shining out of the other." It is hard to deal with that calculating aspect, right? You wish your kids would do the right things for the right reasons and not because there is something in it for them? That would be nice, but that's a long way down the pike!

In fact, expecting children to be able to make unselfish decisions before about the age of 12 is a losing battle. Children are simply not able to reason at that level yet. Once you realize that your child's self-centered behavior is not your fault, and let go of that emotional reaction of guilt or shame, you can tackle this problem behavior head on.

How then do you get your three- or five- or nine-year-old to behave like a civilized, considerate person instead of a barbaric, self-centered beast? Quite simply, you use the 'good ole boy' axiom: You scratch my back, I'll scratch yours.

Children tend to be egocentric (self-involved), and have to learn about the merits of cooperation. It will be a lot easier for your kids to appreciate *your* interests — for example, taste in literature or the arts — if you don't put down theirs. Let them enjoy what they will as long as they are willing to earn it. Force only leads to resistance. For example, your youngster may love to attend those midnight shows where fifth-rate movies are imitated by the audience of teenagers who dress and act like the characters. Instead of putting that interest down, say, "You can go to that show Saturday night if you attend the ballet (concert, lecture, film,...) with me Friday night." At least, then, you are introducing your child to other interests and choices. It's the way the world works. Things "cost."

Keep your expectations realistic, reasonable, and geared to the age of your child. You cannot expect or demand "instant sainthood." For example, unselfishness — willingness to share — starts when Jeremy feels assured that his *own* rights are respected. Give him the right to say No when asked to share, or even when asked to give affection. That's a difficult freedom to permit a child, but if the consequences are clear, it is the best kind of learning opportunity. Sharing a brand new toy, for example, is an unreasonable parent expectation.

Recently, I saw a mother who was very upset with her eight-year-old son. Joey had created a scene at a family gathering because he refused to permit his younger brother to touch a present given to him by his grandfather. "It was so embarrassing. How dare he! He's so selfish!" There was no debating that. Joey clutched tightly to everything that belonged to him and watched vigilantly to see that he got his fair share — even at the dinner table.

It was very difficult to convince his mother that she could help Joey relax and become more generous by giving him the right to say "No, you may not have or touch what is mine" or "No, you may not come into my room" or "No, I don't want to play a game with you." When Joey learns that he has the right to say No, he can also give others the right to say No. Kids have a sense of fairness. They usually understand that concept easier than the more abstract merits of "unselfishness."

Given the right to say No, Joey will learn that to get, he has to give. That kind of learning cannot be forced. Trying to make him feel guilty or "selfish" only serves to build resentment. What's more, if he *does* buy the guilt trip, he may become a "push-over" who is easily exploited by others.

Be sure to praise each tiny step toward unselfish behavior. When Jeremy decides to share his oldest Hot Wheel car with his younger brother, be lavish with praise for his sharing. Point out how much fun the boys have when they play together. Younger brother may even decide to let Jeremy use his "Star Wars" figures. Isn't cooperation wonderful? And, as parents, you can *model* the kind of unselfish behavior you'd like your children to achieve. Do kind acts for one another and talk about it: "You made my favorite lunch for me today!" "Thanks a million for helping me get ready!" Reward good behavior with affection and praise, not material "things." Plan cooperative family activities and games. Emphasize, whenever the opportunity arises, cooperation rather than competition. Remember, *self*-centeredness is a necessary, albeit trying, step toward *other*-centeredness.

Sex Education

WHAT DO I DO WHEN it's time to teach my child about sex? How? When?

''And here's the happy bounding flea -
You cannot tell the he from she...
But she can tell and so can he.''
Roland Young

Your child has to learn a lot more than telling he from she! If ignorance were indeed bliss, there would be a lot more happy people in the world. Many parents approach this inevitable responsibility as a painful chore because of their own insecurities about sex.

It need not be so. In fact, you have been teaching your children about sex, whether you are aware of it or not, from the time they were born. ''There is no way a parent can avoid being the principal sex educator of his or her child — whether the parent is open and candid about sex, or says nothing at all,'' says Dr. Sol Gordon, Director of the Institute for Family Research and Education at Syracuse University. By the time your son and daughter enter school, they have acquired your attitudes as well as whatever information you have given.

Although you are Sean's and Sharon's *principal* sex educator, you are not their *only* sex educator! How can you make certain that they learn only what you want them to know? You can't unless you want to become their shadows, prohibiting them from browsing through magazine and book racks in the stores and library, from watching TV, listening to the radio or playing records. They also must *seldom* enter a movie theater!

You would also have to screen Sean's friends very carefully, probably finding that the two-year-old group is ''safe.'' The three-year-old group may be ''iffy.'' You will have to monitor telephone conversations and never permit Sharon to enter a public restroom. When she becomes a teenager, adolescent peers will be only too happy to convey their own unique versions of sex education.

Some parents do choose to employ extreme measures to control their children's exposure to information about human sexuality. I consider it healthier and more natural to provide clear guidance and information within the family, and to trust Sean and Sharon to rely on that foundation when confronted with ''outside influences.''

You are, of course, interested in protecting your children from misinformation. The best way to do that is to become an "askable parent" when they ask questions. Even though you may secretly wince and feel embarrassed, answer in simple terms. Don't feel that you have to take a crash course in anatomy or go on the lecture circuit. The most important thing is for you to be honest. *Never* tell Sean that you found him on a lily pad, or that the stork dropped Sharon down your chimney on a dark and stormy night. A child who finds that your answers can't be trusted will stop asking questions.

Some children start asking questions when they are two or three years old. Others wait awhile. If your youngster hasn't shown curiosity by age five or six, you can create opportunities to talk about birth and pregnancy. Examples: when a neighbor has a baby, or a relative becomes pregnant, or the cat has kittens. If you feel uncomfortable talking about anything but the birds and bees, get a book for your child and let that pave the way for you. Remember that this is an area in which experience is *not* the best teacher. It's not knowledge about sex that gets kids into trouble. It is ignorance and misinformation. "Tain't what a man don't know that hurts him; it's what he knows that just ain't so," observed writer Frank Hubbard.

(For only 50 cents, you can order a very helpful booklet, "Sex Education: The Parents' Role," by Sol Gordon and Irving R. Dickman from Public Affairs Pamphlets, 381 Park Ave. South, New York, N.Y. 10016.)

Does Sex Education in Schools Promote Sexual Experimentation?

As far as we know, school sex education programs don't promote very much of anything. The only states which *require* sex education in schools are Hawaii, Kentucky, Maryland, Michigan, Missouri, North Dakota, and Washington, D.C. Most of the courses are limited to technical instructions (the "plumbing" aspects of the human reproductive process) and generate about as much interest as bee pollination and the mating call of the moose. Sex education in school *should* answer tough questions openly and, ideally, extend to other courses, for example, art and literature. Kids, then, can learn why Mickey Spillane represents poor taste and Boccaccio and Flaubert represent literature, why the centerfolds in *Playboy* magazine represent unpardonable mediocrity and voyeurism and Rodin's nude sculptures represent art.

Studies show that the *less* children know, the more likely they are to experiment. They tend to indulge in irresponsible curiosity and know enough to get into trouble but not enough to get out of it or to prevent it — as indicated by the unhappy increase in teenage pregnancies, abortions, and venereal disease.

Don't Leave Choice to Chance

Try not to be naive as was the mother of the pregnant 15-year-old girl who said, "I knew that her boyfriend visited while she babysat for our neighbor, but I didn't think that...I thought she was smarter. I never thought to talk to her. I really trusted her."

Don't hesitate to let Sharon and Sean know your opinions, your values and concerns. Teenagers are not sufficiently mature for the emotional commitments and responsibility of sexual attachments. There are moral, medical, and psychological reasons why they should steer clear of premarital sex. Your teenagers may want you to take a stand, thus helping them resist peer pressure.

Sexual activity among teenagers has always concerned parents. Currently it is the topic of much heated national debate over such issues as abortion and the parents' right to know. If your daughter or son becomes sexually involved, I believe your principal task is to stress the importance of responsibility for contraception. You may want to use threats and severe penalties; that will almost certainly alienate your teenager and create even more problems. You may be concerned, however, that by giving birth control information you are implying approval. Pregnancy and venereal disease are now epidemic among teenagers. You really have an obligation to advise Sean and Sharon that while you don't want them to get involved in sexual relationships in the first place, "If you're going to do it anyway, knowing all that is at stake in your life, I insist that you use birth control." Refer your sexually active teenagers to a Family Planning Clinic and see to it that they get there.

As calmly as you can, try to discuss the issues with your teenager, for example, how sexual involvements may affect self-image and future relationships, the possibility of pregnancy, the dangers of venereal disease. Where does love and morality fit into all of this? Ask questions and let your teenager come up with some answers. This is a serious decision that only he or she can make. Your teenager needs to know your limits: you may absolutely forbid having sex in the home, and that you would not raise the baby if pregnancy occurs. (Check local laws regarding your responsibility if your under-age daughter should have a child.) Admittedly, this is a hard-nosed way to go and it can't be easy for you. Clarifying your position and then stepping back is hard to do.

Some inexpensive pamphlets that may be very helpful are: "Is It Love or Sex — and How to Tell the Difference" and "Teenage Sex — Ten Ways to Cool It" may be ordered by sending 50 cents for each to Ann Landers, P.O. Box 11995, Chicago, Illinois 60611.

"Crazy Changes — Tricky Choices," "Straight Talk," and "It Just Happened" may be ordered by sending 70 cents each to New Mexico Family Planning Council, 3207 Matthew N.E., Albuquerque, N.M. 87107.

Three free brochures may be requested from National Clearinghouse for Family Planning Information, P.O. Box 2225, Rockville, Maryland 20852. They are: "Changes: Sex and You"; "Choices: You and Sex"; and "Changes and Choices: Your Children and Sex."

Sexual Abuse

WHAT DO I DO to protect my children from sexual abuse (molestation)?

Although some children are grabbed by strangers in dark alleys, many more are abused by people they know and trust.

Child victims have no special "victim" characteristics. They are not of one age, one sex, one race, or one social class. They range in age from infancy (six months) to young adulthood. The average age of the victim is 11 years, and female victims outnumber males ten to one. Most (50 to 80%) are sexually abused by people who are familiar to them — parents, parent-substitutes, relatives, friends, neighbors.

Over one-third of the assaults on children appear to occur in the child's home, while about 20% occur in the home of the offender. Often a love-starved or frightened child will cooperate, when seduced by a trusted adult, out of a need for affection or attention, a misplaced sense of loyalty, or just fear of disobeying. Adolescents, however, are particularly vulnerable to physical force and violence.

In about half the cases of assault, the child didn't tell anyone about the incident until more than a week later, for fear that the parents would be angry and punish for what happened.

We know only a little about the characteristics of the sex offenders. They come from all ethnic groups and all social classes. They are employed in every sort of occupation/profession and are often widely respected in their communities. Mostly male, they range from adolescents to seniors, with average age about 30. Most had been charged with at least one criminal complaint prior to the child abuse offense, and about 25% have a history of excessive use of alcohol.

How Can I Protect My Children?

A number of very useful recommendations have been made by the Queen's Bench Foundation, San Francisco, in *A Guide for Parents*.

...Be aware of where your children are and what they are doing. Your supervision is their best protection against sexual abuse. You can't be with them all the time, of course. When you aren't there to care for them yourself, make certain that another *responsible* adult will watch them. If you can't find adult supervision, arrange for them to walk or play in a group.

...Know who is with your children. If you are hiring a babysitter for the first time, ask for references and be sure to check them. Inquire about people who offer your son or daughter a job, particularly if it involves working in their home. Get to know your children's friends, especially those who are a few years older than your son or daughter.

...Teach your children to watch out for their own safety. Remind them not to accept money or favors from strangers. Warn them never to accept a ride or go anywhere with someone they don't know. Talk about what they can do if someone approaches them. In their book, *No More Secrets*, Caren Adams and Jennifer Fay of King County (WA) Rape Relief recommend playing the "What if..." game when you're just chatting with your children, for example, during dinner time or when taking a car ride. You might ask, "What if we are separated in a department store?" "What if someone is touching you in a way that makes you feel uncomfortable?" "What if the babysitter asks you to keep a secret?" Children enjoy "What if..." questions, and the game encourages them, also, to ask questions in return. This is an excellent way to find out what they already know, and what they are curious about.

What Can Children Do if Someone Approaches Them?

Tell your children to seek help immediately if any adult

makes them feel uneasy or afraid. Tell them to run away and scream for help. Explain that it's all right to attract attention and create a scene in these situations.

Remember that many children are abused by adults they know. Tell them that they don't have to agree to demands for physical closeness. Assure them that it's all right to say no — even to close friends and relatives.

Encourage your children to tell you or another adult immediately if anyone touches or talks to them in a way that seems strange or makes them uncomfortable.

How Can I Talk to My Children About Sexual Abuse Without Scaring Them?

You have already taught your children many safety rules — how to cross busy streets, what to do when they get hurt or lost, etc. Precautions relating to sexual abuse can be a natural part of your discussion of safety in general.

You don't have to tell very young children about sex when you discuss these rules if you don't want to. Just explain that some adults may try to take off children's clothes or touch them in a way that makes them uncomfortable.

Be sure to use words your children understand. Answer questions fully. Let your children know that they can come to you any time to talk about anything that is puzzling or upsetting. A calm, matter-of-fact manner is reassuring to children.

Won't My Children Become Suspicious and Mistrusting of All Adults?

Children know that adults are not perfect. As with their friends, they have to learn that some people can be trusted and some people should be avoided. They must learn when they must be reserved and very cautious and when they can be spontaneous and affectionate. They learn that by watching what parents do and through corrective feedback and instruction.

How Should I Respond if My Child Tells Me That She or He Has Been Sexually Abused?

(The following recommendations are adapted from guides prepared by the Sexual Assault Center, Harborview Medical Center, Seattle, Washington, and Queen's Bench Foundation, San Francisco, California.)

...First of all, be aware of your own feelings about the incident and get those feelings under control. You will be upset by what happened to your child and feel guilty, angry, or shocked. If you feel angry, make sure that your son or daughter understands that you are angry with the molester, not with the child.

Your first reaction may be disbelief. Children do tell

tales, but they very rarely report imaginary sexual relations with adults. Take your child's story seriously *even if the offender is someone you thought you could trust.*

Your reaction will be the most important factor in how your child readjusts.

...Secondly, remember that no matter how you are feeling, your child's welfare is your first concern. If you are very upset, stop and collect your thoughts and emotions before talking to your child about the incident.

...Go with your child to a private place and ask him or her to tell you what happened in his or her own words. Listen carefully. Don't pressure your child to talk.

...Be patient. Reassure him or her of your love and concern. Explain that you are upset by what happened and understand that he or she may be upset, too.

...Praise your child for telling you about the incident. Emphasize that the molester, not the child, is to blame. Say that you are very sorry that this happened and will protect him or her from further molestation.

...Call the local abuse center (if there is one in your community), your state's children's services agency, or the police immediately. Someone will come to your house to take the initial report.

...If you suspect that your child has been injured, call your family physician.

What if the Offender is in the Immediate Family?

This situation is particularly difficult for the child and other family members. You may have strong, conflicting feelings about the molester, but protection of your child *must* be your first priority.

You can feel assured, however, that the problem will be handled sensitively and with concern for all members of the family if you consult a skilled counselor.

How Can I Help My Child After an Assault?

...Continue to believe your child and do not blame him or her for what happened. Give reassurance and support that he or she is an okay person.

...Instruct your child to tell you immediately if the offender tries to bother him or her in any way again.

...Respond to questions or feelings that your child expresses about the molestation in a calm, matter-of-fact way but do not pressure your child to continue to talk about it.

...Follow the regular routine around the home. Expect the usual chores, bedtime, rules.

...Respect the privacy of your child by not telling a lot of people or letting friends and neighbors question him or her.

...Other children in your family may also be upset by the incident. Without going into all the details, tell them what has happened and assure them that their brother or sister will be okay. Make sure that all children in the family are given enough information to protect themselves from the molester.

...Talk privately with someone you trust — your spouse, friend, relative, a counselor — as a way of expressing your feelings and getting reassurance for yourself. Do not discuss the situation and become emotional in front of your children.

How Will I Know My Child Will be All Right? What Should I Look for After the Assault?

Permanent *physical* damage as a result of sexual assault is rare. Talk with your physician about any possible injuries.

Your child's *emotional* recovery, however, will depend largely on *your* response to the incident. It is the child victim of incest who apparently suffers the most damage, particularly in cases where the incestuous relationship has been prolonged.

Be aware that the first few weeks after the assault may be quite difficult for both parents and child. Many youngsters continue to be frightened and upset for several weeks.

The problems most commonly reported are:

...*Loss of appetite.*

...*Irritability, crankiness, short-tempered behavior.*

...*Bedwetting.*

...*Needing more reassurance than usual; clinging to the parent.* Often children want to talk about the incident over and over again. You can help by listening quietly and answering questions calmly and without a great show of emotion. Don't feed into your child's feelings of betrayal and violation by saying how terrible and awful it was. Children are apt to feel guilty for what happened. Assure your child that he or she is not at fault.

Even if your child doesn't talk about the incident, don't assume that he or she has forgotten. Your affection and quiet understanding will help heal the emotional wounds.

...*Changes in behavior at school or in relating to friends.*

...*Increased fears about everything and anything.* The child may feel that nothing is dependable or reliable for awhile.

...*Behaving as a younger child* (*regression*). It is important that your child know that the incident does not provide an excuse from chores and other household rules and routines. This is a way of giving the message that a lot of things happen to a lot of us. We need time to grieve, but life must go on.

The adolescent may also act out feelings of disgust and anger and self-hatred by running away or skipping school or by being rebellious.

No one knows for sure about long-term emotional effects, but if the situation is handled in a direct and sensitive way at the time it happens, your child is given the best chance of recovering from the assault and the feelings of having been violated.

If your child seems to be extremely upset and hasn't resumed the normal routines within three or four weeks, look for professional help. Your physician, school counselor, clergyman, or mental health center are resources for help. (See "More Resources for Parents" for tips on finding professional help.)

Information adapted from "Guides for Parents Concerning the Sexual Abuse of Children," *Sexual Abuse of Children: Selected Readings*, U.S. Department of Health and Human Services, DHHS Publication No. (OHDS) 78-30161, Issued November, 1980.
An excellent book that provides guidance is: *No More Secrets: Protecting Your Child from Sexual Assault* by Caren Adams and Jennifer Fay. San Luis Obispo, CA: Impact Publishers, 1981.

Shopping

WHAT DO I DO WHEN my child won't behave when we go shopping?

"Children are a great comfort in your old age — and they help you reach it faster," said Lionel Kauffman. He might have added, "particularly if you find yourself the target of cold stares and raised eyebrows when your child has a tantrum in the supermarket because *you* won't buy *that* candy or *this* toy." You have learned that the floor will not mercifully open up to swallow you and save you from embarrassment, and you can't stuff Sammy in the vegetable bin and hope that people will think that he belongs to somebody else! Everyone saw you come in with him. You're stuck with the dilemma. The good news is that there are some things that you can do to alleviate these problems.

First of all, what is it that you want to have happen when you go to the store? If shopping is one of the few times that you get out of the house, it may be that you really want to look forward to this as a time to enjoy, even relax a little — a diversion. If you're in a hurry and feel under pressure, you may want the shopping experience to be quick and convenient. You certainly don't want to have to go chasing after Sammy down the aisles or be a one-note Johnny saying "No, No, No" all the time.

It would have been nice if Sammy had been born with special instructions encoded in his head telling him how to behave on a shopping trip, but, so far, the geneticists have failed us in that regard — so you'll just have to be prepared to train your child.

If you have a toddler, the solution is fairly easy. Put him or her in the shopping basket seat. Remember, though, that your toddler has a short attention span, and being wheeled down store aisles may not be his or her idea of a "big time on the town." How, then, do you keep his or her interest?

Talk, a *lot*. Learn to say out loud what you are thinking, for example, "Hmmm, those oranges look really nice. What do you think? Hey, do you know how they grow? That's right. They grow on trees. Can you see any other fruit here that grows on trees?" or "I need to buy some salt. I wonder what aisle it's in. See if you can help me. Where do you think it is?" Now, you might feel like an utter idiot babbling along like this, but you're doing something very important. You are teaching your child about his or her world. You are also teaching about practical matters — prices and how to judge the quality of things. How else are kids going to learn about these things?

My Child is Too Old for the Shopping Basket

Now you can instruct your child *before* you leave home. It's a very simple process, so be sure to do it every time before the two of you walk out of the door. Call Sammy to you, look him straight in the eye (you're running this show, remember?), and say:

"We're going to the supermarket. There are three things you must do.

—You must stay with me. Do *not* walk away.

— I *will* let you help me, but do not touch anything unless I say you can.

— Don't ask me to buy anything for you because I'm not going to on this trip."

Then, and this is important, ask your child to tell *you* what the three rules are. It's really amazing. Sometimes you think that you have said something very clearly and your child can't *help* but understand, and you learn that only a part of your message got through. You can only find that out, though, if you ask Sammy to repeat what you've said.

Follow the same instructions as with your toddler. Talk a lot about things that you're seeing and thinking about buying. Praise him for walking with you so nicely. Be sure to ask him to help you, for example, "Bring the bag of pretzels, please. Gee, I'm lucky to have all this help."

If Sammy, however, walks away or touches something without permission or starts whining for a treat, immediately go after him or stop, put your hand on his shoulder (no need to hurt), look at him directly, and say softly but firmly: "What was it that you were told before you left home? What are you supposed to do?" Most children will respond to that although tears may well up in their eyes and they may swallow hard, and you may feel like a fiend. The secret is to move in directly and immediately before things get out of hand.

If you have more than two incidents, then Sammy has earned Time Out. Be sure that he "pays his dues" as soon as you get home. You would then say, "Okay, Sammy, you walked once and touched things without asking, so go to Time Out right now. You didn't do what I told you to do."

If Sammy has a full-blown temper tantrum in the store, you may, of course, have to leave off shopping and take Sammy home. Well, that would be really inconveniencing, and it would be hard not to feel really angry and nag all the way home. It's a way of letting off steam, but won't accomplish anything. It's better to bite your tongue and be silent. (If Sammy is accustomed to your yelling and nagging, that'll *really* intimidate him.) Just impose Time Out when you get home and try again in a few hours.

If you have persistent problems with your child even after all of this, you may wish to plan to take your child on training trips, as recommended by the psychologist, Dr. E. R. Christophersen.

Hopefully, you won't have to plan training trips, but, if you do, it's a simple matter of walking your child through the store for about 15 minutes without shopping for anything. Go through the procedure of telling him or her what is expected before you leave the house, and then take a practice trip. It's really a rehearsal. *Do not* buy anything for your child on a training trip, but you might want to celebrate with him or her the first time that you can go through a whole shopping trip without incident. An ice cream cone and praise will do!

Remember that your child learns best and most quickly when you show appreciation through praise and attention —even for those things that you feel should be automatically done "just because"...Discipline in itself just won't do the job.

Shyness

WHAT DO I DO WHEN my child is shy — even with friends and relatives?

Here you are — a vivacious, outgoing person — and you have this shy child! How did that happen? Or you may be a shy person yourself and are really concerned because you don't want your child to go through the agonies that you did in learning to meet people and get involved socially. How can you help?

A lot of research evidence suggests that children are born with different behavioral styles. Babies do indeed differ in their emotional and social responsivity, and that seems to be genetically determined. Does that mean that there is nothing that you can do about your "shy" child? Fortunately, social *learning* experiences — school, church, relationships with peers *and* with adults — can help release your child from her prison of shyness.

The home environment is the first learning experience, and, therefore, the focus of this discussion. Even if you are "blessed" with a shy Violet, it is possible to minimize, overcome, or prevent shyness. Violet has to *learn* to interact cooperatively with others, and to be socially responsive. And *you* are her first and most important teacher.

You may have to make some changes in your own "modeling" behavior (the example you show your child) if you are shy or domineering or hypercritical. Ask yourself: Do you tend to be impatient and do for Violet what she can do for herself (thus shaping dependency)? Do you model the joy of being outgoing and eager to welcome new experiences and new people? Do you project the message of assurance and confidence that says: "You can do it by yourself, and I'm here just in case?" Start early, when Violet is still an infant or toddler. Do not react with unusual interest or alarm when your child "plays coy," and do not permit your friends and relatives to do so. If everyone "oohs" and "aahs" that she is shy and vies for attention, Violet may start playing the "shy person" game. Be matter-of-fact and ignore her when she averts her eyes and hides her face from others. Radiate confidence and behave as if she is not doing anything unusual. Do not force her to say or do anything. As soon as she makes any effort to smile or reach out to anyone, pay attention and encourage that. Violet will learn quickly if you and others consistently ignore "shy" behavior and pay attention to sociable behavior.

Do not "label" Violet as "a shy child," and don't

permit others to do so. Some parents and other adults unwittingly *encourage* shyness ("Isn't it cute?"). The more Violet withdraws, the more attention some will give her. The slow-to-warm-up child should be permitted to adapt to new surroundings at her own speed, but should be encouraged, expected, and taught to interact with others in polite ways.

Simple social skills can be taught, practiced, and praised at home: telephone manners, introductions and departures, "standard openers" and conversational responses, asking for information, ordering in a restaurant. A friendship with a younger child (who is likely to be less demanding and uncritical) may help your child to reach out and form other friendships. Once Violet feels secure enough to try these skills on others, each successful attempt will surely help her blossom. More details on ways to teach these skills may be found in the "Social Skills" chapter.

As Violet becomes more verbal, be sure to allow and encourage her to express herself freely at home, even though you may disagree with her opinions. Encourage talk about feelings and "I" statements: not "Johnny *made me* mad," but "*I felt angry* when Johnny laughed at me." She needs to be given responsibility for her own feelings rather than to learn to blame others for what she feels, does, and thinks. That encourages independence and self-sufficiency. If children learn that they can take care of themselves, they will feel secure enough to reach out to the world, take risks, and care for themselves.

One of the idiosyncrasies of older shy children is that they do not like surprises, so it's important to respect that. When you are going visiting or know when guests are expected, be sure to advise Violet in advance. Tell her how you'd like her to behave; for example, to say "hello," shake hands, pass the cookies, answer questions politely, go out to play or to her room. Practice new situations by "role playing," so your child will feel more comfortable. Even though mistakes may be made, be sure to praise her. Ignore any clumsiness or failures. Provide even more and new social opportunities as Violet learns to assert herself and take risks.

Be as encouraging as possible. Don't offer too much sympathy if Violet expresses fears of failure or rejection. Your message should be, "You can do what you have to do."

Don't worry about becoming impatient sometimes. You can make many mistakes as long as you give Violet many opportunities to practice being sociable. Sometimes, too, the development of special talents — musical, dramatic, or artistic abilities — helps a child move out of the shell of shyness. Nothing succeeds like success.!

Sibling Rivalry

WHAT DO I DO WHEN my nine-year-old is always fighting and arguing with my seven-year-old?

> *"Birds in their little nests agree;*
> *And 'tis a shameful sight,*
> *When children of one family*
> *Fall out, and chide, and fight."*
> Isaac Watts, "Divine Songs"

If that 17th century poet were alive today, we might respectfully ask him when he ever saw a little bird shake its head and close its beak, so sister bird would get the worm?

You probably told your child about the wonderful new friend and playmate you were going to bring home with you from the hospital — and what a big helper he would be with the marvelous new baby. At first, he seemed interested; but then came the big day when you walked in with the pink bundle. You said, "Isn't she just precious? Don't you just love your new baby sister?" Said he, "I think I'd rather have a dump truck. Put it away, Mommy, and let's play."

The loving relationship we parents hope for between our youngsters doesn't come automatically. You may find that, increasingly, you have to engage in policing activities, particularly if your children are fairly close in age. You may wonder what you did wrong. How can you make the situation right? You think that it's wicked and sinful for Steve to even *feel* jealous, much less to *show* it. *Nice* people don't have such feelings. (*Do* they?) You try very hard to make Steve feel wanted and loved — just like before Diana came. But nothing that you do seems adequate. Your "wretched" child wants to be the *only* child you love. He does not want a buddy, particularly a baby sister buddy. He does not want to share you with anyone. Is that terrible? Awful? Is there anything wrong with your Steve? No. He's just human.

Even though three-year-old Steve is fairly self-sufficient and is not as dependent on you as he once was, don't expect him to be terribly thrilled about sharing your love and attention. Don't be disappointed or upset either. He'll adapt eventually.

Prepare your older child for the coming of the new brother or sister by talking about the new member of the family often *before* the baby is born. Say that you are going to need help sometimes, and assure Steve of *his* importance. That may not ease all of the concern, but it may help.

Don't wait for the baby to arrive if you plan to make any changes in your child's life. For example, if you plan to move a toddler from the crib to a regular bed or from an infant car seat to a toddler's seat, do so some weeks ahead of time. Delay toilet training, though, until several months *after* the baby is born; there may be a period of regression, and there's no point in training twice.

Don't try to force love and enthusiasm. Don't be surprised if Steve's behavior deteriorates and he starts testing you. Remain as loving as always, but do not become lax about discipline and overindulge him.

After baby Diana arrives and relatives and friends come to visit, be sure to draw their attention to Steve as well. Brag about big brother. Even that won't guarantee that he will not feel twinges of resentment and jealousy, but, then, your child is human — not an angel. Infants are very demanding, so remember to give lots of attention to Steve also during the period of adjustment.

Celebrating the individual uniqueness of each child is the most powerful way to convince Steve, and Diana as she grows older, that everyone is important and valued in your family. One good way to do that is to spend time alone with each child, every day if you possibly can. (Actually, "invest" would be a more accurate term than "spend." The payoffs are great for both of you!) Take a quiet walk, go out for a treat, read a favorite story together, play a game. Don't use this time for lectures or punishment; focus on achievements, hopes, dreams, warmth.

"...Both (parents) must set aside some portion of the day — even if you are both working — that belongs exclusively to the child," said Ira Gordon, psychologist. "You don't have to put it on a schedule. You don't want to say: 'now, kid, it's 5 o'clock. I'm going to interact with you until 5:15 and then go have my martini.' That child sometimes needs you more than he needs anything else."

Families pay a significant price when children are spaced less than three years apart. The toddler, for example, who is only about one-and-a-half or two years old when the new baby is born is still mother-oriented and resents and resists having to share her attention. If you have children very close in age, you probably find yourself expending a great deal of energy just to keep the peace. That does not mean that the older, school-aged child does not feel twinges of jealousy and experience a sense of loss and of being displaced.

Steve finds it very difficult to understand that you can love more than one person, and all the Sermons on the Mount are not going to convince him that this new addition is not taking up valuable time, space, and attention that are rightfully his.

You cannot force your children to love each other. Will "playing fair" help? Not if that's a compulsive endeavor to give equal or the same things to one that you give to the other to "prove" that you are not playing favorites. For some parents that means if one gets a pair of shoes, so does the other; each gets exactly the same size of dessert; and the same amount of money is spent on birthday and Christmas presents. *That* compulsion to be "fair" may even add to the problem. Each child is unique, and such treatment does not allow for uniqueness.

Should you encourage Steve to express his hostility openly — let it all hang out? Not if you value peace in the house and want to avoid having self-indulgent children. There are other ways to define and solve problems, through family conferences, for example.

The reality is that Steve and all older siblings experience jealousy, but they also learn to cope. Children are more likely to learn to like each other if you don't force the issue but use the practices that are recommended for dealing with fighting, arguing, and other problems. Your goal is to encourage cooperation, and you do that by intervening when you have to and being quick to praise *individual* accomplishments and attempts.

When your children squabble, don't feel that you have to dash in to find the "guilty" party. You may find that the "innocent" one is delighted that the other got caught, and unwittingly teach your children to develop clever and subtle ways to provoke each other into some act that will lead to punishment. Since it takes two to tangle, just impose Time Out on both of them. Eventually, they'll learn that their fates are intertwined.

One way to help them learn to cooperate is to ask them to work on some common goal. You can set up some very simple projects, for example, you might say, "Hey, kids, if you can play all morning without hitting, fighting, or name calling, I'll give you both a surprise after lunch. I won't tell you what it is. If there *is* a fight, neither of you gets the surprise no matter who starts it or why." The surprise can be a walk to the park, special dessert, baking cookies, storytime. *You* know what pleases your kids.

You can set up more extended projects, for example, you might plan some very special event with them — a trip to the zoo or to a restaurant or to the movies. That might be earned by five days of "no squabbling." (If they have to be consecutive, though, they may *never* get to the zoo; so just settle for five peaceful days.) Ask them to help you draw up a five-day calendar. They can doll it up with pictures cut out of a magazine. Then see what happens. Don't be upset, though, if it takes them two weeks to earn the five "peaceful" days.

Using the job charts (see "Chores") seems to help in addressing the issue of "fairness." Then your children cannot complain that the other(s) get more or that you are giving special favors; each gets what each earns. Through negotiation, you are also acknowledging the uniqueness of each child.

Meanwhile, understand that jealousy is a green-eyed monster that has to fade away.

> ***You have only as much control over me as I am willing to give you.***

Social Skills

WHAT DO I DO WHEN I am told that my ten-year-old daughter needs to be taught social skills? She knows how to say "please" and "thank you." What more is there?

"True luck," said the writer, John Milton Hay, "consists not in holding the best of the cards at the table: Luckiest he who knows just when to rise and go home."

"Please" and "thank you" are certainly important skills, but full social competence includes much more — not the least being "when to rise and go home."

You have to know the rules, the rituals of various social interactions and expectations in various places. A meeting is not the place to spend the time talking about aphids on your roses. If you walk down the street animatedly conversing and there's nobody walking along with you, others may look at you with raised eyebrows. If you don't pay your rent, you will probably be evicted. If you don't pay your income taxes, you may land in jail. If you go to school and argue with the teacher and tell her how stupid she is, you probably won't do well gradewise. If you punch your neighbor in the nose because his dog dug up your petunia patch, he probably won't invite you to his next party. There are a million other situations wherein you have to know "what to do when." These are the social competencies (survival skills) that must be taught.

Barney and Carol sit in the same classroom, do the same work, and are of the same intelligence. The teacher, however, is very warm and responsive to Barney and can barely stand to have Carol around. Why? Because Barney sits up straight, looks interested, and asks questions. Carol slouches in the seat, yawns, taps her pencil impatiently on the desk while the teacher lectures.

"Wonderful student and so vivacious and intelligent," exclaims the teacher to the proud parents of Barney; but Carol's parents are called in for a conference and hear, "Your daughter has a *bad* attitude. Is she depressed about something? She seems to have a rather hostile personality." The real explanation, however, may be that Barney has learned how to apply the adage that "Honey catches more flies than vinegar." Carol may have concluded that the social amenities are unimportant, a form of "buttering up." She wants to be judged by her work alone. The reality, though, is that we are judged by *more* than our work. That's one of the reasons that Dale Carnegie's book, *How To Win Friends and Influence People* is still in print!

Some people do seem to have magnetic and dynamic personalities — charisma — that attracts others. It was once thought that this was inborn, that people inherited certain kinds of traits, for example, gentle or strong, serious or humorous, calm or emotional, lazy or hardworking, trusting or cautious. We now know that learning has much to do with these characteristics. Most people are a complex mix — sometimes serious, sometimes humorous, sometimes one or the other of many so-called traits. Healthy and adaptable people have a lot of options. They know when to do what, and that gives them a lot of freedom to be creative, spontaneous, and innovative.

No doubt the differences between Carol and Barney are due to both genetic and environmental factors. Each was born with tendencies to respond in certain ways (shy, irritable, spontaneous). Each then *learned* to express or inhibit those inborn predispositions. If your Carol has a tendency to be aggressive, you can teach her to be self-controlled and assertive instead. If your Barney has a tendency to be withdrawn and inhibited, you can encourage him to be more sociable and self-sufficient.

What Are the Important Social Skills?

What *are* the skills that Barney and Carol (and everybody else) need to learn to get along in the world? One of the first is to develop a *good sense of humor*. "It better befits a man to laugh at life than to lament over it," said the Greek, Seneca. Noted Arnold Glasow: "Laughter is a tranquilizer with no side effects."

Most babies seem to be born with a sense of humor, a desire to smile and laugh. The tragedy is when they stop smiling. If nothing else, children need to learn to develop a sense of irony, to be able to recognize and accept the incongruities of life, when things don't happen the way we expect them to happen. "A taste for irony," said Jessamyn West, "has kept more hearts from breaking than a sense of humor, for it takes irony to appreciate the joke which is on oneself." When we say to someone: Don't take life so seriously, we really mean: Look for what's funny about the situation even though you may end up laughing with tears in your eyes.

To stay out of trouble, children have to learn *how to handle social situations* at home, at school, and in the community. They need to learn *what gets them into trouble* and how to deal with it. (What is it that gets Dad mad? When he's mad, will an apology help? Why does Sonny always want to fight with me and not with the other kids? How can I deal with Sonny and not land in the principal's office?) They need to learn *how to avoid trouble*. (I guess the kids tease me more when I show that I get mad. Being the class clown isn't worth having to stay after school every day. Maybe I ought to save my jokes for recess.)

Learning how to think through and solve problems is critically important. Both aggressive-impulsive children and inhibited-fearful children don't stop to consider the consequences of their behavior. They have to learn to think first and *then* act. Carol, for example, may have to learn that there are other options to hitting another child or throwing a pencil at the teacher when she feels frustrated. Good problem solvers are better adjusted than poor problem solvers; they deal with less frustration. (See "Reasoning")

They must also learn to *control their tempers* and not to jump to conclusions. Each will have many opportunities to practice *that* skill, such as when: Dad or Mom is angry because of something she's done; another kid teases; a kid pushes her; the teacher says she hit someone and she didn't.

To make friends and get along with adults, children must learn to *cooperate*; *take turns* when playing games and in other activities; *speak up or ignore others when irritated* (rather than to haul off and slug somebody); to *smile* (sometimes even they want to cry); to *give and receive compliments*; *when to make eye contact* and when to *avoid* making eye contact; to *listen* to others; to *speak* in a conversational tone rather than to yell; to *express feelings* appropriately; to *handle criticism* without falling apart; to be *personally groomed* (neat and clean).

How Does a Youngster Learn All Those Skills?

"C'mon now! Do you mean I should send my kid to charm school?"

Attending courses in a charm or finishing school is not all that far-fetched, and I have sometimes recommended that for teenagers who needed to develop some self-confidence or smooth off some rough edges. Training in social skills actually starts very early, when you bring your child home as an infant. *You*, the parent, are the most important teacher in this realm and have been so from the beginning. And that's what most of this book is about — to help you teach your child to be socially skilled, to have integrity, to be self-sufficient and responsible.

"Let us count the ways" you teach your child:

...By what you do. Your modeling is a powerful teaching device, and your children are always watching what you do — how you ask for what you want from others; how you deal with anger and frustration; how you greet guests; how you treat your neighbors; how you dress; how you do your job. We learn most of our behavior, including speech patterns, walking, social customs, and more, by watching what others do.

...By what you say. Telling your child what you want and how you want something done is a very simple and straightforward way to teach skills. This is also known as direct instruction.

There are ways to add power to your modeling and instruction, for example,

...Praise a lot. Pay attention, not only to your child's successes, but to the *attempts* (even those that are half-hearted) to do better. Maybe Barney just hung his head when his Aunt Clarisse asked him a question, but he *did* remember to smile and take her coat when she arrived. Praise the smile and help. Remember how excited you were when he first said "Mama" or took his first step? Well, you didn't expect miracles then, why now? Praise remembering to say "please" and "thank you" at Grandma's house or that he asked questions about quality before buying that new model car. Tell him *why* you're pleased, so he'll start thinking in terms of cause and effect ("When I do this, that happens.")

...Rehearse situations. It's very difficult to do some things without practice, and this is a favorite technique behavioral therapists use to teach people skills. Later, under stress, it's easier to behave in the practiced ways rather than to act impulsively.

If Carol comes home from school complaining that Butch the Bully pushed in front of her in the cafeteria line, you can help her to prepare for the next such occasion by "rehearsing" the scene with her. Pretend that you're a stage director and set up a scene. You can take one part, while she takes the other. "Coach" Carol and practice until she feels competent to handle Butch when the next confrontation comes up. Start with an "easy" scene; gradually make it tougher as she gets more skill.

...*Give special assignments*. Just *talking* about problems does little to change people. Counselors give "homework" to help clients practice what they are learning. You can do the same thing. For example, if Barney has a problem talking with his teacher or is afraid to ask questions about assignments, set up an incentive program wherein he is to go up to the teacher each day and ask one brief question or say *something*, if only, "Have a nice day." The important thing is to try to do something that seems really scarey and learn that the world really doesn't fall apart during the attempt. The teacher will probably be surprised and pleased at his interest. The positive response may help Barney feel that he isn't being rejected after all. (Rehearse — practice with Barney — *before* he tries this assignment!)

...*Find a playmate for your shy child*. It is sometimes useful to find a younger child or an older, but socially slow, child to play with your youngster. That provides an opportunity to practice leadership and social skills with those who are not hypercritical. However, it is not recommended that you encourage long-term relationships with younger children to the exclusion of age mates. Your child has to take the same risks that others do — sometimes being rejected or criticized — in the give-and-take of human relationships.

In all these and other methods for helping children develop social skills, it is important not to push them beyond their capabilities. You don't want to force your child into a shell. Remember, as Mark Twain said, "Habit is habit, and not to be flung out of the window by any man, but coaxed downstairs a step at a time."

Special Problems

WHAT DO I DO WHEN I have a special problem? My kids can be really annoying at times! Why can't they just behave themselves?

There was a little girl
Who had a little curl
Right in the middle of her forehead;
And when she was good
She was very, very good,
But when she was bad she was horrid.

An incentive system may get the interest and attention of your offspring. This is a potent approach to changing those behaviors that are very annoying to you. *"I'm all ears!"* Think of your child's problem as a challenge, and that the two of you are going to have fun working this out together. *"Fun? Fun is tennis — fun is peace and quiet — fun is not having a problem!"* If you're going to do this, you may as well enjoy it. It's certainly more fun than fussing and fuming.

(Sigh) *"All right. I'm smiling already! What do I do?"* Good attitude! Congratulations! You can use the Special Problem Chart for children ages three through twelve or thirteen. A plain 5" x 7" card will usually serve the same purpose for your older child, who may prefer a more "businesslike" approach.

You can use the chart for any behavior that you can see and count, for example, crying when going to Day Care or to bed, temper tantrums, complaining, interrupting, bedwetting, arguing, coming home late, teacher's complaints about misbehaving at school, teasing, sarcastic remarks, picking up toys, practicing music lesson, whining, fighting, swearing, borrowing things without asking.

"Ah-hah! I want to start with attitude. My kid has a terrible attitude. He grumbles, growls, makes faces. He acts like he has some kind of terrible disease inflicted by a witch doctor." Sorry, you cannot use "attitude;" that is too general, sort of like trying to put a cloud into a box. When your boss says you have a "good attitude," what does that mean? You say "Yes, ma'am" a lot? Your performance is good? If you were told that you had to *change* your attitude, how would you go about that? What would you *do*? You might dash out and sign up for a charm course only to learn that all you had to do was come to work on time!

"But David is so sullen about piano practice! At least, with the cost of lessons, that boy could practice his scales

without looking like he's being drawn and quartered!'' As long as he's practicing, that's all that's relevant. Praise him for practicing and ignore everything else. Act as if *nothing else is happening* — no matter how agonized he looks. It's unrealistic to expect him to act like a member of the Trapp family, singing, ''The hills are alive...!'' Who knows? He might do that someday — if you don't press the issue. There's nothing like *success* to help change ''attitude.''

All right. I have four kids with ten different kinds of problems. Where do I start?''

...Start with one child and one problem at a time. Arrange an individual conference with each child. One of the great advantages of this approach is that your children are partners in planning. You're giving each child power when you are willing to negotiate, and that's very gratifying to a kid. You are asking David to do something that *you* want, and, in exchange, you are willing to give something in return. Children *want* to ''buy in'' to this system because there's some benefit for them in it. Also, by being willing to negotiate, you are showing that you really care and want to be helpful — not critical. That adds a whole new dimension to your relationship with your child, and can be very gratifying to both of you.

...During the conference, use the Special Problem Charts on pages 159 and 161. You or your child may also design your own. The first thing to do is to write out what you want your child to do. Be very specific and be sure to write it as a ''Please do,'' *not* as a ''Don't.'' This is very important. Most kids know what *not* to do. They don't always know what they are supposed to do.

Example: Practice piano 30 minutes each day at 3 p.m.; *or* At 5 p.m. pick up your toys in the living room and put them away; *or* When I'm on the telephone write me a note (or draw a picture) and deliver it when I get off; *or* Be brave and wave (not cry) when left at Day Care.

...Write out what your child wants to earn. She might choose a game, toy, T-shirt, trip to the zoo, afternoon on the town with you. As long as the request is legal, don't be critical about the choice. Your kid has to feel that this is worth working for!

...That's all there is to the negotiation. You are both now ready to put the contract in action. Each block on the chart represents a *successful* day. Each day that your child *completes* the condition of the contract, let your child paste a star in the block. One mother found that letting her four-year-old son choose from a page of colorful stickers really made a difference. He had the habit of using swear words that he picked up from friends, and he enjoyed his mother's shocked response. Being able to choose the sticker, however, became even more interesting than the shock treatment!

________________ IS REALLY BUZZIN' TO EARN: ________________

THIS WILL BE EARNED BY: ________________

____

DATE: ________________

SIGNED: ________________

(MOM OR DAD)

B Z Z Z Z

YOU GET THE HONEY, HONEY!

WHAT DO I DO WHEN...? © 1983 by Juliet V. Allen.
Impact Publishers, P. O. Box 1094, San Luis Obispo, CA 93406.

Do not skip any blocks. It may take your child five days to fill the first two spaces. Be patient and sympathetic — not critical.

...Continue using Time Out. The chart does not replace regular disciplinary procedures. For example, "dry bed" earns a star, but a child who happens to wet the bed has to strip and remake the bed as usual.

...Praise a lot when your child earns a star. The praise really gives power to that star! If s/he fails for the day, do not scold or lecture. Just say that tomorrow is another day.

...It is important to note that some blocks indicate that you are supposed to provide a special surprise treat. *Don't forget to do that.* A day is a long time to a child, and a week seems like forever, so the "surprise days" are very important. Your treat can be anything from a stick of gum to baking a favorite cake that the whole family can share and enjoy — or even a trip to the park playground. It helps to brag to the family, too, about the progress made.

If the Special Problem Chart is not working for you, you may be asking for too much change too soon. Take another look at your goals; start smaller. Consult with a behavioral specialist to tighten the program if necessary.

When your child has successfully completed two charts, go on to another problem — or another child — if you want.

"Never Use a Cannon When a Fly Swatter Will Do"

When you are dealing with trickier, older kids who are less inclined to be impressed with earning stars, sometimes just *counting* a behavior will change it.

That you've got to see to believe? Try it. You may become a believer! For example, Sara, 14, had a habit of making sarcastic remarks and put downs to her brother and two younger sisters. Her exasperated mother began to simply tally the number of unpleasant remarks on a card posted on the refrigerator. Her mother told her that she was interested in finding out how many sarcasms anyone could say in a day — that she was tired of nagging, and it might be of "scientific interest." The card was labelled "Sara," and had columns for the *date* and *number of sarcastic remarks*. Sara's comment about the card provided the first tally. She was soon eyeing the card, however, and quickly learned to stop herself from completing a sarcastic remark when she saw her mother move toward the card, pencil in hand. Did that resolve the problem? It helped, but sarcasm is a particularly insidious habit that is difficult to curb.

Sara's mother negotiated further with her, and agreed to pay half the cost of a special blouse when the card revealed 30 days without sarcastic remarks. The days did not have to be consecutive, and 35 days later, Sara earned her blouse. Another contract was negotiated then wherein

WHAT DO I DO WHEN...? © 1983 by Juliet V. Allen.
Impact Publishers, P. O. Box 1094, San Luis Obispo, CA 93406.

she could earn a small pendant. *This* time she had to make at least two *pleasant* remarks a day to someone in the family *and no sarcasms*. (That may seem contrived, but change has to start somewhere. Old habits have to be replaced with new ones.)

Then There's the "Cost" Approach

You can use a lot of ingenuity if you use the "cost" approach — and also impress your kids with the "cool" way in which you handle situations. For example, Gary, a bright, attractive 15-year-old son of family-oriented parents, had drifted into the habit of waking his mother or dad in the middle of the night complaining that he couldn't sleep. This had started when he was seven years old, and the family had temporarily assumed the care of a young nephew, who stayed with them for about six months.

Gary continued to waken his parents throughout the years. His mother tried everything — warm milk, tea, flannel pajamas, a medical exam, lecturing, scolding. Nothing worked. He never, however, woke his 17-year-old sister when his parents would sometimes spend a weekend away from home. "He wouldn't dare; she'd *clobber* him!" explained his mother.

Gary had also developed the habit of hauling his sleeping bag into the den and would fall asleep there while watching TV. "I don't know why we furnished a bedroom for him," said his mother. "These may seem like stupid problems. We have no other complaints. His grades are excellent, and he does his chores; but I'm tired of being wakened every night out of a sound sleep and having to put his sleeping bag away every morning."

A program was planned which allowed Gary to waken his parents as often as he liked, but each time cost him 50 cents. He would also have to "rent" the family room for 25 cents a night, and, further, pay his mother a fee of 20 cents if she had to stow his sleeping bag. Gary was not thrilled to hear about that arrangement, but four weeks later, his parents reported that he had wakened them only four times and "rented" the family room just twice. A month later at the final conference, Gary had wakened them once and had not "rented" the family room again.

Some Problems Are Tougher Than Others

Nobody has to tell you that some behaviors are particularly irritating because they happen a lot, for example, teasing, interrupting, arguing. Use Time Out to stop these behaviors, and the Special Problem Chart to encourage the behaviors that you want to substitute. It would be nice, but you can't expect perfection overnight — or even in a month. Try to strive — and generate enthusiasm — for improvement.

For example, Billy, age nine, delighted in teasing his

younger brother and would then excuse himself by saying: "I was only kidding. I didn't mean anything by it. He's such a baby!" His mother negotiated the Special Problem Chart, and he was advised that the only way he could earn a star was to tease one time less than the day before. On the first day that he was placed on the program, he received an "automatic" star, no matter how many times he teased his brother. There were 19 teasing incidents. On the following day, he teased 17 times and received a star. On day three, he teased 12 times. To get a star on day four, he could not tease more than 11 times. When he finally got down to one or two teases a day, it was agreed that he could still earn a star. After serving Time Out, he was assigned one of his brother's chores as a way of "working off" the teasing incident. If you decide to use the Special Problem Chart, make certain that you're a helper, not a rescuer. Be very encouraging — even though you really wish you didn't have to do all of this — but *never* back down on the conditions of the contract, for example, "Well, you only went one tease over the limit, so I'll give you a star." Commitment is a hard way to go, but persistence works!

Stealing

WHAT DO I DO WHEN I find that my son has been taking money out of my purse without asking? I noticed that coins have been disappearing, but I am now missing a $5 bill out of my wallet. I don't want to accuse him falsely.

"That was a real shock," said the depressed father. "My 12-year-old son stole my U-Bank card. Evidently, he found my bank number in my desk, and he withdrew $50 from my account."

"What did you do about that?"

The father rubbed his chin nervously. "I really had a long talk with him. He denied it at first. He finally said that he didn't know why he did it and doesn't know what he did with the money. He returned $10."

"What are you going to do about that?"

"I don't know. That's why I'm here. *You're* the expert. You tell *me*."

"When did that all start?"

He paused. "Oh, maybe a couple of years ago. He would take some loose change lying around sometimes.

There were a few complaints from school about things missing. I restricted him for a month when *that* happened, but now I just don't know what to do. Can't beat the kid. He's bigger than I am..."

If you have a child whom you suspect is pilfering, do not delay — as did this father — to seek counseling. When youngsters get into the habit of stealing from the family and/or the community for a year or more, intervention is more complex and troublesome and the serious implications for child and family are multiplied.

It is very difficult to acknowledge that your own child would steal. You would prefer to trust Tom's word that he "found" the hub cap or that the new-looking pocket knife was a "gift" or a "trade." You would prefer to think that you "lost" coins or bills out of your purse. You may be afraid to confront Tom for fear that he may not like you anymore, or that you may be accusing him falsely and "wound" him deeply.

If the evidence is so obvious that you can't avoid confronting him, you may hope that a lecture about honesty and good citizenship will help him see the error of his ways. You may try to make him feel guilty or experience some pain by taking him to the woodshed and/or restricting him for a week or two or three. But, lo and behold, it happens again. *When* will the boy learn? Will he grow out of it?

No, he won't grow out of it. But if he's lucky, someone will take charge early and teach him that stealing has some very unpleasant and inconvenient consequences and that honesty really *is* the best policy.

Why do some kids steal? Are they "bad seeds" — doomed from the time of birth? As a young child, Tom was like all children — strictly *amoral*. He had no concept of possessions or that he would have to ask permission to use or borrow something from someone else. As far as the toddler is concerned, "What's mine is mine, and what's yours is mine, too, if I want it." Respect for the rights and property of others has to be taught, and that teaching begins the first time the child grabs a toy from someone else. That is when you, the parent, say firmly, "No, this is Ruth's. You must ask before you touch." You — or the other person — may, of course, refuse the request to "touch." He won't like it, but he has to learn to live with it.

As children get older, there are a number of reasons why they start stealing. They may simply not have been properly trained. Some parents set a bad example themselves. They may be seen to cheat or lie. Other parents may be models of virtue but tend to ignore it when they see their child pull or take things from others, or they may simply lecture or punish and let it go at that.

Some children are actually rewarded for stealing when they get away with it or the incident is badly handled by adults. It is critically important that the child be held accountable immediately when caught pilfering. Any shopkeeper or other adult who ignores the act or shrugs and says, ''kids will be kids'' or merely lectures and ''forgives this time'' is doing a great disservice to everyone. If Tom learns that people are ''pushovers,'' he is likely to pilfer again and again, and ''being caught'' becomes simply a calculated risk rather than an embarrassment.

Another child who steals may be seeking status and/or acceptance in the peer world, particularly, when grades are poor and home is a place to avoid. A few do so because they feel deprived and don't know how else to get what they want. And, unfortunately, there are youngsters so angry with their parents, and so determined to prove that they are ''rotten'' parents who have ''rotten'' kids, that they intentionally steal or otherwise misbehave to ''get even'' and publicly discredit the family.

It is very important that you confront your child the first time you suspect that he or she has taken something. If you have gone shopping, and you find that little Alice has taken a package of gum, for example, return with her immediately to the store, tell her to apologize for taking what did not belong to her, return the gum and also have her pay for it besides. You may have to lend her the money, and she can ''earn'' it by doing some special job at home. It could be 15 minutes of yard work or scrubbing the pots and pans. Just make certain that it's something that she *can* do. Also, make certain that the job is done before she can do anything that she likes to do — see TV or play with friends, for example. Such early, fast and decisive intervention will go a long way to discourage any further pilfering.

What do you do if your child can't return the item because it has been eaten or the wrapper has been removed? Again, you take Alice to the store immediately to apologize. Because she cannot return the item, she must pay *double* the cost. As is customary in the courts, Alice should be assessed both ''actual'' and ''punitive'' damages. She can take the money out of her allowance or she may have to do some special jobs around the house to earn the money. Her privileges are not returned until she has made restitution.

If money has been pilfered from your purse or from any member of the family, double the amount should be repaid; again, actual and punitive damages help make the lesson clear. If Tom has taken things before, or your intuition tells you that he is the logical suspect, do not feel that you must ''prove'' that he is the culprit. Trust yourself. You may not always be right, but it is really Tom's problem, not yours. He has to learn that a reputation is easily lost and takes time to regain. Do not label him as a thief. Simply say that money is missing, and you believe that he is responsible and must make restitution. *Do not engage in a debate or ask him if he took something*; that will only invite him to deny it.

In very difficult cases, parents may wish to require that the youngster have a sales receipt for anything new or different that he brings into the house. He is not permitted to justify any item as being a "finding" or a "gift" or a "trade." Trust and credibility, then, can be regained after a period of six months during which no acts of theft have occurred. This is a way of providing a light at the end of the tunnel. To say, "We'll trust you again when you can prove that you're honest" is unsatisfactory because the proof to get the "bill of health" is poorly defined. How long does it take to prove something under those conditions? It could be 20 years! As trust is re-established, it is important that the child be provided with opportunities to earn money to give him some legitimate control over his life.

These recommendations, of course, are only a part of all that may be required to help work out the problems of a troubled family There may be other considerations and issues that have to be addressed in resolving this difficult and complex situation. If you have more than two incidents of pilfering, you will want to seek counseling. Theft and lying are serious problems. I urge you to get professional help early.

Stepparenting

WHAT DO I DO WHEN my 13-year-old son is very jealous of the man I plan to marry? He is so rude that it is embarrassing. I have been divorced for four years, and I really care about this man. I don't want to lose him, but I don't want to lose my son's love either. My seven- and nine-year-old children are more accepting of the pending marriage.

This is a complex problem that is going to require a great deal of understanding on your part. Children tend to be extremely moralistic — particularly adolescents. They want adults to be strong, moral, ethical, above reproach. Maturity comes when they finally learn that all adults have feet of clay — that parents are human, have needs, are social and sexual beings.

The situation may be further complicated. It is quite common for divorced mothers to turn to their older children and adolescents for emotional and moral support — even to seek advice for the practical problems of daily living. Many times, the oldest son is asked to serve some of the functions usually provided by the father and to act in mature ways at an early age. Usually, the younger children are most anxious about the mother's ability to cope with stress and financial problems, and are pleased when someone comes around to share those burdens.

In effect, you are asking your son to forget about being your partner in running the family and to move back into the role of compliant child. That is *not* going to happen easily — and probably will not happen at all. He had you all to himself. He is not going to give you up readily. No one gives up that kind of power without a struggle. The situation will probably not be resolved until your son finds his place in the world of his peers and eventually makes his own life.

What do you do in the meantime? It won't be easy. You cannot stuff toothpaste back into the tube. You cannot expect your son to revert to a role of compliance, so you have to prepare yourself and your fiance for a long siege of resistance — and not take it personally. It's one of the costs of broken marriages and remarriages sometimes.

You have an obligation, however, to expect — and demand — that your son will behave with civility. He does not have to love — or even like — the man that you marry. He does have to behave courteously, and to understand that nothing that he does will break up your relationship with your fiance — that the marriage will take place. You hope that he will accept that with good grace and you love and appreciate him. You must convey the message that you do not need his approval for this marriage. You would *like* to have it, but you do not *need* it. Both you and your fiance, then, must present a united front. If your son behaves well, he is welcome to be involved in family activities. If he does not, he will be excused — no hard feelings. He will be given the opportunity to be invited again and to behave in more appropriate ways.

This is the way that you help your son adapt to the realities of his — and your — life. All the recommendations in this book are appropriate in dealing with your son. The *big* issue: don't take anything personally, and be prepared for a long, long siege of trials and tribulations.

WHAT DO I DO WHEN my daughter refuses to cooperate with my wife, who has done everything she can to show loving interest and concern? My daughter, who is nine years old, has done everything to sabotage our marraige and has even destroyed every family heirloom that my wife owns and brought into our home.

Becoming a stepparent is one of the greatest challenges that can confront anyone. Whereas the natural family has time to work out parents' roles, responsibilities, differences, and ideas as to what a family should be, the stepfamily is in a more complicated situation. A unique combination of elements is brought into play, creating problems unlike anything confronted by the natural family.

The issue of discipline is a common problem to all families but is a particularly acute problem for stepparents.

Teaching a child that there are social limits is one of the most important tasks of parents. The child *must* learn how to behave appropriately if he or she is to live a reasonably satisfying life. In both "natural" and "step" families, that has priority.

There are two important factors that may make a child's adjustment to a new family situation difficult. The first one relates to what the child was accustomed to prior to the new marriage. In a single-parent family, the child may have been left to his or her own resources, and may have had erratic meals and bedtimes. Perhaps the relationship between parent and child was casual and "friendly" rather than parent-child oriented, lacking structure and rules for the child to observe.

With the event of a remarriage, the child is expected to adapt to more traditional family life. Dad is no longer a "pal" but has become a parent. Worse yet, he is a parent who has formed an alliance with a stranger. The child may have liked this stranger before the marriage, but, suddenly, *after* the marriage, "Dad is not all mine any more. The stranger is an interloper who is usurping my rightful place as the only one in Dad's life. This stranger is also making life difficult by telling me what I can and cannot do — when I can eat, when to go to bed — and creating all kinds of problems that appear to be unnecessary. The "obvious" solution: get rid of this stranger by any means, fair or foul (or, at the very least, refuse to cooperate with the new arrangement)."

The child's determination to break up the marriage and re-establish the more casual relationship with the custodial parent is a force to be reckoned with.

The second complicating factor is the myth of "instant love." That is the impossible expectation that "the stepparent must love the child as if he were his (or her) own, and the child must love the stepparent as if he (or she) were his natural parent, and they should love each other immediately...and happily ever after...(tra, la)." That would be nice, but it is unrealistic, and yet it feeds into feelings of guilt when it does not occur. The stepmother may then try to please the natural father by being "rigidly fair," or desperately try to love a child who may represent a financial or emotional burden or a constant reminder of the former wife.

How is this resolved? It is important that the child get the message that the father and stepmother represent a united front and that they are agreed as to methods and goals of discipline. Any disagreements relating to discipline should be discussed privately. Publicly, the message should be that the decision of one parent will be supported by the other. Unless this happens, great stress is placed on the marital relationship, and children are very sensitive to cues of weakness.

What is the role of the natural parent? It is to give emotional support and encouragement to the stepparent in the parenting role, to give economic aid, to provide assistance and relief in household tasks and child rearing, and to serve as a model of love, authority, and nurturance in caring for the children. That serves to enhance the stepparent's feelings of self-esteem and competence, which, in turn, influences the relationship with the child (or children). Natural mothers and fathers must give a message of moral support to their new spouses, and not sabotage reasonable efforts to discipline.

Usually after a brief "honeymoon period," stepchildren try to stretch the limits, "testing" to see if the stepparent has the will, energy, and power to establish his or her authority. They may also try to play one parent against another and feel and express resentment that the stepparent is trying to replace the absent parent.

Stepparents must understand that they *cannot* "replace" the natural parent. They may be most effective as concerned adults who have made a commitment to provide guidance and protection to the child or children placed in their care. The goal is to *add* to existing family relationships, and with the passage of time, to build social and emotional bonds with the stepchild.

Most methods of child rearing assume a bond of affection between parent and child. During the early, transitional period of a new marriage, that bond does not usually exist between the child and stepparent. While that affection grows, it is important that the stepparent be established as a person who has power and whose word *means* something. The burden for supporting that authority falls on the natural parent, who must show trust and support for the stepparent's decisions.

Love and approval are the most powerful forces in relationships, but such bonds are not readily established. They may take years to establish — meanwhile, the disciplinary procedures recommended here are appropriate. When a child becomes as destructive as described in the question above, counseling is essential. Parents must present a united front but must also recognize when to seek help and not wait for the child to literally tear the house and relationships apart. Fortunately, relatively few stepchildren are so determined to create chaos, but when they are, run — don't walk — to seek couseling services.

WHAT DO I DO WHEN my seven-year-old returns from weekend visitations with his father, and it takes me three days to get him to calm down and behave? It's really hard to compete with a "Disneyland Daddy" who indulges and spoils my son.

Understanding and a matter-of-fact approach in terms of discipline are the keys to the resolution of this problem. Almost all children experience pain when their parents divorce — anger, fear, depression, guilt; however, these gradually dissipate if parents do not "feed into" them.

Boys appear to be particularly vulnerable when separated from their fathers, particularly if they have had positive relationships with their fathers. Girls tend to adapt more readily. Problems, however, may emerge during the teenage years for a girl who has not established a healthy, affectionate relationship with her father or a stepfather. She may then have doubts about herself and her desireability.

A child is very apt to experience a sense of divided loyalty and be torn by the question: Am I betraying my mother if I love my father and his new wife? Most children want to have good relationships with both parents, and many want to establish rapport with the stepparent. It is very important that both the natural and stepparents accept the child's feelings and never show resentment. It is devastating to children when their parents quarrel, put down, or recriminate each other. They are then forced to take sides. Don't cause that to happen. Help your child to avoid playing one parent against the other or becoming exploitative and manipulative. A child can become highly skilled at escalating differences and conflict between divorced parents, parents and stepparents.

Visitation privileges offer unique opportunities for tension. Family life is interrupted and readjustments after the visits are often difficult. This gives the mother an unfortunate opportunity to take revenge upon the father. She can manipulate the visitation to the point that it damages the relationship between father and child — and do so knowing that it also damages her child. Revenge may be sweet, but the cost may be very high. When the mother is hostile and critical of the father, the child may begin to view him as unacceptable — or it may boomerang, and the child may reject the critical mother. The father may lose power as a male role model for his son(s). For his girl(s), the cost may be a disruption of heterosexual relationships during adolescence.

How do you avoid that? You have to care enough about your child to stifle your own angers and frustrations. Do not denigrate or unfairly criticize your child's other parent. Find a friend or counselor to whom you can ventilate if you have to. Do not listen to gossip from your child after a visitation. It is none of your concern what goes on in the other home unless, of course, your child is being mistreated or neglected. If you are confident that your child is safe, provide a ready ear only for the *good* news, the *fun* that happened — even though it may hurt and you wish your former spouse and the new partner would disappear. Be very matter-of-fact when your child comes home. Give the message that you expect your child to adjust quickly to *your* structure. Children are adaptable and discriminating. They learn what-works-where very quickly.

Ideally, of course, you and your former spouse will be able to talk with each other in friendly ways and share similar kinds of parenting practices. If not, just let your child know that in *your* house there are certain rules and expectancies. Never, *never* say to your child: ''If you don't like it here, you know where you can go — to your father (mother).'' Do not allow yourself to treat your youngster as a piece of baggage.

WHAT DO I DO WHEN I'm an every-other-weekend father? I love my kids, but it really hurts that I'm left out of a lot of their life. Maybe I ought to drop out altogether?

Some fathers who are very attached to their children do find that seeing their children every other weekend is far too painful and withdraw. Don't. Your kids need you. You have a lot to offer. It has been learned that those fathers who maintain frequent contact and involvement with their children have much influence that is lost when the father visits only infrequently and appears to be relatively detached.

It's inevitable, or course, that the parent who has custody will have the most influence. You, however, can be a friend and an important source of support (*moral*, as well as financial). Hang in there. You are important in helping your child cope and adjust to the new and often unhappy situation of a divided family.

Divorce and stepparenting are very complex subjects that cannot be adequately covered in this book. The following resources are recommended:

E. Atkin and E. Rubin, *Part-time Father,* (written for divorced fathers without custody of their children). New York: Vanguard Press, 1976.

R. Gardner, *The Boys and Girls Book About Divorce* (written for school-age and adolescent children. It includes a chapter entitled ''How to Get Along Better with Your Stepfather and Stepmother''). New York: Bantam, 1971.

S. Kalter, *Instant Parent: Who Are These Children and What Am I Doing Here?* New York: Berkley Publishing, 1980.

B. Maddox, *The Half-Parent* (Discusses adoption, legal obligations, rights, etc.). New York: New American Library, 1976.
A. Richards and I. Willis, *How To Get It Together When Your Parents Are Coming Apart* (addressed to adolescents and discusses the problems and feelings related to remarriage). New York: David McKay, 1976.
J. Stenson, *Now I Have a Stepparent and It's Kind of Confusing* (explains remarriage to young children). New York: Avon, 1979.
The Step Family Foundation of N.Y. is a clearinghouse for information and publishes a newsletter for stepparents. The address is 333 West End Ave., N.Y., N.Y. 10023.
Stepparent News is a monthly newsletter which offers info on new books, commentary on new ideas in stepparenting, and "Stepping Stones Just for Kids." Info: Listening Inc., 8716 Pine Ave., Gary, IN 46403.

Suicide Talk

WHAT DO I DO WHEN I hear my child or teenager talk about dying or threaten to commit suicide? (And what if I occasionally think about it myself?)

"And nothing to look backward to with pride,
And nothing to look forward to with hope."
Robert Frost

Listen:

"I think I am the stupidest kid in class...," says the 12-year-old boy. "I never really try to kill myself, but sometimes I think to drown myself."

"I feel ugly and like a dumbbell...Sometimes I would like to kill my friends or my own stomach or arm...Friends make fun of me all the time," says a dejected eight-year-old.

"It wasn't an accident," whispers the dying five-year-old boy after dashing in front of a truck. "I figured if I died, it wouldn't hurt as much as if I lived."

Can children so young really hurt so much? They can, and they do; they're human like the rest of us.

If you hear a threat of suicide, take it seriously and seek consultation with a mental health specialist. Listen sensitively when the child speaks.

If you have contemplated suicide yourself *in any way at all, please* find a counselor, minister or friend to talk with about the feelings that led you to that point.

What we don't know about suicide *can* hurt us. There are many myths which get in the way of understanding and helping. You may want to check yourself as to what you know about some common beliefs: The following items were compiled by Richard H. Horner, social worker in Marion County, Oregon:

1. True or False. Only a few people ever think about committing suicide.

2. True or False. Thinking about suicide is a sign of mental illness.

3. True or False. Most of those who commit suicide have made previous attempts.

4. True or False. Females are more likely to commit suicide than males.

5. True or False. Males are more likely to use more violent means than females.

The answers are:

1. False. Most people consider suicide as an option at some time in their lives but usually discard it as a passing thought.

2. False. Thinking of suicide is not necessarily a sign of mental illness. It IS a sign that problem solving skills are being challenged and that the negative aspects of life are being emphasized.

3. False. People are often successful on their FIRST attempt. (However, it is also true that people who have attempted suicide unsuccessfully are more likely to attempt again, particularly if there is no remorse about the first attempt.)

4. False. Suicides are three times more common among men. Women make four times more suicidal gestures, but men are more successful.

5. True. Men are more likely to use guns, and women tend to use less lethal means, like sleeping pills.

But Why Would a Child...?

"It doesn't make any sense," you say? "Children have their whole lives ahead of them!"

To the child, the present is everything. In depression and suicide, it is the *message* that kids get from parents and significant others that counts. There may be a genetic predisposition to become easily depressed, but the parent-child relationship is of prime importance.

The child feels rejected and unappreciated. The message is: "You're no good. You're inadequate." There's a lack of respect or caring and a constant barrage of criticism and humiliation. Overprotection also conveys a message of inadequacy and worthlessness. The parent who makes all the decisions and does everything for the child is really suggesting that the youngster can't take care of him- or herself, and that mistakes are unacceptable.

Common to all children, teenagers and adults at risk are feelings of helplessness (the negatives of life far outweigh the positives), haplessness, and hopelessness. The person feels that nothing he or she can do will make a difference. Suicide attempts may occur at critical periods when all the stress of the past and the present come together. There is no relief in sight; and from the depressed person's tunnel vision of the world, the only way out is to commit suicide.

The very young child may not understand the finality of death, but specialists in this area suggest that is irrelevant. Children have *some* notion that the threat of suicide is the *ultimate* threat.

Suicidal children are often trapped in chaotic family situations where they cannot predict when or how something is going to happen or who is going to do what to whom. Divorce or the death of a loved parent adds to the feeling of helplessness. In order to exert some kind of control, to seek revenge, these children often threaten to commit suicide or threaten and attack others. These techniques are usually taught to them by their parents, who may be alcoholics or drug abusers and have a history of frequent marriages and separations.

Very young children are apt to make impulsive suicidal gestures, for example, jumping from a height or running into traffic. Teenagers tend to be more calculating — and more successful.

High risk teenagers usually fall into three types, according to Horner. One is the angry, impulsive adolescent who indulges in self-defeating behaviors. This youngster is quick to take dares, drinks and drives, likes guns and other symbols of violence. Energies are directed toward self-destruction. As children they are often described as being "hyperactive." At a critical time, this teenager may be likely to kill himself or someone else.

The second type is the depressed teenager who has not been a behavioral problem but who has a history of chronic depression and a multitude of ill-defined problems. This is a young person with inadequate coping skills, who feels overwhelmed with these burdens.

The third type is the shy, withdrawn, isolated, virtually friendless teenager who is often totally absorbed in studying or other solitary pursuits. He or she often seeks perfection, but, when faced with loss or failure, has no one to turn to.

The belief that those who talk about suicide never do it is another myth. *Most of those who talk about it make an attempt* that may or may not be successful. The talk is usually a subtle plea for help.

"...Early detection and treatment of...'distress signals' is vital," notes Dr. Allan L. Berman, psychologist. He recommends intensive family therapy and teaching effective problem solving and coping skills. If children and teenagers "aren't taught very good problem solving skills, they tend to resort to suicide as a way of trying to focus attention on their problems or escape them," he notes, but also adds, "If they are living with alcoholic or abusive parents, sometimes the solution is to get them out of the family."

It is important to listen. Don't give advice and don't argue or debate. Don't tell the child or teenager to think about other things or to "forget it." Refer or take the depressed person to a school counselor or other mental health specialist.

There are no sure ways to tell that someone is definitely suicidal, but an ounce of prevention may save a life. With some, the important thing is to "buy time." Dr. Martin Seligman, a psychologist who is renowned for his work with depression, observed that "Suicide usually has its roots in depression, and depression dissipates in time...Often the best gift we can give to someone contemplating suicide is the gift of time, the great healer."

And again, if you've read this chapter looking for some help for *yourself* because depression or life circumstances seem to be pulling you down, *please* ask a trusted friend for help in finding a professional. Talk to your physician or minister. Call your local Community Mental Health Center or Hotline crisis telephone service. "Phone home." You — and your children — deserve the best help you can get.

Some of the most difficult problems are resolved just by the passing of time.

Tantrums and Other Bad Habits

WHAT DO I DO WHEN my child whines, pouts, sulks, cries, and throws tantrums?

"The wheel that squeaks the loudest is the one that gets the grease," observed the humorist Josh Billings.

Whining, pouting, sulking, crying, and throwing tantrums are the squeaks that your child applies to get the grease of your attention. Nevertheless, *you* can decide not to "lubricate that wheel." Ignoring such action is easier when you know what's happening and why.

Children are quite innovative in finding "what works," and they can be *very* persistent. (After all, they have all the time in the world! *They* have few appointments to keep. What's more, you are a captive audience!)

Unwittingly, you may start encouraging this behavior the first time you say: "For heaven's sakes! Here's the cookie. Now be quiet!" or "I just don't have time for this. *I'll* pick up the toys. *You* go and get ready for bed." or "What's the matter, Dear? Why are you sitting there in the corner, sucking your thumb? Come here. Let me entertain you." Years later, you might find yourself handing over the car keys, muttering to yourself "*Anything* to get that kid off my back!"

Your child learns to engage in annoying behaviors *when they pay off*. Either they get the most powerful reward you can give — your attention — or convince you to change your mind about something (that is, to "give in" to a childish demand). Kids don't learn that by themselves. They are *not* born with an "instruction manual" in their heads; these are *learned* messages (and *you* are the teacher!):

"If I whine, pout, sulk, cry, and throw temper tantrums, my parents will feel angry or guilty and I'll get what I want.

"Above all, I have to *be persistent!* I'm young, and parents are much older and usually wear out fairly quickly. It's particularly effective to whine, sulk and do other irritating things in public places or when my parents visit friends and relatives. Grandma is a special ally, who will protest and sigh heavily if my folks do anything nasty like putting me into Time Out. I have to remember to *persist!*"

Of course, if those instructions *were* inborn, we parents could not *change* our children's bad habits. Fortunately, they are learned. Each time you "give in" to a childish demand or pay attention (even *scolding* is a rewarding attention!), you teach your child to be annoying. Be firm and resist that temptation because such behaviors, once learned and "embedded in the personality" of your child, can effect a whole lifetime of unhappy relationships. Even speech development can be delayed if Caspar learns that you or other family members will give what is wanted if he just stands and looks at the desired object. (Appearing helpless and pathetic also works in some families!)

Your attention is powerful. Use it wisely. *Ignore* Caspar when he whines, pouts, or otherwise engages in irritating behaviors; *pay attention* when your child behaves politely and nicely and quietly. (Now admit it. Aren't *those* the behaviors that you usually ignore?!) When Caspar learns that he gets lots of hugs, warm words, special treats and attention without being a pest, he'll feel better about himself — and will behave better as well.

Effective Ignoring

Admittedly, it is very difficult to ignore a child who is making a scene or glaring at you with lower lip protruding. Just remember that as far as little Caspar is concerned, one of the worst things that can happen is to be ignored. Almost *anything* is preferable — even scolding or spanking is *some* kind of acknowledgement of existence and power.

The thing to do is to cut off *all* attention as soon as you notice that Caspar is whining, crying, pouting, or tantrumming — once you have assured yourself that nothing is *really* wrong. To be *maximally* effective, move at least three feet away. Try to keep your facial expression completely neutral because even a frown is a reaction and, therefore, rewarding. Do not respond to anything that he may say — no matter how tempted you may be. The secret is to act as if *nothing* is happening. You might whistle, sing, pretend to read, busy yourself with something. Walk out of the room if you have to. The important thing is to act as if *nothing is happening*. (Nobody said that this would be easy!) Just think to yourself, "I am *not* going to let this kid get to me. I will *not* reward this nasty behavior!"

Be forewarned, however: whatever Caspar is doing will probably escalate — get worse. This is known as the "frustration effect." He will be testing you — after all, this scene worked before. Maybe you've become hard of hearing? Some children become desperate when you start behaving differently. They want you to behave like you usually do — give in or get mad. At least that's familiar. But you're wiser now. You know it's important that you not interfere in the process of your child's learning the "new rules"; what worked before is not going to work any more. Continue to ignore and *act as if nothing is happening*.

The period of testing will probably be brief but intense. Caspar really does not want you to give in — that gives too much power, to be able to control an adult. It gives a child a great sense of security to see an adult act self-assured, to "show grace under pressure."

There's another very important part to the ignoring procedure. Within five minutes after the crying or pouting or tantrumming stops and Caspar has started to occupy himself with something more appropriate — or may be even just quietly sitting — *praise* him for playing nicely, or just chat pleasantly, *without talking about the scene that just occurred.* Whatever happened was irrelevant. Don't take personal offense at his behavior. He is learning about the way the world works. Also, don't conclude that the problem is solved just because ignoring worked once or twice. He'll test you any number of times, and you will probably get a lot of practice in ignoring.

If you *really* want to know how effective you are, keep a record of how often your child whines, cries, pouts, tantrums each day for a week or two. Just tally on a card that you tack up on the bulletin board or refrigerator. If you are doing a good job of ignoring, you will find that more and more time elapses between fewer and fewer marks.

Ignoring is a particularly powerful procedure for young children, since they depend heavily on you for attention and other rewards. As your youngsters get older, and have more social contact with others, you have less control over their rewards. For example, a tantrum in the grocery store may be something *you* can ignore, but it is unlikely that the other shoppers will! A tantrum in public puts a burden on everyone present, and you are forced to make a judgement about ignoring vs. removing under such "emergency" circumstances. If you elect to remove Caspar, be sure to do so without hurting him *and* without giving him any show of warmth. Don't add to the problem by scolding or nagging. It's not the end of the world. He's not a rotten kid. He's just misbehaving and needs to be removed.

Occasionally, Caspar will try the same stunt at home when you have guests — testing the limits to see if you will be consistent. You may need to use Time Out at these points, rather than ignore him to the discomfort of everyone. If your Time Out location is near your visitng area, you may wish to take Caspar to his room or another safe but distant spot in the house.

Plan ahead for such possibilities. They will occur, but if you are prepared they can be handled with a minimum of trouble for you and the bewildered onlookers (who have also experienced the same situation, and are anxious to see if you handle it as badly as they did!). Early intervention, incidentally, will keep the situation from getting out of hand; try not to let it escalate!

Do not ignore a child who becomes aggressive — hits you, another child or adult or animal, or damages property. Teasing and sarcasm are also aggressive behaviors.

Do not, of course, ignore a child who is in *genuine* need of help (for example, an open diaper pin, a cut, an earache). If in *any* doubt, check that out. The purpose of ignoring is to teach your child to seek attention appropriately, not to teach that you don't care!

Television

WHAT DO I DO WHEN my children want to spend hours and hours watching television?

> *"I find television very educating. Every time somebody turns on the set I go into the other room and read a book."*
>
> Groucho Marx

If there is such a thing as a universal phenomenon in American culture, it has to be television. It cuts across all manner of boundaries that otherwise separate us: rich and poor, Black and White, Brown and Yellow, old and young, women and men, north and south, east and west...

Deciding how to deal with the ever-present tube can be a real pain for parents, but the one-eyed monster can also be a real asset in child rearing — if you take charge.

There are two major issues to resolve in handling your children's TV watching: *what* they watch, and *how much* they watch. Since "how much" is easier, let's take that up first.

If your Terry is glued to the TV set, there's a marvelous way to unglue him or her and get a lot of things that you want done. All that you have to do is use Grandma's Rule, the old standby that has come down through the ages.

This is a very simple procedure: "After you wash the dishes, you can see TV" or "After you do your homework,..." or "After you mow the lawn..." Then *make certain* that the set is not turned on until after you are satisfied that the assigned job is well done. If Terry is watching TV *without* earning the privilege, you are throwing away an opportunity to use this in *very* constructive ways. Just think of the incredible power that you have in that one little finger that turns the TV set off!

You can even use TV to help your child improve his behavior at school if that's one of the problems. For example, if you have been getting complaints from the teacher, make an arrangement to get daily feedback from school. Each day that there's a complaint, Terry loses the TV privilege for that night. (If you remove the privilege for a week, he has nothing to lose by misbehaving; so just take a day at a time.) Set clear limits on total viewing time each week. The "right" amount is an individual matter, of course, but do you really favor more than 20 hours?

Which *programs* you allow or encourage is the more difficult consideration in TV viewing. Children, particularly those ages three through nine, take what they see very seriously. Monitor what they view, explain what they don't understand, and talk about concerns or issues that are raised in the program. Help Terry learn to be discriminating. He then has to decide what is worth working for.

TV can be a boon or a bane. It can easily become an addiction but, also, can be used to promote cooperation and good work habits. Unfortunately, some parents spend hours before the TV set themselves — and permit their children to do so — thus losing the opportunity to help their youngsters learn to think, talk, plan activities, to become achievers and doers rather than passive observers.

We live in a complex age of technology requiring highly skilled people. The world keeps shrinking, and we need statesmen and creative, reasonable, and educated persons if we are to survive. Where are we going to get them? Who is going to train them? The Dukes of Hazzard?

Psychologist Dr. Ed Christophersen suggests that most television programming is either a waste of time or is actually detrimental to a child. Soap operas, for example, may be amusing parodies if they are not taken seriously; but viewers who are not analytical may have difficulty sorting out the sham of the fantasy world, featuring characters who model poor judgement, dependancy, questionable morality, immaturity, and, generally nonsensical behaviors. You might want to get worried if your son or daughter stops laughing and starts wanting to imitate one of these characters.

Saturday morning cartoons may *seem* to be fairly innocuous and innocent fun; however, most of them feature an incredible number of acts of violence. Research suggests that children tend to become increasingly aggressive as they watch these, so if you find that your children start rough-housing while viewing these, turn off the set and tell them that they will have another opportunity to see the shows next week. If you have to turn off the set several Saturdays in a row, it might be best for your children to find other shows to view or do without TV.

Recent psychological research gives clear evidence that violence on television leads to aggressive behavior by children. Children are great imitators, and if Terry sees a steady stream of characters shooting, hitting and pushing around others, he's likely to try out those actions on the nearest "other" — probably a younger brother or sister.

Two important research findings on the positive side:

...cooperation, friendliness, delay of gratification and generosity can all be enhanced by *appropriate* TV programs (one often identified as constructive is "Mr. Rogers' Neighborhood");

...parental intervention, through discussion, can help minimize the negative effects of TV, and help increase positive effects.

The bottom line for you, parent, is to stay on top of your children's TV viewing, control the amount and the type, and help your children grow beyond passive acceptance of what they see by discussions with you. Help them sort out and evaluate programs. They should understand that situation comedies are really mindless fantasies, showing a life that doesn't exist and never was. They'll gain little that is constructive from those shows that are pornographic, featuring sex and violence.

Game shows are "mindless trivia, depicting get-rich gimmicks that are beyond practically everyone who watches them," observes Dr. Christophersen. Those teenagers who have serious problems appear to be particularly intrigued with these shows. Those who are more reality oriented tend to be "turned off" by the displays of pure greed and contrived enthusiasm.

It is inevitable, of course, that your child will be exposed to TV programs reflecting poor taste when visiting in other homes, but he or she will learn to be discriminating if *you* insist that only quality programs will be viewed at home. The best example you can set for your child is to turn the set on for a specific program, then turn it off and do something else. You then demonstrate that self-discipline and other interests have top priority in your family.

Toilet Training

WHAT DO I DO WHEN my child needs to be toilet trained?

"*My* child," says your neighbor sipping daintily at the cup of coffee in *your* kitchen, "was toilet trained at the age of six months. It was *no* problem at all. She is *such* a bright child." You both have a perfect view of the sand box where little Christopher, *your* son and heir, completely oblivious to the suspicious wet patch on the seat of his pants, is carefully measuring sand into a dump truck.

That comment is usually known as a "conversation stopper," so you might want to take advantage of the silence that follows by changing the subject to the marvelous buy you found at a sale last week. Refuse to brood. *There is no point in trying to "housebreak" your child before he is ready, and different children are ready at different times.* No matter what any over-zealous mother says, it's best not to be concerned about such training before your child is 24 months old; however, age is not as important as skill development.

When Is a Child Ready for Training?

Toilet training can begin when Christopher

...understands what is said and can ask for what he wants;

...can raise and lower his pants;

...obeys when told to do something;

...can wait to go to the bathroom.

Training Your Child

Admittedly, washing diapers is not high on anyone's list of fun activities; however, try not to initiate toilet training with an air of grim determination. Your child's future and the family's reputation are not at stake, and no awards are given for the quickest toilet trained kid on the block. Training may take two days, two weeks, or even two months. Be philosophical. Soiled pants are just soiled pants — not the end of the world.

A simple approach is to start by making frequent "dry pants" checks. You have to start with small steps, so, at first, check your child every five minutes until he or she asks to go to the bathroom. It's a good idea to set the timer to remind yourself to make the checks.

Once Christopher has begun to ask to go to the bathroom, make dry pants checks every 15 minutes. Again, when he has asked on his own to go to the bathroom, you know that you can move to a more extended period. Make the dry pants checks, then, every 30 minutes. Later, you extend the time to every hour, then every two hours. This can be tedious, but stay with it. *Praise a lot* when you find that Christopher is dry.

Do not get upset when the pants are wet. Just say: "Oh,oh, an accident. You'll have to change your pants. Now where is the place to put your wet pants?"

Expect temper tantrums. Don't get upset. Just impose Time Out (for the *tantrum, not* the wet pants!). Your child will learn that having a tantrum will not delay or interfere with the training.

It's a good idea to post a chart in the bathroom. On each successful visit, Christopher may pick a colored star and paste it on the chart. That way the whole family can notice and praise his progress. Let him hear you bragging about him to friends, neighbors, and relatives. "Imagine that! That boy earned five stars today. He is *so* smart!"

Try to stay as relaxed and casual as you can throughout the process. Toilet training is simply teaching your child a new skill. You wouldn't punish or react emotionally to your five-year-old because he fell down while learning to ride a two-wheeler. You would know that he simply needs more time and practice. The same applies to toilet training.

Time cures almost all parent anxiety about toilet training, so don't be in too big a hurry! If Christopher is ''fighting'' your training efforts, crying and otherwise vigorously resisting — and you have difficulty being patient and encouraging during the course of the training as recommended, put your porta-potty and other paraphernalia away for at least another month. He'll be ready when *he*'s ready! But don't make a habit of giving in. Just prepare yourself for the next training time and follow through.

If you are really convinced that Christopher must be trained right away (i.e. if he is over three, or entering pre-school), there are a couple of additional resources I recommend. Precise instructions are presented in the book, *Toilet Training in Less Than A Day* by Azrin and Foxx (New York: Pocket Books, 1981). However, be forewarned that this is a rather rigorous procedure that requires a real commitment. If you decide that highly organized approach fits in with your life style, you will want to outline the instructions for yourself so that you can follow them carefully.

A system called the ''Potty Pager'' has been developed by Dr. Kurt Mahoney for parents who find it difficult to follow a pants-check routine. With the kit ($19.95), it is claimed that the child is virtually self-trained in about 20 hours. I mention it for your information, not as an endorsement. Information: Wet Control Systems, 2600 East Southern Avenue, Suite C-2, Tempe, AZ 85282.

Toy Pickup: "The Sunday Box"

WHAT DO I DO WHEN my kids won't pick up their toys?

''Thunder is good, thunder is impressive,'' said Mark Twain, ''but it is lightning that does the work.'' And one of the best forms of lightning that I know of is the ''Sunday Box.'' It will save you hours of yelling, nagging, and sermonizing. It is far more powerful than any number of threats of mayhem, and you'll wonder why you didn't think of it yourself.

This minor marvel is simply a cardboard carton (although you can design something more elaborate if you feel creative) that you place in the middle of the living room — or whatever room is to be cleared of clutter. You also set the portable timer for 15 or 30 minutes as the deadline, and you should then see marvelous activity if you remain calm, cool, and collected and follow through. The secret of generating a sudden passion for cleaning by your kids is that when the buzzer rings, *you* will deposit all socks, shoes, toys, parts of puzzles, records, and miscellaneous items in the box; and *nothing* will be returned until Sunday.

The box should be kept in a closet or in the basement and is not to be touched by anyone but you. On Sunday, then, the things that were impounded are returned. Try not to be sanctimonious. Your kids will have been made miserable enough if they had to wear an old pair of shoes to school or do without something precious.

Be sure, though, that you advise everyone about this procedure *before* you institute it, otherwise your kids can justifiably call it a "foul play." Just remind them that to be "forewarned is to be forearmed" — and that's sanctimony enough. They may not believe you the first day, but they certainly will by the third day.

This idea was devised by Kansas educator, Dr. Ogden Lindsley, for his own children. He noted that after his daughter had to go to school wearing either one shoe or battered tennis shoes for one week, she was completely cured of leaving her shoes in the living room. It is very important, he said, that parents, too, be penalized for littering. Kids love to see that they aren't the *only* ones subject to the rules of the house. It's assuring to know that those who make the rules have to keep them too.

To prove the point, Dr. Lindsley deliberately left his briefcase in the living room, and his daughters were only too happy to deposit it in the Sunday Box. "My heavens," he exclaimed to their delight, "my briefcase is gone. What *will* I do! I have tests for the advanced students in it. My day tomorrow will be ruined!" He noted that when he went to work the following morning, he saw the curtains in the window flutter, and eyes peered out to see if he really did go without his briefcase. "That kind of strategy," he wrote, "is what makes the Sunday Box effective. It is similar to the mayor of the town seen in traffic court paying his own $10 ticket. *That* is being a good administrator."

That is also a clever way to clear clutter!

Truancy

WHAT DO I DO WHEN my child starts skipping classes? Could she be school phobic?

'And how many hours a day did you do lessons?' said Alice...
'Ten hours the first day,' said the Mock Turtle: 'nine the next, and so on.'
'What a curious plan!' exclaimed Alice.
'That's the reason they're called lessons,' the Gryphon remarked: 'because they lessen from day to day.'

Lewis Carroll
Alice in Wonderland

You thought your child was an A-1 solid citizen, but the day comes when she enters the seventh or eighth grade, and she becomes the Gryphon whose lessons lessen.

What happens? Why? *Where* is that child you used to know? The sad fact seems to be that if school success is going to start falling apart, it usually starts when the child enters the seventh grade. That seems to be a critical period because most school systems are designed to give more freedom and more choices, and some kids simply are not ready for that. Instead of having only one or two teachers for the whole day, they have to move from class to class, from teacher to teacher. They are given increased independence and responsibility, along with having to contend with more sophisticated peer pressure.

All of your previous training is now put to the test. If you have had a good relationship, it will pay off. This is the time that your power begins to erode, and can be a difficult time for all concerned. If you learn that your Gryphon is skipping classes, this is a cue that you should not ignore. Seek assistance as soon as possible.

A child may decide to become truant or skip classes for many reasons — boredom, academic problems, peer pressure, depression, anger. The problem is further compounded because the truant is going to do *something* with her time, and the something usually ends up to be mischief.

Could it be that your youngster is not a truant but is simply extremely fearful of going to school? "School phobia" is rather rare and occurs only in about 17 cases per thousand. The phobic child is often a good student while the truant is more likely to be a poor student, or to have a history of good grades which dramatically drop. Phobics do not want to leave home and tend to remain out of school continuously. Truants usually leave home on schedule, then avoid school or home and attend only some classes, playing the game of deception and secrecy.

If your child is diagnosed as being school phobic, you will have to consult with a mental health specialist who knows how to deal with phobias and develop a plan with the school counselor to gradually phase your child into the school system. The process can sometimes be rather complex. What it really adds up to is a way of gently nudging and building self-confidence.

If you have a truant on your hands, get down to the school counselor's office as quickly as you can and work out a cooperative arrangement. Arrange for *daily* feedback from the school so you'll know when Gryphon has not been attending classes. She has to learn very quickly that truancy will not be tolerated, and the powers that be (you and the school) will work together to close any communication gaps.

To counter truancy requires a real collaborative effort, among you, your child, and the school staff. The counselor, of course, will want to evaluate the situation by discussing it with you and your child. Is the work beyond her capacity? Are there problems at home? Are there unusual peer pressures? Special programs may have to be developed, or your family may be referred for counseling — but, meanwhile, Gryphon has to attend class until things are straightened out. She can't wait for solutions, and *then* attend class! (Nobody would ever do anything if all the problems had to be worked out first.)

It is critical that you get daily feedback about class attendance. That will determine whether your child gets any privileges at home each evening. If one or more classes are skipped, she may not use the telephone, see TV, use the radio or record player, or be given free time to go anywhere. Those are privileges that must be earned by attending all classes, one day at a time. If you withdraw *all* privileges for a week, Gryphon may as well skip *all* classes. She has nothing left to lose, and can figure out the cost/benefit ratio just as well as you can!

Weekend privileges give you a lot of power. You can teach her that free time and other privileges may be earned at school. Your role is to set up the conditions, and she makes the decision as to whether she will meet those conditions. I usually recommend that parents require 85% class attendance (for example, attending 21 of 25 weekly classes) for the youngster to earn privileges for one weekend day (starting Friday), 90% class attendance for two days' privileges, and 100% attendance for full Friday-Saturday-Sunday privileges.

After several weeks of that program schedule, you may improve performance by "upping the cost" to 90% class attendance for one weekend day, 95% for two days. And stick to your standards: when you say 21 classes a week, you don't mean 20!

Would getting a weekly report from the school substitute for the daily report? That is not recommended because there is too much room for slippage. A little inconvenience now will save a lot more later! Incidentally, if the school report says that Gryphon skipped a class and she denies it, the report wins out — right or wrong — unless she can present "hard evidence" that she was there and the school report is mistaken. "That's the way the money goes. Pop goes the weasel!"

A consistently applied feedback-attendance-privileges program such as this will get Gryphon's attention, and let her know clearly that the problem is important, not to be taken lightly. Now that you have the crisis under control, take a look at the truancy question in more depth.

Spend some time talking with Gryphon — and the school counselor if you need some help — to explore her *reasons* for cutting classes. No third degree here, parent, just a concerned interest in her life and growth. Try to listen more than you talk. Are there attractions outside of school that are tempting her away? Is she anxious about the social demands at school? Many adolescent groups are *very* hard on those who refuse to conform, and those who do not meet the peer norms. Are certain teachers particularly difficult to get along with? Does she lack the academic preparation needed to handle certain classes successfully? Are there special problems on the way to and from school?

Difficulty with the routine, regimen and requirements of school has been the beginning of a lifetime of "coming up short" for thousands (millions?) of people. Do all you can to intervene quickly, firmly and sensitively to help your child get back on a positive course. The school system we have is far from perfect, but it is essentially the only route your child has to developing the personal, social and vocational skills needed to get along in the world!

Video Games

WHAT DO I DO WHEN my kid spends all his time and money at the video game arcade?

> *"It is good to be without vices, but it is not good to be without temptations."*
>
> Walter Bagehot

Oh, for the good old days when the pool hall in River City was considered to be the primary den of iniquity and corruption! (Whatever *did* happen to those boys who hung out at the pool hall?) What devilish contraption now wreaks havoc on the morals and discipline of our youth and sets adults' teeth to gnash? It's right down the block in the middle of Main Street? See those lights blinking and flashing? The tense bodies standing with eyes riveted to a screen? If anyone yelled "fire" would anyone hear? Care? "It," of course, is the video game arcade.

Is Pac-Man (the leader of the pack of video games) truly a device of the devil — a Pied Piper leading the youth astray? Should all temptation be removed?

It's really not the game, you say? You're concerned because Tony spends all of his allowance and then some? He's undependable? Not doing chores at home? Grades are dropping? He's getting fat and flabby from lack of exercise? You think that he's addicted? He was a fairly good kid until the arcade opened?

An interest or diversion becomes an *addiction* when someone spends time and attention on it to the exclusion of almost everything else. Addictions are nothing new to the history of humankind. The ancient Greeks felt compelled to caution, "Moderation in all things." When the life of anyone becomes a video game, that person can be said to have an addiction.

Admittedly, electronic games are fun and challenging and require unusual coordination, timing, and concentration. They seem to meet some innate need for novelty and feeling of control and competency. They are also a privilege and a pastime. You know that, but how do you convince Tony? Maybe it's those kids that he runs around with who are unduly influencing him?

Blaming others is not going to teach Tony to be responsible for himself. Removing temptations will not teach him to exert self-control and set priorities. Forbidding him to play computer games at the arcades will only complicate things by setting up a challenge that Tony can't refuse!

Addiction to the games is really a symptom — not the main issue. It is a symptom of the need to learn to set priorities, to use money wisely, to broaden the horizon of interests. Electronic games are fun, but so are tennis, volleyball, camping, hiking, basketball, and numerous other activities which add variety to life and contribute to good health and enjoyment. Most youngsters who get into trouble with the law or who feel inadequate do not involve themselves with organized activities, for example, sports, school projects, scouting, and recreational activities with their families.

How does Tony fill his time? If Tony spends two hours at school and six hours at the game arcade, his judgement is suspect.

You can start to address the problem of addiction to computer games by sitting down and discussing your concerns with Tony. Don't start out by saying: "Look, kid, it's time you stopped playing those stupid games and started doing some work around here. And, furthermore, about your grades...!" That would only convince Tony that he had to "prove" to you that he could do whatever you didn't want him to do. Instead, let him know that you can understand his interest in the games (whether you *accept* it or not), but you are concerned about other issues that need to be worked out; that is, negotiated. There is the issue of priorities, for example. School work, school attendance, and home responsibilities are most important, and satisfactory performance in these areas will be required to *earn* free time — to go to the arcade or do other activities. Work out a system together for earning an allowance so that he will learn what energy it takes to earn a dollar, and learn to be discriminating in how he spends his money. Encourage him to consider other interests, and plan to do something *with* him — go to a ball game, go fishing or bowling, go to the museum or zoo. (School problems, chores and allowances are discussed in other chapters of this book.)

You cannot make a *rule* about how much time Tony can spend at the arcade or how to use his allowance because you cannot enforce that rule (unless, of course, you plan to glue yourself to him!). Free time is very important to kids. Having to earn it helps them decide whether certain activities are worth all the time and energy. Trust your youngster. He'll figure it out eventually. You can help best by being sympathetic but, also, by setting up a tough schedule to earn free time and allowance.

You have a special advantage if you *own* the equipment for electronic games. Access to the equipment can be earned by completing all chores for the day — if that has been a problem — or by controlling nuisance behaviors — teasing, swearing, sarcasm (see "Special Problems").

Purchase of new games can be another negotiated goal. If Tony wants a game to be purchased and has a problem with temper tantrums or some other behavior, you can negotiate. If you know that you can afford to buy the game in 30 days, you can say: "Fine, I'll be glad to get the game for you, but the cost is 30 points. You will earn one point for each day that you don't have a temper tantrum. Let's keep a chart on the refrigerator so we'll know how many days it takes you to earn the game."

Educational programs (learning multiplication, spelling, grammar, etc.) are also available, and kids enjoy learning through the computer, which is a remarkably patient tutor that gives highly individualized attention. Some discussion of these programs can be found in the book, *The Personal Computer Book* by P. A. McWilliams (Prelude Press, 1983). This is also a good reference book for those families who are considering the purchase of a home computer.

Working Parents

WHAT DO I DO WHEN I have become a working parent and no one is at home full time?

"Man for the field and woman for the hearth;
Man for the sword and for the needle she;
Man with the head and woman with the heart;
Man to command and woman to obey;
All else confusion."

Alfred Lord Tennyson

Sorry, Lord Tennyson old bean, *au contraire,* "All else" makes *more* sense, particularly since women have worked in the fields for years! It's only recently, however, that they decided that a *paycheck* should come along with the job! If you, Mother, have gone to work outside your home, or are planning to do so, you are participating in one of the most significant changes that has occurred in our society within the past 20 years.

Television would still have us believe that most women are concerned with "ring around the collar," the shine on their dishes, and comparing the merits of floor waxes with neighbors. The reality is that work away from home has become important in the lives of most women. Over half of the women in two-parent families with school-age children and almost 42 per cent of those with preschoolers are employed. Rates for single-parent families are even higher.

Fathers are also turning from traditional roles in record numbers. Not content with the field and the sword, many dads are now working at home. And it's not just the writers, artists, and musicians. Microcomputers are allowing businessmen to stay at home and be fully as productive as they were in the office. Craftsmen of all varieties, and owners of cottage industry businesses are successfully breaking the nine-to-five mold. An important "side effect" — though also a major motivating consideration for many men — is increased time with their children and responsibility for child rearing. What's more, these fathers usually take on more household chores as well — planning meals, running errands, even (bless their hearts!) waxing floors.

How Does it Affect the Children?

It would be nice to be able to tell you, but nobody knows. Since women have entered the labor force enmasse only within the past 20 years, there's little research; and the findings are scanty. It does appear now that, under certain conditions, the mother's employment is beneficial. "The family with the working mother," observed Dr. Lois Hoffman, psychologist, "may be better suited than the traditional family for preparing children to fill new adult roles" in our changing society.

If you're a full-time parent, she notes, you may even become *too* protective, unwittingly fostering dependency in your child. Some kids have more "mothering" than they can handle when parenting is a full-time job. The Greeks, as usual, advised us wisely long ago: "Everything in moderation."

Preschool children of working mothers have been noted to be more socially competent and self-assured than those of non-working mothers. Daughters of working mothers appear to thrive and tend to be more outgoing, independent, active, highly motivated, score higher academically, and reflect good adjustment on both social and personality measures. They are more likely to admire their mothers and hold the female role in high esteem.

The effect on sons is more complicated. Those who come from middle or high income families are less likely to stereotype the roles of men and women. They view women as being competent and men as being morally supportive. Those boys who are reared in low income families, however, may conclude that mother has to work because father is a failure as a provider. That places a strain on the father-son relationship. Otherwise, they tend to adjust reasonably well both academically and socially.

No strain on the father-son relationship was found in

© Masters Agency, Capitola, CA

"Occupation? Well, if you promise to keep it under your hat, I'm the kingpin in an international spy ring."

average income families, but, academically, these boys tend to perform poorer when mother is working than when she is not working. Laxities in expectations and monitoring school work may be involved.

Some Questions to Consider

Organization, needed at some level in all families, is particularly important when the parents work outside the home. If you consider the family members' basic needs, you won't have to feel wicked for working. This can be a real opportunity for your children to develop independence, self-confidence and cooperation.

...What arrangements can you make for the supervision and care of your children?

...Have you worked out a schedule with your spouse and older children as to "who will do what when" in regard to household tasks and child care? Mutual assistance is important, and *writing out* the arrangements helps to avoid misunderstandings.

...Instead of nursing guilt, can you generate enthusiasm? Feelings are contagious! Tell your children that you are all entering a new and interesting life style and you need their help. They need to know what is expected of them, for example, cooperating with the babysitter, keeping up with school work, doing household chores. They need to be involved in the planning. Even more will be expected of children in single parent families.

...Will you schedule family outings or activities at least once a month? A weekly family conference to review problems, plans, and accomplishments can be a big help to everyone.

...Will you schedule a "date" with your spouse once a week? Or give yourself some "personal time" if you are a single parent?

Research confirms that the family adjusts best when firm house rules are established and children are encouraged to be self-sufficient rather than expecting to be waited on. Working parents must avoid overindulging and underdisciplining their children when they feel twinges of guilt.

In seeking alternative care, the focus should be on the children's needs at their various stages of development. That issue is discussed in the "Day Care" chapter.

Remember that to develop a sense of responsibility, children need opportunities to make decisions and mistakes but must also be held accountable by reaping the rewards and penalties. Assigning household responsibilities to them helps build their esteem and assure them that they are making important contributions to the family.

Teenagers need responsibilities, guidance, love, understanding, *and* the freedom to make critical decisions when challenged by peers and numerous temptations. Justifiably, parents feel much anxiety during this period, which often coincides with their own crises — concerns about aging, the imminent empty nest, and, perhaps, marital difficulties. Working parents can be more "psychologically free" to show trust and encourage teenage independence because they are more likely to feel self-sufficient and competent themselves. That is much more difficult to do when your self-worth is based only on your role as a parent.

Our society has been slow to acknowledge that women are an important part of the work force, and that many men are adopting home-oriented life styles. These new needs of the family have resulted in a scarcity of resources. Community services, social institutions, government policies, jobs, children's literature, and public opinion are lagging dangerously behind the temper of the times. Someone needs to post the warning that "The mills of the Gods grind slowly, but they grind exceedingly fine."

If you have joined the ranks of those who receive a regular paycheck for your daily labors, congratulations! There will be inevitable adjustments for your family if there is no longer a parent at home full time, *or* if the at-home-parent is Dad instead of Mom. But if the family prepares well, communicates a lot, and pulls together as a team, it can be an exciting adventure which will benefit everybody.

Worrying

WHAT DO I DO WHEN my child is a worrier?

"To him who is in fear, everything rustles," observed Sophocles. These words are as true today as when written during the 4th century B.C.

We are all apt to be concerned about the possibility of failure or rejection when we try something new or apply for a job. We have to take those risks if we are going to do anything with our lives.

Worry, however, goes beyond mere concern. Psychologist Dr. Albert Ellis notes it is a composite of anxiety, lack of self-confidence, and a feeling of personal responsibility for failure or rejection. The worrier is convinced that any error or unfortunate event is not merely unfortunate, it's a catastrophe, and that the worrier is at fault because he or she is a misfit — a really rotten person. After all, why else would it have happened?

Worriers "exaggerate the difficulty of things and then elect themselves as the cause of all the difficulties," notes Ellis. Further, when they don't have any current worry, they indulge in "What if..." thinking: "What if I fail;...if I make a fool of myself;...if my father loses his job;...if I'm orphaned;...if I have to recite in class and my dress (or pants) falls off;...if the bus comes late;...if the sun doesn't shine."

Fear of disaster is a constant companion, and the worrier also acts as if a phantom reporter is haunting her footsteps, only too eager to release a newspaper headline reading: "Helen Smith is a complete, utter failure. That was proven yesterday when this dolt..."

The philosophy of worriers tends to be quite simplistic. They believe that the world should be well ordered and safe, with everything in its place and highly predictable. They don't like surprises and want the assurance of certainty. They believe that this is a "just" world, in which just rewards are given for honest efforts, and that rewards and punishments are dispensed in systematic and rational kinds of ways; therefore, good things happen to good people, and bad things happen to bad people.

Not even worriers, however, can avoid the realities of daily living; and, at some point, worrying assumes some kind of magical power. Unwittingly, the child (or adult) starts believing that worry has the power to control situations. ("If I worry enough, I won't make mistakes or be rejected or bad things won't happen.") It is very difficult to convince the worrier differently, and to directly challenge that belief system only puts the worrier on the defensive and confirms the conviction that others "simply do not understand."

I love this story: A man went into his yard at midnight each night and banged drums and cymbals. His neighbors became rather distressed about this and visited him one night and asked: "What *are* you doing?" He stopped briefly and said: "I'm chasing away the tigers and protecting the neighborhood." "But, Sir," exclaimed his neighbors, "There *are* no tigers within 5,000 miles of here." "Ahah!" said the man. "You see? My technique is working!"

Worrying tends to be a complex behavior that is supported by a unique rationale very convincing to the unhappy worrier. In a crazy kind of way, worrying purchases a sense of control and security; however, that security is bought at great cost. No one can be happy if he or she must worry all the time in order to keep the world revolving properly on its axis. Also, so much energy is diverted to this useless activity, there is little left for more creative endeavors. Ironically, the worrier often brings on the very things that are feared because judgement is affected. He or she then concludes: "I *knew* this would happen. Maybe I didn't worry *enough*."

The most effective way that I have found to help a worrier crawl out of the hole that he has dug for himself is a three-pronged approach: *total agreement, satiation,* and *diversion*. I'll use a case study to show you how it works.

In a consultation with a concerned but frustrated mother and her 11-year-old son, it was learned that David has been a worrier ever since he entered school six years ago. He did not want to leave his mother for fear that she would get sick and die or be run over by a truck while he sat in a classroom. He worried about his work, his friends, any mistakes that he made. He worried about worrying, and his parents worried about his worrying. They had done everything they could to reassure him and had tried to convince him that his worries were irrational. They found that the more they debated, the more he worried.

David was a bright, verbal youngster who readily admitted that he was a worrier, and his litany of worries was nonstop for about ten minutes. He was still worried about his mother's daily survival although her health had always been excellent. He worried about his father's job, nuclear war, a scolding by his teacher for talking with a classmate, forgetting his homework, doing it all wrong, or losing it. Those were among his chronic worries. His current worry was the anticipation of entering junior high school in the fall, and he feared that he would not be able to find his classrooms and that teachers would yell or laugh at him if he asked for directions. On the very first day of school both teachers and other kids would conclude that he's a real dunce. He was also concerned that he might not find the front door to escape to his home and might wander throughout the school for weeks, lost and hungry.

I listened patiently and agreed with him that (almost) all of these things *could* happen. I also suggested some worries that he hadn't thought of, for example, that the teachers might stand outside their classroom doors and kids line up along the hall walls to laugh at and watch him dashing madly around looking for his classroom. David did not know whether to take me seriously. I was very interested to watch what he would do with *new* worries that were being proposed to him. He appeared to make a very important decision — the first step. He decided not to worry about *my* worry proposals and smiled instead. He began to learn that *he can decide* whether or not to worry about things.

To give David full responsibility for worrying, his mother was advised that both she and her husband should stop being concerned because David's share of worrying was enough for any household, and, therefore he was relieving his family of the burden of having to worry. David's mother readily agreed to that recommendation. The family's concern had reinforced the worries, and the attention maintained the worrying behavior. David did not discuss his worries with his friends, for example, because they were completely disinterested!

The second step in intervention was to convince David that worrying is a burden and a nuisance. Telling him that, however, would not be convincing. Instead, he was given a homework assignment wherein he was asked to rate his worrying each day on a scale of 0 to 10 and to make a note of all his worries for the day. If he rated his day as a 10, he had to list 10 worries; a 6 required a listing of 6 worries; and so on down the scale. It was suggested that he really concentrate on worrying. Most children (and adults) do not like this kind of assignment because it takes a different kind of energy than simply complaining about free-floating worries. They are caught in a bind, however, because if they don't follow through, others may not take them seriously any more. The real goal is to help them decide that it's less of a nuisance to cope with an unpredictable, fairly disordered world than to have to go through this exercise week after week after week. David's family was advised not to discuss his worries with him but to refer him to the counselor, with whom he could discuss any number of worries.

The third step in helping the worrier to a happier state is to find another interest to occupy his or her thinking. One cannot think of two things at the same time. The worrier is then able to say to himself: "There I go worrying again. That's dumb. I'm going to think of something else." The diversion for David was chess, but it could have been athletics or building models or electronic games or any number of things.

Concerned lectures, debates, scoldings will never convince the worrier that he can cope with an uncertain world, rejection, pain, failure and still enjoy life. The message has to be positive: "You handled that really well when your teacher scolded you today in front of the class! What are you going to do for fun today as a way of treating yourself for a job well done?"

David's worrying began to diminish in about two weeks. After two months, he was worrying only once a day or so, and his parents had completely relaxed. Six months later I spoke with David's mother, who assured me the problem was resolved. When David found it more trouble to worry than to take each day as it came, he gave up the unproductive habit!

The worrier can gain much from the words of George Bernard Shaw: "People are always blaming their circumstances for what they are. I don't believe in circumstances. The people who get on in this world are the people who get up and look for the circumstances they want, and, if they can't find them, make them."

To live is not so much to achieve goals as to participate in processes.

More Resources for Parents

No More Secrets: Protecting Your Child from Sexual Assault by C. Adams and J. Fay. San Luis Obispo, CA: Impact Publishers, Inc., 1981.
Important guide for parents and child care workers. Is thorough and specific. Used in a number of training programs.

How to Deal With Your Acting-Up Teenager by R. T. Bayard and J. Bayard. San Jose, CA: The Accord Press, 1981.
Serious problems of teenagers and parents' rights are addressed. The goal is for parents to enjoy their own lives more and help their teenagers in the process.

Parents Are Teachers by W. C. Becker. Champaign, IL: Research Press, 1971.
This book has long been used as a training manual by parent training groups. It is basic, and a classic in the field.

Successful Parenthood: How to Teach Your Child Values, Competence and Responsibilities by W. C. Becker and J. W. Becker. Chicago, IL: Follett Publishing Co., 1974.

Little People — Guidelines for Common Sense Child Rearing by E. R. Christophersen. Lawrence, KS: H & H Enterprises, Inc., 1977.
With wit and wisdom, the author presents specific recommendations for common behavior problems for children to age five and general guidelines for parents.

Effective Parents, Responsible Children by R. Eimers and R. Aitchison. New York: McGraw-Hill Book Co., 1977.
Presents detailed descriptions of how and when to use specific parenting skills and how to develop special incentive systems.

Solving Your Child's Behavior Problems: An Everyday Guide for Parents by Jeffrey Kelly, New York: Little, Brown and Co., 1983.
In addition to addressing problems of children to age six, makes recommendations for dealing with fears, decision-making, day care, and entering school.

Caring About Kids is a series of pamphlets written to help parents care for their children and themselves in ways that promote good mental health. For free single copies write to: Public Inquiries, National Institute of Mental Health, 5600 Fishers Lane, Rockville, MD 20857.

Public Affairs Pamphlets, 381 Park Ave. South, New York 10016.
Offer much valuable information about child development and family relations. Send for information or subscribe for 15 issues for $3.50 (30 issues for $6).

Child Management by J. M. Smith, and D. E. P. Smith. Champaign, IL: Research Press, 1976.
Focus is on rule setting and enforcing and on moral training to help children make wise decisions by considering alternatives and their consequences.

The First Three Years of Life by Burton L. White. Englewood Cliffs, NJ: Prentice-Hall Inc., 1975.
The child's experiences during this early period determine, to a large degree, emotional and intellectual functioning. The author offers a number of suggestions for making these productive and stimulating.

"Help! We Can't Handle It Anymore!"

What to Expect from Professional Counseling

"It is part of the cure to wish to be cured."
Seneca

"I'm not going to say nothin'," said the boy. "I don't want to be here. Only crazy people go to see a shrink. I'm not crazy."

"Nobody said you are crazy. What do you think happens in counseling?"

"I dunno, and I don't wanna know. S'pose my friends hear about my coming here?!"

"They won't unless you tell them yourself. Let's talk about what happens here and why your mother brought you here."

It took a while to assure this youngster that nothing terrible was going to happen to him — that no one was going to crawl into his head and say, "Ahah! Just what I thought. A screw is loose!" He began to relax only after he felt confident that the conferences would be confidential, that no one would do anything *to* him, and that he would be a part of the discussions and planning. The problem, he was told, "is that you're doing some things that create unhappiness for you and your family. Maybe *they're* doing things that you don't like either. The goal is to work things out so that you can get along better." He decided to take a "wait and see" stance. Some weeks later, he was glad that he did. He particularly liked learning how to negotiate with his folks, and his parents were gratified to find that he was not all that unreasonable and arbitrary.

Admittedly, that story had a happier ending than some others. Commitment to change is critically important. "It is part of the cure to wish to be cured."

Most children and teenagers are not eager to consult with a counselor, and it is a good idea to discuss with them beforehand why you have decided to seek outside help. Emphasize that the purpose is to resolve problems, not to blame or criticize: "We're all in this together, and we're going to work things out together."

Children must be involved in the counseling process from the very beginning. Be open and honest about the counseling appointment. Instead of simply telling the child that he or she is "going to see a doctor," say where you are going, why, and what you think is going to happen.

Be prepared to talk about what you *like* about your child as well as the behaviors that concern you. No one enjoys hearing a litany of misdeeds without *something* positive. The counselor will probably excuse your child from the room if the discussion becomes too negative. You may need to ventilate your feelings of frustration and anger — just to express the strength of your concern before you get on to the business of doing what must be done — but it's best to do that in a private conference.

Do not expect any magic. There is no miracle pill. Some parents drag in their reluctant offspring and, in effect, say: "Here's the wretch! *Do* something with it." They sometimes feel betrayed when they learn that *they* are the ones who have to do things differently.

When Should I Seek Counseling?

There are three main reasons why people decide to see a counselor. One is when they feel out of control of their child's behavior or find that family, marital, or other personal relationships are unsatisfactory. A second reason is feelings of depression, fears, anxiety, or anger which seem out of control.

The third reason is the failure of a personal philosophy of life. Feelings of confusion and frustration often result when one's system for explaining the way the world works breaks down.

All three reasons relate to feeling out-of-control. If you experience such feelings in some aspect of your life and don't know where to turn or how to handle the situation, you will want to consider counseling help.

How Do I Find the "Right" Therapist?

No one therapist is skilled in every problem area. Some have expertise in working with child-parent problems, others with marital problems or sexual dysfunctions, still others expertly treat emotional control (anger, depression) or phobias, and more.

An advanced degree (M.D., Ph.D., M.A., M.S., or M.S.W.) and state license or certification, while desireable, do not assure you of the experience and skills needed for your particular problem. Be extremely cautious, however, before you consult with anyone who has minimal training, for example, no graduate degree or a diploma from some unknown (or "mail order") school. If your problems were all that simple to work out, you'd be checking in with your next door neighbor instead of a high-cost professional. (In some instances, that might not be such a bad idea!) Complex problems, however, are more readily resolved by consulting with an objective and skilled counselor. Parent-child problems can be difficult and complex.

To save yourself time and money, don't hesitate to ask questions of the practitioner. Before you commit yourself, ask how much the sessions will cost, how many sessions may be required over how long a period of time. Most qualified and ethical professionals will have a pre-printed statement describing their qualifications, their point of view, the therapy procedures you can expect, and a fee schedule. It may not be possible for a therapist to tell you exactly what procedural methods s/he will use until your problem and needs are assessed. However, you should be given some idea as to whether the approach and point of view are *psychoanalytic, cognitive, behavioral,* or *humanistic*. Mental health professionals represent many different schools of thought, but most fall into one or a combination of these four major camps.

As you have seen from this book, I work within the behavioral framework, in which interventions are direct and aimed at behavior change. I also find that Rational Emotive Therapy (RET — a cognitive approach) appears to be quite effective in helping people change their thoughts and feelings. Behavioral therapists usually are members of the Association for Advancement of Behavior Therapy; perhaps your local library has the AABT directory so you can easily look up practitioners in your area.

While I make no pretense that behavioral psychology and RET are the *only* approaches to problems, I do recommend that you seek a therapist who is trained and qualified in these skills. Many therapists use a number of procedures and are knowledgeable about various approaches. Ethical professionals know their own limitations and should not be reluctant to refer you on to another counselor who has the skills you need, if necessary.

What Should I Expect?

Short-term interventions should yield results for most of the child behavior problems identified in this book. Do not commit yourself and your child to more than three months of therapy until several shorter term procedures have been tried. I find that 12 to 18 sessions — sometimes stretched across six months — are usually adequate for difficult cases. Less complex problems may require only two to four sessions, and parents are always welcome to call back as needed. If any changes are going to be made in parent-child problems, improvements will be noted in six or fewer weekly sessions — unless, of course, the family situation is very complicated and other factors are involved.

Therapy should be problem oriented. You and the therapist need to delineate the goal. What do you want to accomplish? "Rap sessions" may be fun — and often can be prolonged over a very long period of time — but a problem-oriented intervention is of much greater immediate value. Don't worry if you don't know exactly how to state your problem; one job of the therapist is to help you clarify the issues.

Once you and the therapist have clearly defined the problem — whether it is dealing with yourself or your child (or both) — therapy should be directed toward that problem. Expect that you will be given homework assignments. There is *no* way that effective and lasting changes can be made simply by talking about problems. If you have any concerns about any of the recommendations, be sure to discuss them with your therapist. If, for example, your child is referred for play therapy, ask what is to be accomplished and when you should be able to see results. Also, if you or your child is referred for a psychological evaluation, clarify the purpose and how the results are to be used. Ask for and get a full explanation of the results.

Counseling, I believe, is a process of education — not an act of self-indulgence (although some people do make a "hobby" of self-analysis that goes on for years). If you knew what to do about your problem, you would probably be doing it. If you're *not* doing what you want to do, you will certainly want to see a therapist who will help you define your problem, suggest — and teach, if necessary — the alternatives, and provide encouragement and support while you are trying to create more happiness for yourself.

Finding a therapist is not an easy task, but you will improve your chances of finding one who is right for you if you follow the guidelines I have proposed here. Incidentally, do not hesitate to change therapists if you are not getting the help you think you need, but be sure to tell your counselor why you are changing. No professional can be successful with every client, but even therapists need reality feedback!

To learn more about counseling services, write to the American Psychological Association, Public Information, 1200 Seventeenth Street, N.W., Washington, D.C. 20036 for a copy of their brochure describing professional counseling and how to get it.

"Guidelines for Choosing a Behavior Therapist" can be ordered through the Association for Advancement of Behavior Therapy. Send 25 cents to AABT, 15 West 36th Street, New York, N.Y. 10170. Detailed information is given on: What is Behavior Therapy? Qualifications and Training Necessary for Particular Mental Health Professionals; Practical Information About Therapists; Questions to Ask When Deciding On a Therapist; What To Do If You Are Dissatisfied With Your Therapist; and How To Get The Names of Behavior Therapists.

Your local telephone book or the library will help you locate your nearest Community Mental Health Clinic and various private practitioners. Look for psychiatrists (M.D.), psychologists (Ph.D., M.A., or M.S.), marriage and family counselors (Ph.D., M.A., or M.S.), clinical social workers (M.S.W.).

How Well Do You Know Your Child?

There's no understanding kids these days. It seems to me that *we* were different — more responsible, more polite, more self-disciplined. My son, a big-shot junior in high school, thinks he knows everything. He never listens to me. I never thought that I would be arguing with my own son.

When people are arguing, they are not listening to each other. Some other cultures, for example, the Japanese and Chinese, understand the importance of talking about mundane, little things with another person before they tackle big issues.

It's the same way with a family. It's a lot easier to discuss things with your son or daughter — even though you may disagree — if you really know each other. How well do you know your kids?

To test your knowledge, see how many of the following questions you can answer in this questionnaire compiled by the California Family Life Education program. Remember that only your children can grade this for you. Only they have the right answers!

What is your daughter's/son's favorite game or sport?
What is your daughter's/son's height (within one inch)?
Who is your daughter's/son's closest friend?
If your daughter/son could choose to do anything for a day, what would it be?
What is your daughter's/son's favorite color?
What was the last movie your daughter/son saw?
What is your daughter's/son's preferred dinner: steak and salad, macaroni and cheese, or chicken and corn?
Would your daughter/son rather ride a bike, ride a horse, or ride in a car?
Who is your daughter's/son's favorite singer or musical group?
If your daughter/son had a choice to buy a pet, what would it be?
Which would your daughter/son rather do: wash dishes, mow the lawn, clean her/his room or vacuum the house?
Do your daughter's/son's friends call her/him by nickname? If so, what is it?
In the evening, would your daughter/son rather play a game with the family, go to visit a relative, or read alone? her/his room?
What was the last problem your daughter/son came to you for help with?
What gift would your daughter/son most like to receive?
What does your daughter/son do that s/he is proud of?

If you get more than 15 right, congratulations...you really know your kids!

From 11 to 15 right, not bad, but you might want to show more interest and pay more attention.

If you get less than 11, you need a crash course called, "Getting to Know You!"

From: *Family Life Education: Parent/Child Homework Assignments*, Planned Parenthood of Santa Cruz County; Network Publications, 1983. (Used with permission)

How Well Does Your Child Know You?

There's just no way that I can talk to my folks. They're always bugging me to talk to them, but what is there to say to them? They don't understand the younger generation, and they certainly don't understand me! Anytime I *do* say anything, they cut me down.

Maybe they just want to be heard. Maybe they just want you to show some interest in them and their opinions and are a little heavy-handed in the way they go about it. Parents are people, too, you know. Maybe the place to start is to try to understand them. After all, what do you really know about them?

Many of us know very little about our parents, what they really think or like or dislike. Knowing — or wanting to find out — about someone shows that you really care. One of the best ways to get parents to listen to you is to let them know that you are interested in them.

See how much you've learned throughout the years of living under the same roof. Remember that only your dad or mom can grade your answers to the following questions.

How did your parents meet?

What color are your father's eyes?

If your mother went on a trip to a foreign city, would she head first to a historic site or museum, the shopping streets, or a cafe?

For a vacation, would your father prefer a luxury resort, a rustic mountain cabin, or resting at home?

What presidential candidate did your mom vote for in the last election?

Does your mother believe in love at first sight?

For a pleasant evening, would your dad rather watch TV with the family, sit alone and read, or go to dinner with your mom and another couple?

Does your dad gas up the car as soon as the tank is half empty or when the fuel is nearly gone?

Does your dad usually carry a photo of your mom in his wallet?

How old was your mom on her first date?

If your mom turned on the TV and found these choices, which would she pick: a football game, soap opera, old movie — or turn off the set?

Which of these can't your mother do: touch her toes, do a headstand, rewire a lamp, replace the spark plugs, sew a shirt?

What was your dad's first full-time job?

What was your mom's first full-time job?

Which of these can't your father do: touch his toes, do a headstand, rewire a lamp, replace the spark plugs, sew a shirt?

What gift would your dad most like to receive?

If your folks could have you do anything for three hours, what would it be?

If you get more than 15 right, congratulations…you really know your folks!

From 11 to 15 right, not bad, but maybe you could show more interest and pay more attention.

If you get less than 11, you need a crash course called, "Getting to Know You!"

From: *Family Life Education: Parent/Child Homework Assignments*, Planned Parenthood of Santa Cruz County; Network Publications, 1983. (Used with permission)